MY UNCLE THEODORE

In every epoch there are a few lives that finally come to represent its real historical significance. Dreiser's was one of those lives, principally because his novels consisted of the search for an ethic for America that could not only be publicly institutionalized but privately lived by.

Arthur Miller

My Uncle Theodore

by

VERA DREISER

with

BRETT HOWARD

NASH PUBLISHING

NEW YORK

Nash Publishing Corporation
1 Dupont Street
Plainview, N.Y. 11803

Library of Congress Catalog Card Number: 75-30392

International Standard Book Number: 0-8402-1366-2

Printed in the United States of America
First Printing

To my Parents
especially my father,
Edward Dreiser,
who deserves to be remembered here
not only
for his contribution to this book
but also
for his loyalty, kindness, and devotion
as a husband and father.

Contents

Acknowledgments

My sincere thanks goes to the following people: Neda Westlake, University of Pennsylvania, who has been a help and inspiration to me since the first time I talked about this book; Doris M. Reed, Elfrieda Lang, and David Randall, Indiana University, Humphrey A. Olsen, Vincennes University; Mrs. Leo Vogt, who gave me her permission to use the courtship letters written by my uncle to Sara White; Max Morath and John W. Ripley for the wonderful song slides of "In The Baggage Coach Ahead"; Stephen Kanych of Shawnee Press; Camilla Anderson, M. D., for helping me to confirm my feelings regarding my grandfather, and to express it in proper terms; members of the Lambs Club who knew Paul Dresser; Joseph Lash for permission to use a quote from *Eleanor and Franklin;* Harold J. Dies, trustee, the Dreiser Trust; Elsie Holsman and Bernice Walther for expert secretarial assistance.

Conversations, as sources, included those with

My father, Edward M. Dreiser,
My mother, Mai V. Dreiser,
My uncles, Theodore and Rome,
My aunts, Mame, Emma, and Sylvia,
Sara White Dreiser (Mrs. Theodore),
Gertrude Hopkins, George Nelson, Sr.,
and Harold J. Dies.

Certain pictures were given to me by Paul D. Gormley, Gertrude Hopkins, and the Theodore and Helen Dreiser estates.

Funeral picture–*Life* Magazine; Black Star Photographers

". . . to keep Life's heart from breaking,
I–
With my cap and bells
My tambour and my gestures,
My capers and my leer.
Because of dullness,
Greyness,
Want,
Misery.
To keep Life's heart from breaking,
I–
With my cap and bells."

Theodore Dreiser

Prologue

Men of genius do not need
to pay attention to style,
they are good in spite of
their faults and because of
them, but we, the lesser ones
only prevail by perfect style.

Eleanor Roosevelt

As far as I am concerned the above says all there is to be said about Theodore Dreiser's style, although much of the criticism leveled at him was based on that theme. I am more concerned here with trying to show my uncle in the family setting out of which he grew, and the influence it had on him. What I have to say is primarily intended to clarify misinterpretations and omissions in previous biographical material, including his own. My contribution is drawn from what I saw and heard over the years as a member of the family: the stories my father told me; my personal contacts since childhood with, and later observations of, the rest of the family, especially my Uncle Theo; my long friendship with his first wife, known to me from childhood as "Aunt Jug"; my thirty-year friendship and correspondence with "Aunt" Louise Dresser; my fifteen-year acquaintance with Helen Dreiser; plus bits and pieces gathered from so many conversations with friends and admirers of both Theodore and Paul.

As I am a psychologist by profession I hope to be able to give some insightful glimpses of the underlying causes and motivations for the way he lived his life. A critique written for *The New York Times* about one of the recent biographies of Theodore Dreiser was titled "A Giant Still Asking to Be Accounted for." That really sums it up.

No one who knew Theodore Dreiser or his work is able to discuss him dispassionately. He is either adored or thoroughly disliked. His books are among the best, or not even worth mentioning. No one who reads, however, seems to be indifferent. This is greatness. A man who arouses such controversy is a man who didn't go unnoticed through life. Right or wrong he tried to find answers for himself and indirectly for others. A man who goes through life looking for answers, disagreeing with things as they are, saying so, and challenging the status quo, pays a high price. Theodore Dreiser knew he was thoroughly distasteful to certain critics. Wrote H. L. Mencken:

> While Dreiser lived all the literary snobs and popinjays of the country, including your present abject servant, devoted themselves to reminding him of his defects. He had, to be sure, a number of them. But the fact remains that he was a great artist, and that no other American of his generation left so wide and handsome a mark upon the national letters. American writing, before and after his time, differed almost as much as biology before and after Darwin. He was a man of large originality, of profound feeling, and of unshakeable courage. All of us who write are better off because he lived, worked and hoped.

He would have been surprised at that paragraph, even from Mencken. According to my father: "We were all down by the river one summer day, jumping from barge to barge, when Theo fell in. He couldn't swim, and with the help of another boy I hauled him out. Years later, Theo laughingly told me that if certain critics knew we had dragged him out of the river they would never have forgiven us." (From *My Brother, Theodore* by Edward Dreiser, *The Book Find News,* March 1946).

My father was an inveterate storyteller, reader, and frequently singer of little-known romantic and comic songs. The comic songs, for the most part, were written by his brother Al. The stories and plays I remember most vividly from childhood were Shakespeare's *Hamlet, Richard III,* and *Macbeth.* Longfellow and Poe also stand out in my memory. He always had a great interest in Indian lore, and that has influenced me to this day. He was an actor, a good one, and therefore was impressive when he read or recited. As a matter of fact, at age seventy-two, after one of the many memorial programs in New York after the death of Uncle Theo, I heard the then program director of WNEW say, "You have a wonderful recording voice, Mr. Dreiser..." and, jokingly, "If you ever need a job let us know." I loved to listen to him tell stories about his family, and until I read *Dawn,* my Uncle Theo's autobiography, my vision of the grandparents I had never known was quite different.

Those who knew the Ed Dreisers were aware that we were a close family. While socially very active during my father's theatrical career, after his serious accident which terminated his stage career and sent him into textiles, my parents were home-loving and togetherness was prevalent. We were all devoted to my maternal grandmother and her sister who lived with us as long as I can remember. I was as close to them as I was to my parents. So while I was without doubt an "overprotected" child, I unconsciously developed a strong sense of family unity. Consequently, in spite of the often-strained relationship between my mother and the Dreisers, I was anxious and ready and *did* in fact cultivate a warm friendship with father's brothers and sisters. I was most devoted to my Aunt Mame, although I knew well my Aunts Sylvia and Emma, and my Uncle Rome. My Aunt Claire died while I was still quite young so my memories of her are somewhat blurred, though pleasant.

It is necessary to mention here that my mother was a Roman Catholic. As I look back I realize she never really let it interfere with her own thinking unless it was convenient to do so. However, I remember well her attempts to use it to control me, since after all I was part Dreiser and needed strong limits set for my own well-being. As I grew up I broke away, intellectually at least, from the indoctrination I was subjected to but I believe in all such cases remnants haunt us like a distant voice through many adult years. I mention this because it may have been in some way responsible for my reaction to my Uncle Theo in later years. To this day I am *not* sure, and would not accept even Dr. Freud's voucher for it!

We do not have to be clinicians to know that we are greatly

influenced by our early environment, and that it contributes in varying degrees to what we are and ultimately become. No matter what school of thought professionals subscribe to, I believe we all go that far together.

Everyone, it seems, is now writing psychohistory and dissecting the great. With Dreiser subject matter, one has a tendency to concentrate on his sexual life, his "atrocious style," and his liberalism, without considering the integrity he had in probing for reasons. Asking one to be objective in this age of emotionalism is too much, I realize, but can't we at least be expected to be fair? Perhaps if we could show those who are peeved because he had both genius and women, that he never really had the women, they might come round to the viewpoint of writers like Fitzgerald, Anderson, Hemingway, and others who found Dreiser immensely useful. Sherwood Anderson even went so far as to call him the first American to tell the downright truth. Much of the recent biographical material written about Dreiser has been for Dreiser scholars, and not of general interest to the reading public. I can back up any claim I make in this book, heretofore disputed, by material in my possession. My objective, therefore, is to write this book for the reading public and to acquaint the youth of today with Theodore Dreiser, the uncle I knew, and his struggle to *understand* and be *understood*.

This is no easy task, due to my own involvement, my desire to avoid being too clinical, and the amount of material that needs to be included to set the record straight. Perhaps that is why I have started this book four different times! This time I intend to finish it.

When John Dos Passos heard of my plan, he said in a letter to me a few years before his death, "I hope you will look at him objectively but with affection."[1] That is my greatest wish.

Vera Dreiser

I

Vera and the Funeral of Theodore Dreiser

"Oh what is this that knows the road I came?"[1]

I had never before been in an embalming room. My attendance in the room at Forest Lawn on New Year's Eve with the sculptor Edgardo Simone was for the purpose of standing by while he made a death mask of my recently deceased uncle, Theodore Dreiser, and cast a mold of his right hand.

I was the only Dreiser present, having come from New York upon the receipt of Uncle Theo's widow, Helen's telegram on the morning of December 29, 1945, announcing his death, December 28. None of Helen's family was there.

I was with Simone because Helen Dreiser asked me to handle this task. Helen, my Uncle Theo's second wife, whom he had married only a year earlier, at my mother's insistence (although Helen had lived with him for twenty-three years as his common-law wife), was beside herself and emotionally in no state to cope with the realities involved in the burying of Theodore Dreiser. My own father, Ed Dreiser, who had been "the playmate and boon companion" of Theodore way back in Indiana, at seventy-two was the only brother still alive. The other boys and the five sisters were all dead. Since the trip was not an easy one, as war-time restrictions were still enforced and flight reservations were almost impossible to procure, he and my mother were unable to go. In addition, it had been an unusually cold winter. There were several feet of snow on the ground and the physical and emotional ordeal would have been too much for them. Consequently, the family duty fell to me. I discussed the plane problem with my husband, Alfred E. Scott, and somehow he and his brother managed to secure a seat for me on a plane scheduled to leave La Guardia Airport at 8 A.M., December 30. However, it began snowing hard again, and all planes were grounded that morning. I was told to wait nearby and that the airline would call me as soon as it was possible to take off. It was 10:15 P.M. EST before we got going and ours was the first flight to go. We landed passengers at Tri City, an unscheduled stop, then had wing trouble and landed in Phoenix, Arizona. It was my first flight and to say I was a bit edgy is quite an understatement. I arrived at Burbank Airport at 9:00 A.M. Pacific time on December 31. I expected to find Helen's sister, or other members of her family, but there were only a few good friends.

My composure deserted me as I approached the embalming room. I suddenly felt numb and possessed of an acute awareness of self. All the years of stored-up hungers, of loves and fears, of hostilities and unanswered questions welled up inside of me. For forty-eight hours I had traveled toward this destination, and now that I was on the threshold, I felt weak knowing I was to go through a strange ordeal. I steadied myself and prepared to enter when Simone turned to me, stopping abruptly in his walk, and said, "I will have to return to Hollywood, I've forgotten some special material. Do you mind waiting for me?"

He showed me his case with his equipment as if I would be able to know what was missing.

"I'm as helpless as a surgeon without a scalpel." He was a living portrait of frustration. "I'll only be gone a short while. Just relax and wait." He rushed away leaving me standing in the doorway, watching him go back down the long corridor until he turned a corner and disappeared out of sight. I knew he had to go now, as the following day was a holiday and all the stores would be closed. As in a trance, I turned the knob; it moved in my hand and the door slid open. I was inside.

The embalming room was very large and cold. It was in utter contrast to the outside of the building where the architect and the landscapers had outdone themselves to create an atmosphere of physical beauty and warmth to house those who were officially dead. In this embalming room, nothing had been done for those temporarily in limbo between their earthly home and the resting place selected for the grave. I walked around the stone-gray floor which resounded with my footsteps in sepulchral echo. In the left-hand corner of the room stood a concrete plinth. On the stone-gray slab, a white sheet drawn to his shoulders, lay Theodore Dreiser, my uncle, my friend. Death had requisitioned him.

Standing there, I looked *down* at him, at his calm face. It seemed strange, since in life I had always had to look *up* to him to see his eyes, his smile, his expressive massive brow. In death, he looked as I had never known him—young, virile, and possessed with a curiosity that was inscribed upon his face. Tears filled my eyes and although I was alone, I was embarrassed at my inability to hide my sorrow. I turned away and through the door which I had inadvertently left open, I saw two attendants rushing past with another corpse. It was a woman—her long black hair literally flying from her head. Like someone mesmerized I stepped from the room and watched until I saw them open large double doors and place her in an enormous room filled with the other waiting dead. I stood back in awe at the sight, frightened that I would be discovered witnessing something I possibly should not be, when suddenly a thought momentarily crossed my mind: "The dead ... are not alone!"

I walked back to the embalming room and entered, this time fearlessly closing the door behind me. It was my lot to be alone with my dead. I returned to the corpse and stood looking at the back of my uncle's head, at the neatly groomed snow-white hair, just beginning to thin on the top. For some unknown reason, I touched his bare shoulder, and then I touched his forehead. It was cold; the chill of his flesh met the dampness of my own fingers.

Slowly I turned back the sheet until the hand which had written his words was exposed. It was this hand which Simone had been commissioned to cast. I lifted my own hand and laid it upon my uncle's in a simple gesture of sympathy; in a final effort to feel some physical contact with someone I had dearly loved, someone who was a part of myself and my progeny, and someone with whom I would never again have physical communication. There were many questions which had to be answered. Why had I not sought him out earlier and learned to love and understand him as a man, a human being, my Uncle Theodore—the dead genius? I was seized with the sorrow which is customary when one is in confrontation with the dead. My feelings revolved around the fact that I had not answered his summons when he had begged me to come and work with him on his last project—*The Bulwark*. Perhaps, as a therapist with a record of success in dealing with the emotional problems of disturbed people, in addition to being his niece, the child of his favorite brother, I might have been able to alleviate some of his emotional problems.

Theodore Dreiser had been a very natural man and he came to a natural end, December 28, 1945, when he died at his Hollywood home of a heart attack preceded by a flare-up of kidney trouble. Although he had not been in the best of health, death came unexpectedly. He had been suffering from fatigue for quite some time. In June, 1944, during his last visit to New York, I persuaded him to visit my friend and colleague, Dr. Shailer U. Lawton. But Uncle Theo had not been a good patient. He had been more concerned with completing his work than keeping himself in proper physical condition. The following year, the last correspondence I had with him was a personal note which followed his formal Christmas card. In it he complained of feeling constantly tired and apologized for not writing more often. His words worried me but I still was not prepared for the telegram announcing his death: TEDDY WAS TAKEN ILL AT 3:00 A.M. AND RALLIED FOR A WHILE BUT PASSED AWAY 6:45 P.M. TODAY. WILL NOTIFY YOU OF FINAL ARRANGEMENTS. HELEN.

I was startled from my thoughts by a noise; Simone had returned. It had been two hours since he had departed and I had been left alone. He had his necessary materials and I stood back to watch him go to work, unhampered by my curious stares. I had never seen a death mask made. It was with something of a jolt that I saw him prepare a mixture which he applied to the still face of Uncle Theo. Simone was the artist at work. He watched the pasty substance harden and then he removed it with a sigh of contentment—it had not broken. When he pulled the hand mold and put it in the light for inspection, I stared, a little horror-stricken. The hairs from the forearm and the fingers of my uncle were visible in the plaster form.

At that moment my thoughts wandered back to another New Year's Eve in 1922 when I was a adolescent girl of fourteen years of age. We had been invited to a soiree given by Mame and her husband, Austin Brennan, at their home at 119 West 11th Street. Uncle Theo was residing in a nearby apartment.[2] My mother, who was not lacking in manipulative powers, had decided we should all be together, and arranged our invitation. I was tall for my age and had determined for quite some time I was going to wear one of my mother's dresses—a pale lavender, spangled frock. I had long, coppery red hair almost to my waist, which my mother took great pains to curl and properly coiffure. I had managed to slip the dress into my closet and when we left for the party I was wearing my mother's gown and—incongruously—Mary Jane strap slippers! When we arrived at Mame's and I presented myself, my mother, instead of being annoyed, was amused with my attire. Shortly after our arrival, Mame announced, "I think Theo and Helen are going to drop by." There was a moment of silence. I suppose everyone was tense, not knowing what either my mother or father would do. My father had not seen Helen since he had first met her and called her an "adventuress." My mother knew of Helen and her relationship with Theodore. When she visited Mame and I was with her, I was cautioned against mentioning Aunt Jug, Uncle Theo's first wife. Mame would talk to my mother about Helen and how she was hanging on to Theo and in the next breath she would criticize Jug for not divorcing Theo and giving him his freedom. To which my mother would always reply that it was her opinion that Theodore *did not want to be free!* She felt that Jug was his legal "ace-in-the-hole" against a matrimonial commitment with another woman.

When it was announced that Uncle Theo was coming, I was tingling with excitement. I had heard a great deal about my uncle, and although I had previously encountered him when I was a child, I now had great curiosity about him. I knew he was famous, and with the precocity of a half-child, half-woman, I was inquisitive as to why his life's affairs were unmentionable in our home, and why my mother disliked him so intensely. I was very excited over the prospect of our New Year's Eve encounter. I think I was the first to see him coming down the stairs in the house near Washington Square, escorting Helen who was to meet my father face to face for the first time since her liaison with Uncle Theo had begun. I do not know if she knew of his opinion of her, and I am not certain if she was ever aware of the fact that he never altered his original judgment.

I remembered there were records playing, and dancing. The atmosphere was festive and once the discomfort of the arrival of Helen and Theo had passed without incident, the mood of all of the guests was that of conviviality. There were no recriminations or censures. Uncle Theo was a quiet man, seated apart, removed from the activities. I urged him to dance and he said he couldn't. (This confession was true; his coordination was awkward and his sense of rhythm static.) But I was persistent and—used to getting my way—I would not be content until he finally satisfied my whim by getting on the floor to dance with me. We must have made quite a sight—me, in my grown-up dancing frock, and he in his rigid, well-tailored attire. He stepped all over my shoes, but I kept telling him what a good dancer he was. Contrary to popular opinion about him, he had a fine sense of the ridiculous and the unique, and possessed an individualized sense of humor which only a few people of his acquaintance ever appreciated. In a few moments cavorting around with me, he was no longer the grave, serious-minded man with deep-set eyes, heavy brooding eyebrows, and an eternal expression of gloom and despair. He was bumbling about with a niece in a lavender frock which belonged to her mother.

Uncle Theo and Helen left before midnight. Mame said he was going to a private celebration at the very exclusive White Rats Club. When he left, the party ended for me. I was very impressed with myself and my Uncle Theo. I talked about him all the way home. Perhaps as many children do, I sensed his inner loneliness, his shyness, and the true kindness which lay beneath his gruff exterior. From that night, I identified with him, protecting him and defending him against the vocal onslaughts of my mother, who, I believe, from that night resolved that our social contacts would be seldom, if ever.

When Simone had packed his gear and prepared to leave, I walked away with him, my mind still filled with the acute visions of the past New Year's Eve in contrast to the present one, when my Uncle Theo lay dead.

The rest of that day is almost a blank in my memory due, no doubt, to the constant flow of adrenalin helping me to perform what was expected. I know Simone took me home where I had to talk to those who were concerned with funeral arrangements, substituting for the shattered widow who said she refused to argue over the type of service. All aspects of death, as those of life, have moments of comedy as well as tragedy. It becomes the acting out of the theatrical dictum—the show must go on. Helen was

Charles Chaplin and Will Durant were among the pallbearers at Theodore Dreiser's funeral

preparing to attend the funeral of her husband in a borrowed coat. I remember insisting how inappropriate this would be and finally convinced her to buy a handsome broadtail jacket (which I told her she could wear in New York when she came to talk to my uncle's publisher and also when she went to visit her family in Oregon). She was so pleased that I had encouraged her to make this necessary purchase, that in gratitude she bought me a stunning black wool suit.

A gravedigger's strike delayed the funeral for a few days. This was an ironic note in view of Uncle Theo's sympathetic view toward strikers, which must have gone unnoticed by most of the mourners but which I have always felt would have struck a cord in Uncle Theo's organ of humor. In addition there was a great deal of arguing over the form the actual funeral service should take. It was finally determined that it should be a Congregationalist service conducted by Dr. Allen Hunter, who had been friendly with my uncle in his latter days. Helen picked "a beautiful dark rich red mahogany casket lined with a beautiful delicate shade of velvet." (Helen's own description.)

The next remembrance I have is of the funeral itself held January 3, 1946, at Forest Lawn's Church of the Recessional. Handel's "Largo" was played, as was Bach's "Come Kindly Death." Dr. Hunter conducted the services while John Henry Lawson delivered his tribute to Uncle Theo. Then Charles Chaplin, who had been a good friend, delivered the final requiem, reading aloud a poem Uncle Theo had written a few years earlier:

> O space!
> Change!
> Toward which we run
> So gladly,
> Or from which we retreat
> In terror—
> Yet that promises to bear us
> In itself
> Forever.
>
> O what is this
> That knows the road I came?...

The narrow cradle in which his casket was placed was covered with flowers and held open for a last glimpse of Theodore Dreiser in his black lecture suit with the stiff, white-starched shirt, the familiar bow tie—an attire which accentuated his snow-white hair and his face "made up" by the mortuary cosmetician. Before the lid was lowered over the body, Helen laid her poem, "To A Poet," beside him. The final home of the man who had been born in poverty, who had been spokesman for the poor and underprivileged, was an expensive burial lot, number 1132, in the Whispering Pines section of Forest Lawn, California.

2

John Paul Dreiser, Sr.

"For I have made me a garden under the shadow of swords"

The massive ship was being guided into New York harbor to deposit its weary travelers. Among the passengers was a young man from Mayen, Germany. He stared with his two dark, deeply set eyes. Through the steerage porthole he caught a glimpse of the statuesque welcoming bronze lady atop her pedestal on Liberty Island. Beyond was the Battery with the etched outline of the strange new skyscraper city of Manhattan. The stack blows announced as Ellis Island, the port of disembarkation for the immigrants. The man's slender, sensitive face was strained with fatigue and nervous worry. To calm himself and reassure his tortured stomach which had been victimized with constant retching since his departure, he clutched his simple rosary and began to pray silently to himself.

The step of disembarkation was one of the many giant steps being taken by the throng of voyagers seeking a new "fatherland." For the young man, my grandfather, John Paul Dreiser, it was perhaps the most important step taken since his very first because it was a step designating independence not only from the land of his birth, but from the protection and comfort of the prosperous German family who had adopted him shortly after his birth on September 9, 1821. Who his own parents were he had never known, never sought to know. He had matured in the environment of his adopted family and contented himself with the relationships offered to him, including visiting French cousins from Alsace-Lorraine, who taught him a smattering of French patois.

Many Germans were fleeing Germany, seeking the protection of the United States. If one were going to make the break it was well to do it while one was still young, while one had a strong body and a facile mind. Work, he had heard from the relatives of those who had gone in advance, was not hard to obtain in the new country where riches were beyond belief. John Paul reassured himself that for a man with a trade, and a trade as useful as his, employment would be easy to obtain. That he would have to cope with another language did not deter him for he, under normal circumstances, had an innate courage and a degree of self-confidence which at times bordered on stubbornness.

The mill town to which my grandfather went in search of a job, a home, and a new future, was quite unlike any environment he had ever before been exposed to. A small community, it was controlled by the owners of the mill. It was completely Anglo-Saxon in design, having been imitated in every detail from the machines to the operation of the management. The employers were all either of Anglo-Saxon descent, or poor, illiterate Irish who were willing to work for minimum wages in order to remain alive in the "new country." John Paul had come from a conservative German home which was not affluent in any sense of the word, but which had never lacked more than the comforts of life. That way of life consisted of good food, body warmth and comfort, and a style of living which induced good health. In his new home he encountered a parsimony he had never before experienced and he was almost totally without means of communication. He spoke very little English and those few words he knew were uttered with an unmistakable foreign accent. The only person with whom he had any identity was the head of the mill–the weaver to whom he had been recommended–and he found this man, transplanted, to be arrogant and demanding: He did not wish to talk about Germany and resented any attempt on John Paul's part to start a conversation in their native tongue.

John Paul was confused, and he was lonely. Being somewhat shy by nature, he withdrew more and more into himself and his ability to learn another language became stunted in his misery. And there was the matter of his religion, his inner faith.

The mill was in a Calvinist-oriented locale. The only church in

John Paul Dreiser

the community was a Congregationalist church. It stood in its stark white simplicity like a little white clown, its peaked tower reaching above the trees and buildings like a thrust of purity against the bleak New England horizon.

From the Irish girl workers he discovered where the nearest church of his faith was. He soon learned that to be a Romanist in the area was not an easy task. To travel to Mass was an ordeal and to arrive there and be a part of an Irish-Catholic congregation talking, talking, talking, inside and outside the church, was not consistent with his past remembrances of the solitary comfort and the physical beauty of the church he had previously known.

He became disenchanted and one day he learned through a casual acquaintance that there was a predominantly German settlement in nearby (or so he thought) Indiana, where they were hiring German workers and paying good wages and where the German settlers were establishing a sort of little Germany in the country they had adopted. This time John Paul did some investigating, and the more he learned the more Indiana seemed to be the ideal spot for him. Indiana ... he liked the sound of the word. There was rhythm and vigor and the youthful spirit of colonization he had dreamed of. New England was already old. One day he collected his pay and departed.

It was a long haul to Indiana. It was a journey of physical labor for John Paul because the distance was much greater than he had imagined and his funds were limited. He stopped and worked until he had accumulated sufficient money to move farther westward. By the time he reached Kosciusko County near Silver Lake, he was ready to accept any way of life that was tolerable and offered some degree of security. He had come a long way from Germany. He was still a young man, but he was tired. The rich Indiana countryside, with the rolling green farmlands on the banks of the Wabash, reminded him of his homeland. The people jogged his memory with recollections of the family he had left behind—frugal, healthy farmers who lived well. It was a community of good neighbors who specialized in handcrafts. They were bound together in their farming projects, their friendliness, and their acceptance of the native Indians and their religion. The place to which John Paul Dreiser had come in his wanderings was a Mennonite community.

It was here he met Sarah Schnepp (a contraction of Schanab), twelve years his junior, born May 8, 1833. For John Paul and

Sarah it was indeed love at first sight, love for eternity. Sarah possessed all of the physical beauty which is associated with the sign under which she was born. She was earthborn with an innate zest for life and a true love of nature. In his words she was "as lovely as a garden of roses." Her natural personality was in open conflict with the obdurate life of her religious parents, but she had no opportunity for open rebellion. In the world into which she had been born and reared, children were seen and not heard. Mennonite girls were not allowed to learn to read or to write, their pursuits being confined to household chores in which they were all proficient and many quite skilled. Sarah possessed too vivid an imagination to be classified in the latter category and upon occasion she had to be reprimanded for her negligence in the timing of her baking. Her mind wandered into other places; she was listening to other voices. She admittedly believed in "fairies."

When John Paul Dreiser entered her life he was as close to a young girl's idea of a romantic hero as she was ever to encounter. He was tall, lean but muscular, and he had the haunting eyes and the musical voice of a poet. Even his thick German accent gave him a quality of mystery. There was an immediate rapport between the two people. Paul's long period of silence ended. He told the girl of the many experiences he had already encountered in his travels. To her John Paul seemed a Gulliver, a Marco Polo. Perhaps she would never see the places he spoke of–but if she chose him for a mate at least she would have visited a large part of the world through his eyes. She fell asleep one night after a long talk with John Paul–he had told her he loved her!

"I will have to leave, first–to go and find work where I can practice my trade ...," John Paul had said. And so he left to find work in the woolen mills in Dayton, promising to send for Sarah as soon as possible.

John Paul had not reckoned with the impetuosity of Sarah nor was he aware that the repressed spirit of the girl would inspire her to leave her home and parents without asking permission. Nor could he imagine the wrath her action would incur. Her father, although not openly defiant, had been apathetic toward the advances John Paul Dreiser was making because of the age difference, and because of the religious barrier. Sarah's father was anti-Catholic to the degree of fanaticism. When he learned that his daughter had eloped with the German-born, German-speaking, German-Catholic John Paul Dreiser, he closed his doors, and in the

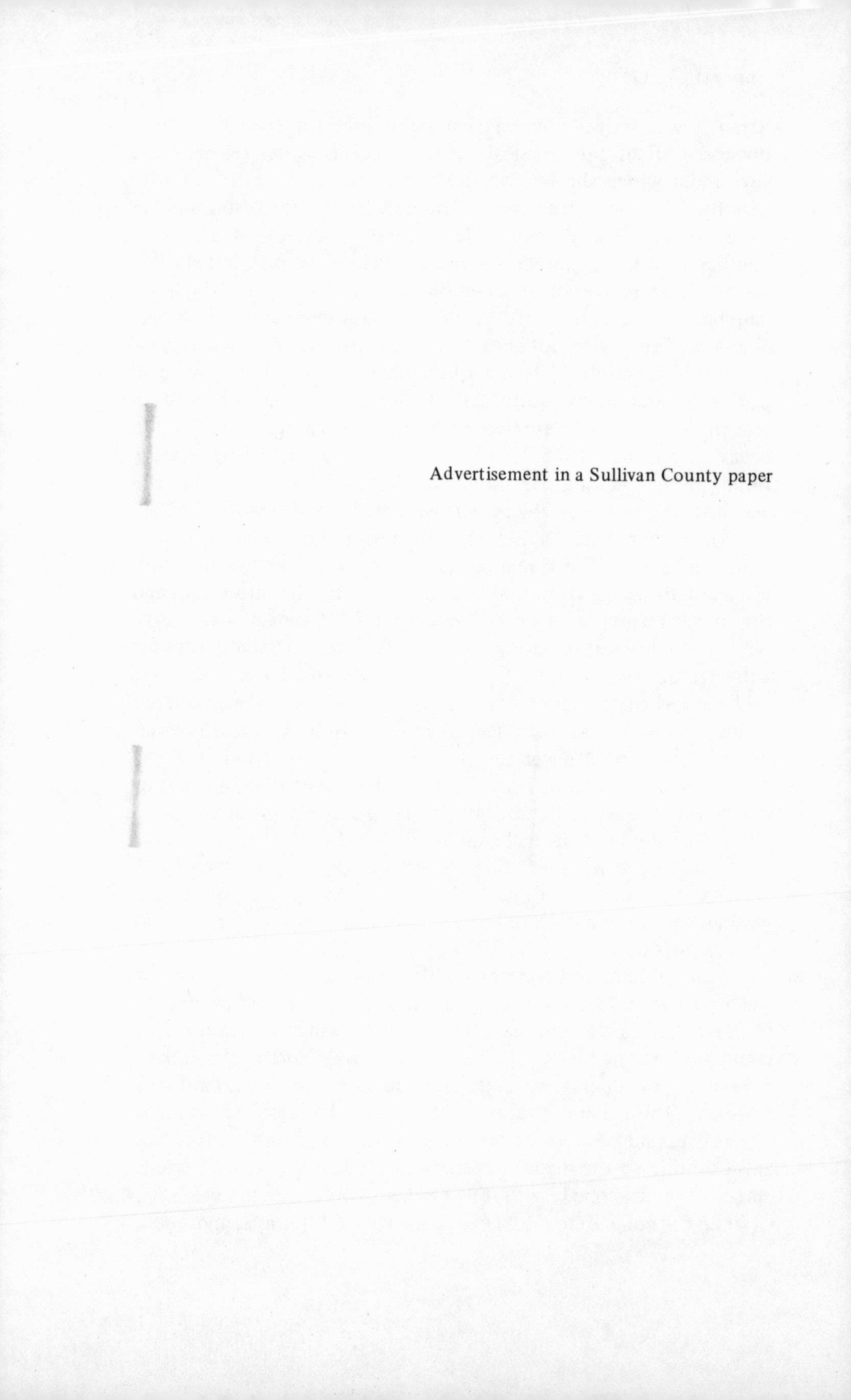

Advertisement in a Sullivan County paper

nal visit to his
ns us that he

—

the only rain
ntire month of
t. The drouth
ning the wheat
had been very
ard by early
ite promising.
will help the
ass were much
n was still do-
n late was very
medy these de-
thers in better

—

that hereafter
unty collectors
s for sale. An
ween Mr. Har-
hich the latter

—

rs ago, Mr. Mi-
ed his life for
Life Insurance
three months
y a draft for
. Stewart, the
the following

ay 21, 1870.
ce Co, at New
Dr.
.....$2500 00
..... 45 37

.....$2545 37
36 12
9 75
145 87

Sullivan Woolen Mills.

—

PAUL DREISER,

Woolen Dealer and Manufacturer of Woolen Goods,

Sullivan, Indiana.

—

Keeps constantly on hand, and for sale at the lowest cash prices,

JEANS AND SATINETS,

Cassimeres, Blankets, Coverlets, Stocking Yarn, &c.,

Or, I will take wool in exchange for any of the above articles, or for custom work, at its cash value. Particular attention given to

CUSTOM CARDING AND SPINNING,

Which we will do on as short notice, and as well as any Factory in the State, and at customary prices.

The Highest Cash Price Paid for Wool.

PAUL DREISER.

June 2, 1870.–3mo

DIVORCE NOTICE.

The State of Indiana, Sullivan County, In the Common Pleas Court, August Term, 1870.

FAI

I hope to rec
Cash paid fo

Sullvan, I

APPLI

NOTICE
the tow
of Hamilton
diana, that c
1870, (it bei
make applic
missioners of
license to sel
intoxicating
quart at a ti
it to be used
scribed prem
A one stor
Scott's Liver
south-west c
of Sullivan,
tween Wash
by John Sec
I will pro
that I posses
entitle me b
may12 3t.

HAR
S

NO. 9, CO

Shingles
AGENT
BUCKEY
HO

three lights, bobbing lightly to and fro, processional wise. They approached very near her—almost intentionally so, it seemed to her, then fluttered on, thistledown wise, over a rail fence and into the woods beyond."[2]

Sarah gasped, "My three children! They are going to die!"

She left her brother's house as suddenly as she had come. She returned home, quieted and considerably more considerate and apprehensive. In a very short time the deaths came—one, two, and three. When the third child had died and was about to be removed from the house by the undertaker, Sarah threw herself on her knees beside the dead body in the little pine casket and wept inconsolably as she vowed in prayer, "Forgive me, O God. Forgive me and let me bear again and I promise with all my heart, with all by body, I promise even if I have ten more children I shall never complain! Never! Forgive me, Father and give me one more chance to prove my worth to be a good mother."[3]

The prayers of Sarah were answered and in the course of the years ten children were born to John Paul and Sarah Dreiser: Paul, born 1859; Rome, 1860; Mame, 1861; Em, 1863; Teresa, 1864; Sylvia, 1866; Al, 1867; Claire, 1868; Theo, 1871; Ed, 1873.[4]

John Paul Dreiser was a man of driving ambition, seeking success and gradually achieving it. In 1867 when there were six children, he moved his family from Terre Haute to nearby Sullivan where he went into business on his own. The building was owned by Chauncey Rose, the Terre Haute capitalist who approved John Paul's enterprising plan. John Paul was to persuade the farmers in the territory to bring him their fleece for storage. He would transform the fleece into wool and they would realize their money much more rapidly than under the present system. John Paul had it all figured out, and the farmers with whom he talked were enthusiastic and agreed to store their fleece with him. John Paul invested heavily in machinery.

John Paul grew in eminence in the little town and his dream of wealth seemed about to become a reality until early one spring day when within the shed of his mill, crammed to bursting with good fleece stored by the neighboring farmers, a fire broke out. A careless millhand lighting his corn pipe did not see the tiny spark that fell as lightly as a snowflake and buried itself in the folds of young lamb's wool. It smoldered until a brisk March wind blew ferociously and strengthened the ember into a roaring blaze. Dawn was approaching in the sullen sky of the raw day. Sarah was asleep in her warm, comfortable feather bed, when she heard the voice of her husband crying the most anguished scream she was ever to hear.

She saw John Paul run like a crazy man in his long woolen underwear, barefoot and barehanded, waving frantically, as futilely against the wild fury of the fire as Don Quixote battling his formidable windmill.

Helpless, Sarah clothed herself in a woolen wrapper and rushed to the side of her husband who was throwing buckets of icy water against the burning shed. She tried to get him to put on the jacket and the boots she had brought out. But he was a man possessed until his energy was drained and he collapsed by the mass of ashes which had been the foundation of his fortune.

The full meaning of the tragedy did not register until the realization that the bounty had been uninsured. John Paul assured his trusting neighbors they would be repaid–*dollar for dollar!*

The reverses incurred heaped upon the family two decades of living hell. Sarah watched John Paul attempt to rebuild his little kingdom. He worked twenty hours out of the twenty-four, instructing his workers in the architectural design of the new buildings which would be nonflammable. Just as the work neared completion, and he was standing, shouting orders for the installation of a ceiling beam, the beam slipped from the worker's hand and fell, crashing with a mighty thud upon the skull of John Paul, knocking him unconscious.

For weeks he lay in a coma, hallucinating or sleeping. All of his spoken words were German, but nevertheless, Sarah knew he was in deep conversation with his God. For his life on earth he was bargaining with his soul in the hereafter. Never again would he be concerned with the now, the present. He would exist in dreams of the hereafter into which he ultimately would escape in death and one in which there would be rewards for his prayers, tithes, and faith.

My Uncle Theodore was born one year after this accident when his father had become a man almost crazed by the sin and shame of debt. The ambition he had once known was replaced by a wild craving to appease the God of his faith. Although he was in the prime of his life and expert in his trade, he gave up hope for the future, turned his thoughts solely to his debts, and hoarded pennies for his salvation and the salvation of his family. He was obsessed.

What happened to John Paul Dreiser was *minimal brain dysfunction.* At the time his accident occured medical science did not have any comprehension of how to cope with a patient suffering from such a catastrophe. Years after my Uncle Theo's death, I had the privilege of meeting and working with a remarkable woman, Camilla M. Anderson, M.D., a psychiatrist who made a special study of minimal brain dysfunction (MBD) and who has authored many books on the subject. I described my grandfather's accident and the resultant change in his behavior and she rendered me the following opinion: "There seem to be two possible effects. One would be that as a result of the head injury there was a resulting pattern of preservation or endless preoccupation with one thing or another—what might resemble a 'repetition compulsion'—and religion was the area selected for preoccupation. Preservation is a kind of 'stickiness' and it is felt by those affected as being a nonacceptable, disturbing factor.

"The other possibility would be that having been spared by God from death due to the blow on the head, it was incumbent on him to 'pay God back,' so to speak, by keeping God ever in the forefront of his mind and trying to influence others to do the same."

John Paul Dreiser awoke from his long sleep deaf in one ear. It was almost as if he had closed this organ of hearing to all sound except the command of God. He moved his family back to Terre Haute where he obtained work sporadically. During his prolonged illness, in addition to the debts he had incurred due to the fire, Sarah had inadvertently handed his deeds and trusts over to business associates who came and pretended to be helping. In reality they were swindling her out of possessions that were legally John Paul's. Poverty was now their accepted identity and survival depended upon individual wits to ward off outright destitution.

Both John Paul and Sarah were psychic to a large degree, and it was this extraordinary contact with the supernatural that helped bind them together. The house they occupied in Terre Haute just before Theo was born seemed haunted with "supernatural occurrences and visitations." Not only did Sarah see the strange visitors, but John Paul also saw them. They were disturbing visitors. They tumbled tables, they spilled food, they entered into the children's beings, causing them to speak in unfamiliar tongues, words of the devil. John Paul sent for the local priest to exorcise the fiends which had moved into the Dreiser household.

The holy water was splashed, here, there, everywhere, and the holy words reverberated throughout the frame building. John Paul was satisfied. He no longer saw the evil, nor heard the evil. But Sarah did. She was frightened. There was a new creature moving within her womb and when he was born, "puny beyond belief, all ribs and hollow eyes, ailing and whimpering," Sarah was terrified. All of her other children had been beautiful, healthy beyond all expectations, giggly and gurgly, the way newborn cherubs should be. What had God wrought in this ugly duckling, named Theodore Herman?

In her distress Sarah disobeyed her husband, and sought the help of an old crone who was believed to have occult powers. Her advice was pure witch-doctor cant, but Sarah was convinced that her son, Theo, survived by the use of a piece of string, an incantation—*"was ich hab, nehm ab; was ich thu, nehm zu!"*—and a secret ritual performed in the light of the moon!

Two years later, Sarah gave birth to the last of her children, my father, Ed.

The Dreisers were a chaotic, hard-pressed family. The atmosphere was loaded with superstition, fanaticism, ignorance, poverty, constant humilitation. The day commenced as the family knelt around the father who sought from God a blessing for the day, and the day ended as they again knelt in prayer and asked for a blessing for the night.

John Paul had become so out of touch with the children he had fathered that his only recourse to control was a physical punishment. Family quarrels were frequent and tensions affected all of them. Young Theo developed a nervous stutter and he cried easily. It was during this period that the foundation of his neurosis was laid. In the parochial schools he encountered the same Hell-Fire and Damnation existence he knew in his home with his father. The nuns terrified him, and the discipline almost stunted his fine brain. For the first years of his life, in Terre Haute, the family was always moving, moving, moving out of necessity. In seven years they lived in five different houses.

These were not the homes John Paul Dreiser had envisioned, or struggled to procure for his Sarah and their brood. But there was no way he could know or be advised that the brain damage he had suffered had removed his controls, paralyzed his ambition. It is probable that the basic tragedy of the Dreiser family was the accident suffered by John Paul and not understood by either medical science or his intimates. Neither his children nor his contemporaries were ever able to provide an explanation for his strange life. John Paul Dreiser, one of the genetic sources of the genius genes of Paul and Theo, has always been an enigma to all the biographers of both of his gifted sons.

But the importance and strength of these genes cannot be denied, nor overlooked. Their manifestation survived in the music of one man, the written words of another.

3

Sarah Schnepp Dreiser

"A Vision from a Mountain Top, Maybe"

Theodore Dreiser was born and spent his childhood in that period of American history which saw the country change from an enormous undeveloped wilderness to a giant of technology. Terre Haute, the scene of the formative years of his life, was atypical of the small town that emerged throughout the country following the Civil War. The Midwest population was a composite of factory workers from the East, refugee farmers from the New England states, and immigrants from Europe, all seeking a new way of life in the industries that were rapidly developing. Things were changing swiftly, almost too swiftly. In forty years the population increased from thirteen million to forty million. It became apparent that if farming were going to survive, it too would have to be industrialized. Gone was the concept of farmers such as Sarah Schnepp's own father had been—a man who tilled the soil with his own hands, housed, fed, and clothed his family with the results of his own labors. In time there would be no more of those communities where neighbor helped neighbor and the group was molded into a solid identity through common interest and religious belief.

To accomplish the mechanization of farming, the reaper, the threshing machine, the twin bindery, and mechanical planters were invented and put to use. The Midwest—the corn belt—was the hub of the factories which manufactured these implements. During this period the United States Patent Office granted more than 500,000 patents–the telephone, the Kodak camera, the typewriter, the sewing machine were but a few of the inventions which soon became household commodities. But more than any single force that affected the lives of the people born in the latter half of the nineteenth century, the railroad was the most influential. Small towns such as Terre Haute overnight altered from homesteading communities to a site for factories processing and packaging food for America. Nearby were the coal mines, and when the railroad connected Terre Haute with Chicago, the "first city of the plains," its destiny was carved.

It was Theodore Dreiser himself who exclaimed, "What a period!"

It was a period which was to temper his memory with personal impressions and opinions:

> I can never look on crowded tenements, or small shabby cottages in cheap, mean streets, or poorly clothed children, men or women with grimy hands and faces and a weary troubled look without reverting in thought to this particular period of my life and wishing without quite knowing how to point out a way by which life might be better organized, wishing that it would not permit the untrained or the inadequate to stew in their own misery.[1]

As John Paul Dreiser's inability to provide a living for his family became apparent, Sarah took in boarders, but since skill in matters of economy were not one of her virtues, her ventures failed. The words of Dickens's "Mr. Micawber" were to have significance: "Annual income twenty pounds, annual expenditure nineteen, nineteen six, result happiness. Annual income twenty pounds, annual expenditure twenty pounds eight and six, result misery!" In due time Sarah took in washing, did household cleaning, anything to keep her and her brood from starving. Obviously the mother assuming the role of head of the household had a severe psychological impact upon all of the children. It had permanently damaging consequences for Theo.

If the father had been impaired by his accident, Sarah was impaired by a dramatic role she created for herself–that of a martyr. It was a role she imprinted upon the mind of Theo by constantly telling him of her sacrifices, and denying him any opportunity to identify with his father. Later he referred to himself as a "mother-child."

A child receives messages from his mother that program him for his later life. She is the pivot, the pace-setter, and she is the first female image known in life which has far-reaching implications for the manner in which other people are perceived. Sarah had some interesting notions about the rearing of her children. If she had not been as she was, Theodore Dreiser would have been a lot more comfortable with himself and with life; but he might not have written such books as he did—all related to his creativity and neurosis.

Sarah Dreiser bore thirteen children; ten lived. Theodore Dreiser said that of the ten the only one who could classify as a "normal child," was my father, Ed, who was from birth very active—played baseball, swam, climbed fences—created a world away from the Dreisers. Sarah would send him on errands, but he would get involved in something and forget his assignment, or forget to come home. By so doing he escaped many of the things which ruled the others and consequently became a fine husband and father.

Theo was enormously sensitive, shy, and withdrawn. Of all the boys he was unfortunate in being, not only the weakest, but the most unattractive. This made him the most vulnerable and the most receptive to Sarah's complaints. She lured him with her eerie charms, such as her ability to tame wild birds, tell tall tales. I am convinced from the stories my father has told me (confirmed by Mame, Sylvia, and Rome) that she was a sweet, charming women, and a passively controlling woman who, unfortunately, had a disturbing influence on most of her children's lives. Whenever any problem arose, instead of weathering the storm with her husband and family, she moved the children away to greener pastures, to someplace designated by her dreamy conception of life as a better, happier place. They were never allowed the security of roots, friends, consistent schooling, and, most important of all, a chance to observe, firsthand, the struggles of their father. Their father was viewed as a failure; she, the mother, was the focal point and constant star in a hostile world.

> Never have I known a man more obsessed by a religious belief. In short, the endless vagaries and complications of mood and

> conduct which followed upon [his] accident succeeded eventually in impressing me as not only fantastic but pathetic. I looked upon him as mentally a little weak.[2]

It would appear that Sarah never got exactly what she wanted out of her marriage, or what she imagined marriage was going to be like when she ran away to marry a man for whom she must have had some respect. After his physical impairment and failures, she constantly communicated to her children that their father was not a good provider and that he—and he, alone—was responsible for their misery. She need not have said this in so many words, but she conveyed the thought to them.

Young Theo continuously heard her say that she was "accursed" and "wished she were dead." He would cling to her and try to be "good," so she would not disappear. She had made him feel responsible for her *life;* if he were bad she would die; if she died, he, too, would cease to exist. The strain and tension on a child caught in this type of vise is almost unbearable to consider.

Sarah has been credited with showering Theo with love, and making him her favorite because of his physical weaknesses. It is more logical that Sarah's emotional needs were so great that she used all of her children to fulfill them, but Theo, because of his sensitivity and shyness, emerged as the object of her special attention. For example, Theo as a small child sat at her feet while a toe was protruding out of her slipper, and she said, "Aren't you sorry for your poor mother's shoes?" Theodore Dreiser, in describing this incident in *Dawn,* says that it was the birth of "tenderness and sympathy" in him, that he was moved to tears. It is far more likely that he must have been frightened to tears by a message that conveyed clearly that there was little joy in wifehood and motherhood, and there was no particular good in being a man. It could have made him feel that the impregnation of woman by man was evil, for look what it had done to his mother. She was shabby and unhappy and wished only to die!

Theodore Dreiser became to some extent an extension of Sarah, and from this she derived her emotional satisfaction. My father, Ed, in describing Sarah, seemed to feel she became depressed when her dreams did not become reality. She depended upon fantasy and lacked a sense of responsibility. How can one be responsible if the world will not allow one's heart's desire? Undoubtedly, she incorporated young Theo into her system and he very nearly didn't get out. In fact, he probably didn't escape but was strong enough to survive in spite of her unconscious crippling influences.

Sarah is usually portrayed as a helpless, gentle, vague, and misty woman, but from today's point of view she doesn't seem to have been so very helpless. A close look at her approach reveals a controlling mother who was quite self-preoccupied, to the extent that she could subject her children to difficulties beyond the scope of their sensibilities. Once when things were bad financially and they were threatened with eviction, she sent her young daughter to beg from a prominent lumber dealer. Of the fifty dollars the girl succeeded in obtaining, the drunken brother, Rome, took all but fifteen, but that is unimportant compared to the picture of a mother who could expose her daughter to such a humiliating experience.

She seemed to control subtly, with charm and seductivity. She could be gentle and lovely, and she could be cruel. Occasionally she would threaten to leave home and abandon them all. Once she packed her bag and took off into the cornfield at the side of the house, while her children stood by crying and watched her go. My father recalled that Theo fainted. Such actions were the double message system of a woman who could treat her children as extensions of herself, on one hand, and as disassociated implements, on the other. To a child plain rejection is easier to explain and handle than rejection under the guise of love. The child must believe in love, and when it is suffused with insecurity and anguish, it becomes an unstable factor through life. In Theo's case, his mother's behavior did great damage to his masculinity. He was always with her; while some of her other children managed to become physically disengaged. His identification with her was such that in later life he was in competition with women, resentful of them, disappointed in them while under the pretext of being in love with them. He was able to write identical love letters to two women at the same time. Yet he confessed to me he did not think he had ever really been in love.

Every normal little boy loves his mother in a *forbidden* way, but passes through this phase easily when other family relations are normal. In Theo's case they were not. Sarah burdened Theo as a young child with her dependent and possessive love. His mother was seductive while he was still a young child. He developed a *fixation*.

According to Karl Menninger, "This attraction to the mother is not comparable to the adult sex interest of a man in a woman, but depends upon infantile attachment which is partly dependence and partly hostility, but very little *love.*"

The women these men consort with later are treated as protecting mothers or as simple diversions. Sexual impotence (either all or partial) represents a way in which fear and resentment are expressed by involuntary reactions. This is an unconscious mechanism.

In a way most of Theo's sexual endeavors were either unconsciously seen as *forbidden,* or they were the direct expression of resentment. In any case his impotence protected him.[3]

The sources of Sarah's problems are mostly confused and complicated, but regardless of whether she felt betrayed in her marriage, or guilt in abandoning her own family by running away to marry (although she never made any attempt at reconciliation with her parents) is unimportant. The fact is, she deflected her resentment of her husband, and the message of his neglect was communicated most loudly to Theo. My own father remembered his father warmly and had no recollection of the abject suffering Theo describes in his writings. In fact, Theodore's perception of John Paul seems to have been determined by his particular relationship with his mother.

There is no question that John Paul was floundering in his desire to implant discipline and dignity in the home to which he was unable to make any substantial financial contributions, and that his religious obsession was catastrophic to the rudderless household.

> I have described my father as a religious enthusiast. At that time, he was a morose and dour figure, forlorn and despondent, tramping about the house, his hands behind his back and occasionally talking to himself. One of his worst phases was his conviction that there was refuge in religion, more and more self-humiliation before a Creator who revealed Himself only through the forms and ceremonies of the Catholic Church. At any rate, here was I at six years of age, installed along with my younger sister and brother in St. Joseph's German Catholic School–a pay school, although right around the corner was a free public school.[4]

Children are usually confused about whom to blame in parent difficulties. The fusion of love and hate is difficult to handle. It is ironic that in the Dreiser household, the father's quest for order and obedience was bypassed, and the greatest unkindness, Sarah's laxity and permissiveness, was perceived as desirable.

By today's standards, there is no question that the Terre Haute Dreiser family would have been regarded as a community welfare problem, a chore for a social worker. Both parents would have been criticized for their behavior, the older boys, Paul and Rome, regarded as juvenile delinquents; the younger would possibly have been placed with relatives or in foster homes. The Dreiser girls were certainly "choice morsels," sought after and waited upon, but their social activities brought forth wrath and indignation from their father. They were considered "shameless."

When Al, Claire, Theo, and Ed were very small, Sarah plotted and executed one of her major attempts at bringing reality to one of her fantasies. Paul had been sent to St. Meinrad's Seminary to study for the priesthood and to atone for his early encounters with the law; Rome had left home for good, heading west for a career of ranching, mining, gambling, drinking, and carousing with women; John Paul, Sr., had managed to obtain employment for himself in a nearby carpet mill and the older girls were working in the same factory as loom hands. To Sarah, it seemed the ideal time to move with her little ones and start life anew. Escape had always gripped her imagination and she dreamed of a new chapter of adventure and happiness. For a reason which has never been explained, she literally dumped the oldest remaining boy, Al, on her sister. The result was a trauma of such proportions that he eventually became the "lost sheep" of the family, disappearing entirely as time passed. The story of Al is significantly poignant and tragic because he remained in the memory of both my Uncle Theo and my father as the most talented of the Dreisers when a child.

Sarah's breaking up of the family was sad. John Paul, seated in his Windsor chair with his children gathered around him, sang to them in German, "Now we are about to travel out of the gate of the city, I sit down to say good-bye, good-bye, good-bye, good-bye, farewell!" My father remembered the scene and often sang the old German folk song but Theodore erased all such memories from his brain. He could not bear the pain of his childhood experiences. He wore his scars in the manner of a junkie whose flesh tells the story of a life so unbearable that the only hope is an injection of a miracle drug of happiness mainlined through his veins into his life bloodstream.

The trip to Vincennes left an indelible print upon the mind of young Theodore. Physically, Vincennes was quite different from Terre Haute. The streets were narrow and winding and the French love of red and white prevailed in the architecture. The tall french windows in the houses were shuttered, and when night fell, the wooden blinds closed the interior completely from the outside world. The little town had been settled by the French and the streets were cobbled and narrow as in a small French provincial village. They had been invited to stay with an acquaintance of Sarah's until she could find employment and a home of her own. In a very short time Sarah noticed gaily painted ladies arriving at odd hours and was puzzled until she found seven-year-old Theo watching one of the ladies through the keyhole. When she realized what was transpiring she acted swiftly and moved again. But she moved out of moral repugnance as much as from a distinct sensation that attention was being drawn from her as an object of emotional absorption.

This time she moved to Sullivan, twenty-five miles from where her husband and daughters were living together and working. To Theodore this locale was always to be remembered as a place of charm and delight. It was here that he and my father developed their deep fraternal love, and it was certainly in Indiana, where the roses bloom until October and the honeysuckle, morning-glory and Gideon trumpet vines wind themselves intricately about the fences and the trees, that Theodore developed his love of flowers and nature. Theodore and Ed were put to work gathering chips and twigs to build fires, pulling weeds from the garden, and running blocks to the nearest store to procure soap, bread, or a jug of molasses. Into the little house there came some furnishings to entice uncomplaining boarders and a collection of mongrel strays, dogs and cats, each named with a great stretch of imagination, Rover, Hound, and Snap, Theo's favorite who was so commonplace that he was almost unfit for association with children, even those on so low an economic scale as the little Dreisers. It was in this environment that Theodore Dreiser composed the portrait of Sarah the literary world has come to know—the hard-working mother whose work was never done. For it was here she managed to create, if only for a brief moment, for

Theodore, at least, an atmosphere of home and idyllic sweetness which he sought throughout his life, an atmosphere which in his own words was "never equalled."

Of all that is being said now of Sarah, it must be remembered that the circumstances of her marriage and her upbringing did not especially prepare her for the acceptance of love and marriage, and they certainly did not predispose her to sensitivity and awareness of her own motivations regarding her children. Her charm and grace were not facade, they did exist, and the children remarked on her ability to completely quell their fears after they had injured themselves in some manner or were simply afraid of the unknown, as children are.

Very few mothers, even today, could honestly give their daughters the comfort Sarah gave Mame when she became pregnant, although it was Sarah herself who had originally been remiss in failing to instruct her children in any of the facts of life. When Mame came home with her predicament, Sarah's first reaction was that she must marry the man, but he was already married. So she said, "Never mind, I will see you through this, you will be a better girl for it." And she saw her through it. The child was stillborn and Sarah took and buried it in a corner of the garden, protecting Mame from the facts until she was stronger.

But it was these very combinations and contradictions within Sarah that exerted such tremendous influence and that made her such an indelible and inexorable force, especially when she employed it with her favorite child, Theodore.

It was this particular mother-son relationship which made it possible for Theodore Dreiser, the author, to describe with terrific, almost feminine sensitivity a woman's agony over her shoes, and at the time place herself consistently in predicaments and positions that would only bring her unhappiness.[5]

As most of Sarah's dreams vaporized from lack of practicality, in time the Sullivan menage began to collapse. She was consumed physically, mentally, and spiritually and had reached that pinnacle of despair in which she sat in a state simulating catatonia–waiting, just waiting for something to "turn up." It did. It came in the now full-grown form of her firstborn, Paul, the junior, the original Dreiser to fly on the wings and song of a bird. He had changed his name to Dresser for his budding theatrical career and because it was easier to pronounce and spell.

When Paul rejoined his family, he was like the warm winter's

Sarah Schnepp Dreiser

sun slipping through the murky clouds of a February Groundhog Day, such as the one on which he crossed the family threshold, exuding an aura of cheer. Tears flowed as easily as laughter, and after much embracing Paul proudly and generously handed Sarah more money than she had ever before seen. He implied there was much more from whence the token gesture had come. To the little ones, in his joviality he was the personification of the mythical Kris Kringle or Santa Claus with whom they had had little personal experience, and he was to assume that role in the family until the end of his life although Theo did see Paul as a Falstaff, a Don Juan.

Paul gathered the clan around him and unfolded his wondrous tales of success which he had found in the enormous and exciting world that lay beyond the confines of the paltry towns of Indiana. He handed Theo and Ed a pamphlet which contained a tintype of himself: "the Paul Dresser, Songster." It contained all sorts of comic and sentimental jingles under which was printed "Copyright, Willis, Woodward and Company, New York."

When he became cognizant of the impoverished conditions of his family, Paul moved his mother and the small children to Evansville, where they lived–unbeknownst to Sarah–off the bounty of Paul's mistress, the madam of a popular bordello and later the subject of one of his most successful song hits, "My Gal Sal." Paul was a member of the local stock company, but at nights he played the piano and sang for the customers in Sal's "salon." But Paul had a roving eye and in time he and his mistress quarreled and a new homesite was selected for Sarah and the little Dreisers. The site was Chicago, where the older girls and Al were now living and working. Paul agreed to contribute to the family support, and then took to the road with Rice and West's Minstrels as an "end man." He was not to be reunited with his family for several years.

When the little Dreisers moved to Chicago, it was already a dream city in Theo's imagination. He had heard of it from the lips of Rome, who reported the magic of the city's temperament, and Al, who had gone and returned, talking of Halstead Street, State and Madison, and the lake, the great factories, and the rivers. Then the girls had come home with more tales of the wonders of the city to which came the children of the old world and the new, "avid for life and love, seeking a patrimony."

Sarah came with her customary enthusiasm–her eyes cast on

the future where there would be fame and riches for her children. The apartment in which they lived was across the street from a theater which in the summer was an open-air beer garden. Music and applause rang forth at night and in the morning it was a site for roller skating for the young. Hope flared up in the hearts of the Dreisers, hope inspired by the spirit of the young city of Chicago.

This move meant a radical change, for the city was filled with a variety of interesting things. There were hucksters calling out all manner of wares from kindling to vegetables, and collectors of rags, iron, bones, and gumshoes. These street salesmen drove rickety old wagons drawn by rickety old horses. They peddled their goods in sing-song dialects. They had come to Chicago from Russia, Poland, Ireland, Germany, Sweden—and some from the eastern coast of America. It was a teeming city of 600,000 or 700,000 people—and millions of rats. At that time it was called the City of Rats, all of which thrived in the decrepit garbage and deficient sewer systems. Raw-boned, ignorant American backwoodsmen and illiterate European immigrants were pouring into the city at the rate of fifty thousand a year, most in possession of little more than ambition and courage.

For Theo, Chicago was a mirage he would never forget, it was so different from anything he had ever known.

> I was lost in a vapor of something so rich that it was like food to the hungry, odorous and meaningful like flowers to those who love. Life was glorious and sensate, avid and gay, shimmering and tingling.[6]

It was my father, Ed, who attempted to make "hucksters" out of Theodore and himself. Ed, who was personable and quick to associate himself with his peers, soon discovered that the current thing to get into was the selling of newspapers. In those days there was no organized distribution of periodicals such as we know today in modern-day newstands. The void was filled by young boys who went to the nearest distributing centers for the newspapers and bought the papers at half price and sold them for the full value stamped on the paper. The price for most of the papers was one cent. The investment of Ed and Theodore was ten or fifteen cents a day in a supply of papers. If they were lucky, the end of their day of selling represented an additional ten or fifteen cents to save, or invest the profits in candy. (The Dreisers were notoriously fond of sweets and there was a confectioner's shop near their home where tempting cream caramels and ice cream could be purchased. The selling of newspapers for the young Dreisers did not portend a merchandising future with a fortune.)

The stay in Chicago was made remarkable by a prolonged visit from the father, John Paul, who was completely captivated by the hourly visible growth he was able to see occurring everywhere he turned. He was so impressed by the enormous size of this young city, this "first of the daughters of the new world," that he spent most of the days of his visit haunting the sundry areas of the new metropolis. He always took Theo along, and it was during this period that the only really intimate relationship between Theodore and his father existed. The impact was such that Theodore always felt that his father conceived a fancy for him—an "affectionate admiration"—which lasted until the day of his death.

At the time of their walks and talks the streets of Chicago were new and attractive. They were lined with red, yellow, gray, and cream-colored brick apartment houses (or flats as they were then called). Father and son were fascinated by the Chicago River, a stream dirty, narrow, and crowded with tugboats and masted vessels, large and small, and steamboats—steamboats far superior to anything young Theo had seen on the Ohio River. Theo discovered his father's love of nature and his ability to study and analyze his fellow man. John Paul had humor and understanding to a point, but then his religious obsession intervened and he reverted to the dogmatic stance, with his dictatorial voice of authority completely obliterating his normal comments about people—their abilities, weaknesses, eccentricities. However, young Theo came to realize that his father was a man of considerable experience. He learned that his father had traveled extensively—for a man of that era—before coming to America, and he was not a man who lacked a trade or profession. He could qualify as a manager of a woolen mill, a buyer or tester of wool, and even a master machinist insofar as wool-weaving machines were concerned. When he visited the family in Chicago, John Paul was still a man of physical strength and energy. Success—even a little recognition—would have helped create the necessary father figure the family required. And he could have achieved that success in the new city of Chicago which was screaming aloud with opportunities. On Water Street there were many woolen merchants, and in Illinois and northern Indiana several woolen mills with which he could have associated himself. But the loss of his mill in Sullivan, the subsequent brain injury, and the religious obsession which overcame him made him psychologically unfit to assume his proper role. He was lost in religious zealotry and was almost totally lacking in courage and initiative. The jobs he held he performed well, but if the mill closed he merely sat and waited until there came another call for his services. The wages he earned went to the repayment of debts and contributions to the Roman Catholic Church and school tuitions in the parochial schools. The brunt of his religious fervor is attested to by a stained glass window in St. Joseph's Roman Catholic Church in Terre Haute which bears his name as the donor—a gift presented at a time when his wife and children were suffering privation.

Obviously the emotional conflict was too severe for a sensitive child. To his dying day Theo never understood why his father lacked the ability to appreciate his own worth, to assert his value and his rights as a human being. The best that resulted from this time spent in Chicago was that Theo managed to feel a bit sorry for the man who was his father. Pity was the only durable emotion Theo ever experienced for his father.

Nevertheless, it was but a short time before the Chicago commune was dissolved. It depended upon contributions from all of the family, and the contributions were not forthcoming. When John Paul came from Terre Haute and was unable to find work, the burdens of the household were oppressive. The older children, who had long suffered at their father's critical hands, and who had made substantial contributions toward the upkeep of the home, were no longer willing to sit by and listen to his diatribes, and so they fled. This again left the responsibility largely to Sarah who, after holding a consultation with her own family brood and her neighboring sisters, decided the only solution was to return to a small town in nearby Indiana, where rent was cheaper, education for the young children available, and occasional work for John Paul in the mills obtainable. The big city was too complex.

The homesite selected was a little Indiana town, Warsaw. In contrast to most of the ugly, prairie towns and cities of the Midwest, Warsaw was a lovely rural community. It lay in the center of an area containing three small but beautiful lakes, two of them so close that they formed an integral part and the houses bordered on their shores. The town was designed around the public square, in the center of which was a white sandstone courthouse with a clock tower one hundred feet high. The hugh clock had four faces which could be seen from the north, south, east, and west and its bell tolled for miles around.

In this small town, through the financial efforts of the older girls and Paul and Al (still in Chicago), Sarah set about to provide for the younger children the atmosphere of a simple, well-mannered, conservative home. There was no immediate sense of worry or strain although there was work to be done—grass to be cut, flower beds and walks to be weeded, a kitchen garden to be planted and harvested, fences to be mended, a house to be cleaned and refurbished, as all of their furniture had been repossessed in Chicago. But when these chores were accomplished, there was an atmosphere of peace and a reasonable degree of security.

To young Theo, the most important area of change was in his education. For once the youngest children were enrolled in the public schools where Theo first sensed most clearly that he had been hampered, delayed, and oppressed by the dogmatic and threatening dominance of the German Catholic schools. It was in this new environment that the genius of Theo evolved to the degree of recognition. Of all the children he alone was the natural intellectual. From the very first moment that he relaxed in the atmosphere of formal education he was a creative student, leaping beyond the confines of the textbooks and the limited boundaries of the learning of his teachers. His young mind was intrigued and he began to speculate on his personal relation to people, animals, life, the stars, the universe—the mystery of origin and continuation. He was possessed with a passion for learning, and the results were so spectacular that his teachers took a personal interest in him, in his future. In this atmosphere he was wanted, appreciated. Through the efforts of his mind, coupled with hard work, he was reassured he could succeed.

The charm of Warsaw was intensified by the fact that this was Sarah's family's home country. Nearby were her relatives who were prosperous, respectable citizens, and for once the little Dreisers were elevated in spirit by their link to respectability and a degree of affluence on the part of their mother's relatives. It was with pride that Theo read in school that Warsaw was considered the most beautiful place in all of Indiana. "I sat up with pride, *we* were living in Warsaw! More, this was my mother's home region, if you please!"[7]

Not only was the town beautiful, but it was prosperous and

becoming famous for its scienic beauty. There were excursions planned by the railroads, from Fort Wayne, Indianapolis, South Bend. It was during this time that Theo discovered books, books books! Dickens, Thackeray, Scott, Shakespeare, Carlyle—the pages opened another world to his young eyes, while Ed threw all of his energies into sports. Girls interested Ed very little. He appeared to like them well enough although they had crushes on him, while to Theo girls represented a fury burning within his body.

When John Paul would visit the family in Warsaw he would lament on the type of nonreligious schooling his children were obtaining—but to no avail. He became filled with impotent rage, bitterness, and grief as he thundered against the education his children were getting—coeducational, boys and girls together! Disaster was bound to follow.

Unfortunately, John Paul's prophecy came true. Sylvia became involved with one of the more dapper young men about town—a man whose family held a prominent social position in Warsaw. On the belief that he loved her, and would marry her, Sylvia became sexually involved with him and soon found that she was *pregnant!* Where earlier Sarah had been able to handle the similar situation of one of her daughters, she was helpless in this incident, and in a very short time the case of the Dreiser girl became common gossip. This could not have occurred at a worse time for the young Dreisers. Theo, Ed, and Claire were just beginning to be accepted in the social order of the town. The boys of good homes sought the friendship of the handsome, sports-loving Ed; the pretty girls friendly with Claire longed for Ed's company; and Theo had already been recognized as "outstanding" by virtue of his prize-winning essays. Then Sylvia's disgrace and plight became the tattle of all the busybodies. In addition, Rome chose this moment to reappear—the drunken brother who cried out his inbred hostilities, cursing the town as a "rube," calling its citizens "duds." The doors which were just beginning to open to the three little Dreisers were to close with a loud slam! Sarah was distressed, the children confused, while drunken Rome ranted, "Who in the Hell are they? Mother is always worrying about them [the townspeople]. A lot of cattle and jays!"

In time Sylvia was sent to New York City where Emma now lived. Rome moved on for futher adventures. Even though John Paul was never informed of Sylvia's unfortunate predicament, saving the children from the trauma of his outrage, the damage had been done. Only through his intellect and hard work did Theodore see a possibility to carve for himself and his family something special. Through his superiority in his studies, Theo was able to sustain himeself. What difference did it *really* make if the people of Warsaw pooh-poohed the Dreisers? When he walked and talked with his teachers he began to "feel much braver, stronger." Within him there was a trifle of vanity swelling. His security blanket was his intellect. Had not the superintendent of the schools taken him aside and assured him that "No accident of birth or condition can harm or delay a determined individual." Theodore was determined, but the environment was more than he could cope with, and like his mother he sought salvation in physical flight from any restraining situation. To him, the road to success lay in the big city. Since Chicago was the only metropolis he had ever visited, he borrowed the fare from Sarah and left Warsaw.

The Indiana the Dreisers inhabited was a state whose components were commonplace: boys and girls who attended the local schools; the graduates taking positions in the town and others finding employment beyond the boundaries of their hometown; the comings and goings of older citizens of repute, married or unmarried, who comprised the solid bulk of the population and conducted the sundry business enterprises of the community. The unique feature of the Dreisers was the fact that they possessed none of the requirements for community identity and social status. They were—even at their peak of family contentment in Warsaw—on the outside, looking in. However, despite their lack of material or social requirements, they felt immensely superior. And indeed they were, possessing as they did a very special charisma. They differed from the masses by having and exhibiting emotion, imagination, and almost a *frenzy* for existence. Not one remained untouched by the beauty of life. No one failed to identify with books, plays, poetry, art—the true dramas of life. As a unit they were in open rebellion against the communal life they saw organized against them. They were the original anti-establishment children. Iconoclastic was the word. That the marble godheads of the nineteenth century were going to be revealed as idols made of plaster of paris which would collapse in the twentieth century was an unpredictable factor. But the Dreisers were among the first to crack the mold, and the pen of Theodore Dreiser writing the intimate story of his sister would be the first to alert the world to the literature of realism. It was indeed the parents, Sarah and John Paul, who in their own confusion and disillusion with life, radically influenced the lives of their children—especially Theodore. It is interesting to note how time alters reactions to human behavior, as witnessed by the inscription on the red granite stone in St. Boniface's Cemetery in Chicago, where Sarah and John Paul lie side by side. The epitaph reads, "A good father and the best of mothers."

In death, the pains of life are forgiven—if not forgotten.

4

The Chicago Dreisers and Theo's College Days

"Suns and Flowers and Rats and Kings"

> O my dear Vera I am so glad you are writing a Book on him. I class him with Walt Whitman and Edgar Poe and Henry Miller as our greatest—and Emerson—of all American writers. Oh yes! I must include *Longfellow.*
>
> Dreiser had a strange vein of weird mysticism and magic mingled with his childlike humility and shyness. When he had got glory for one of his books he came to see me and cried "I am opulent, opulent! What can I give you?" and I mentioned some very expensive and famous old Book and he bought it for me.[1]

Of all the Dreisers, Uncle Theodore in his teens was the least employable despite his high intelligence. He arrived in Chicago at sixteen, gangly, skinny, and awkward. The year was 1887. Although his sisters Mame and Teresa lived there, he was determined to find employment before contacting them. In his fantasy he wanted to árrive well dressed and fully employed as a young clerk working in an expensive office such as a prominent Chicago millionaire like Charles Yerkes might occupy. However, his efforts to gain employment were fruitless and he became terrified by the city's inclement harshness. He finally did get a job as a dishwasher in a restaurant on Halstead Street, run by a

Levantine, John Paradiso, where he earned five dollars a week, plus his meals. His skinny arms were immersed in dishwater and he emptied the slops in a garbage can until he almost vomited in the dreadful odors. He managed to survive and in time he sought out his sisters and told them he was working in a haberdashery, making seven dollars a week. This little white lie seems insignificant, but it was the basis upon which my uncle often functioned, apparently for his own reassurance. He was attempting to live out his own fantasies, regardless of the consequences of his untruths in the lives of other people.

A letter from Sarah, who had now wearied of Warsaw, suggested that it would be possible with contributions from the working family members for her to make a home in Chicago with eighteen-year-old Claire and fourteen-year-old Ed. After a family conference (with the usual enthusiasm the Dreisers possessed when led by Sarah's intuitions), the family, with the exception of the father, John Paul, the brother Paul, and sisters Emma and Sylvia, who resided in the East but were helping financially, the Indiana Dreisers were now the Chicago Dreisers. Al had returned from Milwaukee in hopes of obtaining employment in the haberdashery in which his brother reputedly worked. All soon had steady employment, even Uncle Theodore who after many trials and tribulations with menial tasks finally found employment in the large wholesale hardware firm of Hibbard, Spencer, Barrier and Co. on Wabash and Lake streets. He was a stock boy earning five dollars a week. He contributed three dollars to his mother and the remaining he splurged going with Al to the Chicago Opera House.

The period in which Theo was spending his adolescence in Chicago was one in which the city itself was developing as a metropolitan area with the resultant growing pains. There was corruption and there were prodigious fortunes being accumulated—all of which would be narrated in later years by Theodore Dreiser, the author. At seventeen, he worked at a job in which he was extremely inefficient, a job whose chores he loathed, but a job which he did not dare complain about for fear of dismissal. His bright moments were undoubtedly those spent with Al and Ed going to see such popular theater of the day as *Ali Baba and the Forty Thieves.* But there is no evidence that he was contemplating a stage career. He was suspended in the spaceship of his dull, plodding job at the hardware store, a job from which he momentarily expected to be fired. This had once happened on

Christmas Eve but by summoning his courage and collapsing in tears he managed to get his employer to keep him in the job he so badly needed. From that night when he was temporarily reinstated the dread fear of being "sacked" haunted him and he survived in the manner of a robot–performing without emotional or intellectual awareness.

It was at this dark moment in his life that the identity Theo had commenced to create for himself in the public school in Warsaw where he had attracted the attention of his teachers–two especially, May Calvert and Mildred Fielding–came to fruition. One day at work he was summoned to the front office where a caller awaited him. It was Mildred Fielding, now a principal in a Chicago high school. She had, by some predestined command, carried Theodore in her mind and thought him more deserving than any of the hundreds of pupils she had taught. She wanted to do something for him–send him to the University of Indiana, at Bloomington, at her expense. With parental permission, she had him registered; the cost was enormous–$300. But she believed in him to the extent that she paid every cent herself.

In the fall of 1889, leaving his family in Chicago, a tall, shambling Theodore Dreiser matriculated at Bloomington. At Miss Fielding's suggestion he registered in Latin, geometry, English literature, and history.

In retrospect, it was not Uncle Theodore's intelligence that was so startling, but the unique qualities of this intelligence that separated him from other students. He had no practical aim in life, in contrast to the other students who had specific careers outlined in teaching, law, and medicine. What made Theodore a somewhat unprecedented college student was his passionate zeal, his almost savage ambition, coupled with a feminine understanding, a freshness of outlook, and an eye for detail.

If nothing else, Theodore's year at Bloomington was an emotional one. His roommate was a sociable lad named Bill Yakey whose interests were primarily football and girls. In these two fields Yakey excelled and in due time he undertook to indoctrinate Theodore in both of his competitive sports. He put Theo through an ordeal of sitting-up exercises in an attempt to make him more physically attractive and a more logical candidate for social success. It was an odd friendship yet not unlike the fraternal love between Theodore and my own father who possessed many of the same qualities with which his college friend was endowed. In Theo's words: "His was a light-hearted, swashbuckling nature of that western day and world, fair in his studies, and genial as a companion . . . possessed of many popular or college charms—looks, strength, grace, means, which made him a hero and idol, yet he never took an undue advantage of me or made any base, let alone rasping, comment on my inferior skill in these various matters." That Yakey left an indelible impression upon my uncle is evidenced in the attention Theo paid to the care of his body in later years.

No fraternity sent a bid to Uncle Theodore and he reacted in the same manner as many bypassed young men have done. He was bitter, hurt, rejected, and not totally honest in his reflections. He resented a social order from which he was excluded because he was not affluent, and he became self-conscious about his appearance, although, despite the cast in one eye, his buck teeth, and his innate sense of inferiority, he somehow was not unattractive. He had many social assets, had they been pointed out. He had the warm smile of Sarah, and the poetic, cadent voice of John Paul, along with the aesthetic, slender hands. He also had the Dreiser family characteristic of personal interest in people.

Theodore was like most creative people in his wildly ranging moods. When he wished to, he had great moments of humor, but without forewarning the turn of the emotional screw of his makeup could cast him into a Stygian gloom. Obviously such adolescent contraditions are difficult to surmount or to understand—even with today's psychological knowledge. When my Uncle Theodore was suffering such a period of adjustment, the task was much more complex. In his feeling of exclusion, he found it hard to adjust to the world of the Bill Yakeys. In the cast-off clothes of his brother Paul and the husbands of Mame and Teresa, he felt uncomfortable. The cast-offs were much too large for him. He was convinced that there was no entrance for him into the group Yakey represented, the one which in his daydreams was identified with college life. Determined to make friends among those campus members who were as poor or almost as poor as he was, he sought out two young men who had a tremendous influence upon him: Howard Hall, who despite a speech defect was determined to become a lawyer, and Russell Ratliff, who spent many hours with Theo discussing philosophy and introducing him to Tolstoy. In later years, Uncle Theodore felt that Ratliff's influence was intellectually one of the most important in his life.

There was a side to Theodore that was inherited from his mother, a fun-loving, sex-hungry side. But all during his college life he experienced frustration in pursuit of these needs. It was the era in which dancing was at its peak, and the fraternity houses were filled with bright lights, gaiety, music, and couples dancing in the gas-lit rooms. Theo could never be a part of all this.

The normal pangs and anxieties which accompany adolescent loneliness were intensified in Uncle Theodore's situation as he suffered under the pressures which his mother had imposed on him as a young child when she showered him with her attention while at the same time reminding him of the sacrifices she had made for his sake. He may not have heard or encountered all of the seeming horrors of childbirth but he had come to equate it with descending into the valley of death—all because of a man! In adolescence his troubles grew more serious as he secretly resorted to masturbation (as most youngsters do) but experienced feelings of guilt. As a matter of fact, he masturbated with such frequency as to harm his future sexual ability. His mother's sufferings in childbirth *because of some man* so affected his masculinity that it had a serious effect upon his early attempts at sexual intercourse. There was a mixture of desire, and unconscious fear of consequences, frequently causing an inability on his part to maintain an erection long enough to perform this deadly deed. He was twenty-two before he had the courage to attempt sexual intercourse and his first effort was a miserable failure. He could not maintain his masculinity long enough and ejaculated prematurely before penetrating his partner.

The long search for fulfillment that would never come began with his fear of an intimate relationship, no matter how great the desire, the "transition from a normal to an agonized state was instantaneous. In each case this pain endured for months."[2]

The pain was, in fact, his deep sense of inadequacy. At this very important period of his life when he should have been coping with sex and the companionship of his peers, he withdrew further into himself, and fantasizing the "sweet dreams of youth"—the first joys of physical contact between boy and girl—and retreated into the lonely act of masturbation.

When the year came to its close he had not distinguished himself intellectually. Socially, he regarded himself as a failure, although not Yakey, but another student, Day Allen Willy, had tried to help him fulfill his social and sexual needs. As the freshman term was about to end, Theodore fell passionately in love with the daughter of a doctor. He watched her from afar, he wrote love letters to her which he tore up before delivering. One day he handed her a note requesting that she meet him near her home. She did not do so. He left the university, exclaiming: "They can all go to Hell!"–meaning all of the structures of campus life that had excluded him. But the memory of the halcyon days, the visions of the beautiful university town, and the agonies of his first hopeless romance never left him. He could etch the fine emotional details until the day he died.

To say that Theodore Dreiser was in a blue funk, a cowering state of dejection, when he boarded the train to return to his family in Chicago is an understatement without equal. Now, oddly, the family was in much better financial condition than usual. Paul was beginning to attain quite a reputation for himself in the theatrical world and was appearing in Chicago in the leading comedian role in *The Tin Soldier.* He was living with his family who were enjoying his bounty as well as the contributions of the married girls, and Ed and Al who were working. Theodore alone was unemployed. Despite his bad first year Miss Fielding offered him a second year at college, but he declined it. He set about to find a job with Asa Conklin, a Chicago realtor, who promised him three dollars per week and a commission. Theodore was allowed the use of Conklin's horse and buggy, and the young man showed considerable enterprise in getting listings. Under normal conditions Theodore should have made money, but his employer, a Civil War pensioner, had no business ability and failed to follow through on any of Theo's leads. As the summer wore on, Conklin was not even paying him his salary, but Uncle Theodore continued on because he had a "buggy to ride in, a good horse to ride" and the appearance of success in his new working clothes.

However, there was a black cloud descending over the Dreiser household in the form of an illness which had embraced Sarah. Although she was only fifty-seven, she was daily getting more and more listless. Theodore had no compunctions about using his employer's rig to take his mother riding in the fresh air, hoping to revive her waning spirits. But the superstitious Sarah had a premonition of her approaching death in a dream in which her mother and father appeared beckoning to her. Soon after, she took to her bed. The Dreisers, prone to family arguments, were silenced by her illness. John Paul, now sixty-nine, took refuge in prayer. Various doctors came to try and fathom the nature of the chills and fevers from which Sarah lay dying. Teresa, who had married Ed Davis, left her husband to manage for himself while she waited hand and foot on her dying mother, at the expense of her own health. (She suffered a deep depression following her mother's death and was several years in recovering.)

One day in November Theodore came home for lunch and Sarah, who was in one of her better moods, asked him to set her upright. He lifted her now heavy, bulky body to a sitting position and as he leaned her back among the pillows, he felt her grow limp. Her eyes flashed with that moribund brilliance which quickly diminishes into a blankness of expression. She was dead!

He screamed. Teresa and John Paul came to her bedside. John Paul, overcome with grief, kept crying aloud, "It should have been me. I should have gone first!"

The death of a parent is a trauma of no limited proportions and the death of his mother must have not only frightened Uncle Theodore beyond all realms of imagination but it must have harkened back to his childhood which was spent almost entirely in her company, when his pattern of play was different from that of a normal child. When his mother was not watching him, he would slip away to a neighbor's house almost daily. He was such a regular visitor that the old lady provided a special stool for him to sit upon and he considered it exclusively his. When Ed would go looking for him to play marbles or "catch" he knew exactly where to look for Theo—at the home of the old lady, listening to her tales, eating her cookies. One day, suddenly, without any explanation, he was told he could not go there anymore. He would steal away, peep through the curtains and watch the old lady's home, hoping to see her, but she never came out of the house and the shades were drawn. He thought she was angry with him, but he did not know why. What had he done? What had he said? What had he managed that was BAD? A few days later, while he was keeping watch, he noticed people gathering at her door. Finally a large black box was carried out by some men and place in a wagon drawn away by some horses. No one ever told him anything except that she was no longer there. She had left him and had not even said good-bye!

The terrible sense of inadequacy which welled up in him so often was here again. What had he done to make his friend dislike him? She was his friend. His childish mind was filled with thoughts of his mother's continued threats of abandonment. Now

Theodore

Paul

Rome

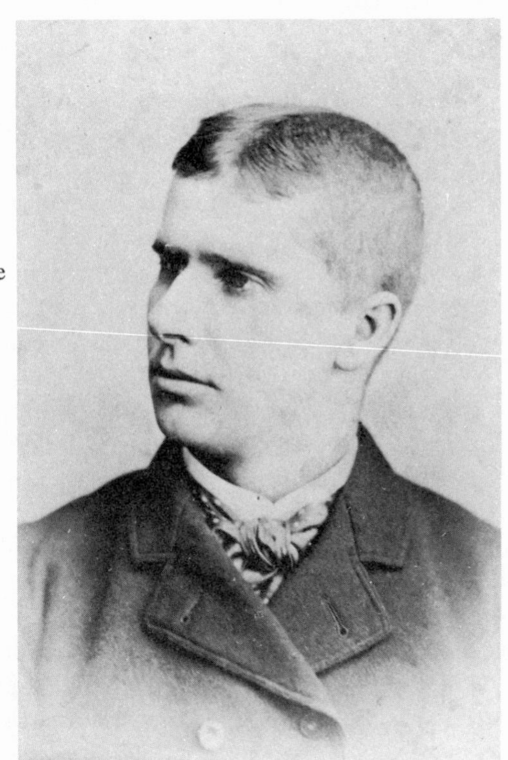

Ed

It was here and in association with the men who made the newspaper fraternity of Chicago, that Uncle Theodore fell in love with writing. By normal reportorial standards he was not a good news reporter, but when he was allowed the freedom to do "special" features, he was in his element. He wrote about the slums, prostitutes, drunkards, dope fiends. It was here that his gift of observation drew favorable praise and he is credited with writing some of the first exposé stories of modern journalism. His newspaper career took on a special identity when the *Globe* hired a brilliant but alcoholic newspaperman, John T. McEnnis, as city editor. He took a special liking to Theodore and was responsible for his obtaining a much better job on the *St. Louis Globe-Democrat.*

At the time, Theodore had imagined himself in love with a girl named Lois Zahn who had been introduced to him by Claire. Lois dreamed of marriage, and Theo let her dream, but when he accepted the offer from the St. Louis newspaper and was unable to find Lois to tell her of his plans, he gave vent to his irrational jealousy and left after writing her a curt note. It was the first of a series of such epistles.

When Theodore Dreiser arrived in St. Louis he contained within him two separate individuals. One was the son of John Paul—ambitious, wishing to be a tycoon, longing for a place in the power structure, dogmatic and serious; the other, the son of Sarah—an iconoclast, a lover of humanity, irresponsible in performance, a seeker of personal security at any cost, a dreamer, a poet. It was an inner conflict which tortured him. Moments of self-acclaimed genius were catapulated into hours of self-doubt and stabs of inferiority. He was lonely, homesick, and miserable. He toyed with the idea of asking Lois to join him, marry him (he acknowledged that he had been a scoundrel in jilting her and was deeply touched by a letter from Lois in which she wished herself dead). But his driving ambition, his yearning for success, and his commitment to his now chosen life work—WRITING—superseded all other considerations.

Uncle Theodore encountered many different types of human beings in his new world. His interviews ran the gamut from John L. Sullivan, the world's heavyweight champion, to Annie Besant, the metaphysicist. He became intellectually involved with each of his assignments for he was in the period of his life when he was concerned with making a personal adjustment to God, creation, and justice—the subjects to which no matter what questions he asked he got no satisfactory answers regardless of what source he selected for questioning. In his daily work he came upon senseless murders and attended fancy dress balls. It was all routine for a young newspaper reporter. In 1893 he got a tip of a train wreck in nearby Alton, Illinois. His eyewitness account of the disaster gave him a name among the reporting elite of St. Louis and a raise in salary.

With his additional income he purchased some decent clothes. His pride in his sartorial appearance was urgent. Like most people who have suffered an impoverished childhood and worn hand-me-down attire, he developed an interest in clothes, and as an "ugly duckling" he set about to compensate for his lack of good looks with good taste in dress. He also intended to use his increase in pay to change his abode. He was living in a boarding-house where his snooping landlady discovered some hairpins on his pillow one morning after he had unsuccessfully attempted to seduce a young woman he had met while covering a church social. His landlady was extremely aggressive, and as a token gesture for not tossing him out of her house demanded *services rendered.* Aside from the lodging facilities, the affair was of little significance except that it calmed his doubts about his ability to perform the sex act. He regarded his sex partner as an individual who "was very much beneath me mentally and in every other way." This attitude decreased the tension usually accompanying a desire to please, captivate, and possess.

At that period in American literature, the names of newspaper writers were beginning to appear. Such authors as George Ade (whose work Uncle Theodore greatly admired), Eugene Field, Augustus Thomas, and William Marion Reedy were among those who got their first start in St. Louis. In short, a writing job which had been merely a means of making a living was also becoming an open door to an art career,[2] a creative area for self-expression.

When Uncle Theo got his job replacing the former dramatic critic of the *Globe-Democrat* he became intrigued with the idea of writing a play. He loved the theater which was the center of the works of Pinero and Oscar Wilde, and the acting arena for de Wolf Hopper, Richard Mansfield, Eddie Foy, and many other noteworthy thespians of the day who tread the boards in St. Louis under the young, critical eye of Theodore Dreiser.

Fate played a trick on Uncle Theo (which has happened

subsequently to other prominent writers) when he was given an assignment which prevented his attending the openings of three new plays. He resorted to using the reviews given by the advance press agent. Much to his horror he learned in the morning newspaper that train service had been cut off and none of the traveling companies had reached St. Louis.

Theodore was so insecure, so sensitive, that he could envision nothing but ruin. He slipped into the newspaper office, collected his pay, left a note of apology, and went into hiding. He felt "the dice were loaded," and not in his favor. However, the target of this debacle was not Theo but his editor, who had evidenced some interest in psychic phenomena, and the other papers taunted him with the reviews citing them as evidence of his powers of clairvoyance.

Dreiser fell into a deep depression and longed for his family, but he had no money saved for a return trip to Chicago and had to weather his humiliation until he was salvaged by the editor of a semi-yellow sheet, the *Republic,* one of the papers that had enjoyed the joke on the *Globe-Democrat.* Theo returned to his working profession at a reduced salary, and in time was a valued feature reporter. Although he worked well and hard, there was no financial remuneration in the form of increased wages due to the 1893 panic which was paralyzing business, but there were other compensations. To promote circulation, the *Republic* staged a popularity contest among Missouri schoolteachers, selecting the twenty who got the most votes and paying their way to the Chicago World's Fair which was the center of attraction of the day. Theo was to accompany the group, attend the fair with them, and record for the home readers the reactions and delights of the twenty ladies. Theo was delighted at the prospect of a free trip to Chicago to be reunited with his father and his brothers, even though he was somewhat appalled at the prospect of squiring twenty spinsters, most of whom he presumed would be old and ugly.

Once again Theo's fantasies had misled him, for when he met the group he was surprised to find most of them young and attractive. One of them especially so in her starched white dress which set off her girlish figure to every advantage and accentuated the beauty of her abundant coils of coppery, red hair highlighting her creamy, flawless skin. She was demure and shy, and with embarrassment admitted she had never been to Chicago—never had been farther away from her home than St. Louis. To the painfully timid Theodore trying to make conversation her admissions were an opening wedge, and he thought to himself, "What a delightful girl!" Her name was Sara Osborne White and she came from Montgomery City, seventy-five miles west of St. Louis, but taught in Florissant, a St. Louis suburb.

In Chicago, Theo quickly contacted his father, whom he found pitiably weak and frail. But it was with considerable pride and joy that Theo was able to take him to the fair. In the German Village, John Paul found happiness and recounted some of his memories of the old country to Theo. Once again Theo was filled with deep sympathy and a love for his father. He met with his brothers Al and Ed. Both were working, but Al had aged and already appeared broken in spirit and in health. Theo was disturbed and persuaded both of his brothers to quit their jobs and join him in St. Louis. The total impracticality of such a move, in view of a national depression which saw hundreds and thousands of people unemployed, never presented itself to the Dreiser brothers. The urge to change scenery, make a new abode, had been implanted in each of them by Sarah.

Theo caught up with the family news, including the birth of Sylvia's illegitimate son in New Jersey. The child was a boy and had been named Carl. But Chicago was filled with haunting memories for Theo, painful recollections such as the time when he was dismissed for holding out twenty-five dollars from Frank Nesbit, for whom Dreiser worked briefly earning fourteen dollars per week to collect for the household gee-gaws Nesbit sold on the installment basis. The torment of the idea of being imprisoned for his indiscretion never left Theo, and suddenly Chicago exemplified the jungle into which a young man could be lured and trapped. He was not unhappy to return to St. Louis where he had a job, and, once again, a sexual relationship with his landlady—a relationship which, even though it lacked emotional values, satisfied his sexual needs and released some of his tensions and frustrations.

From this vantage point, Dreiser persuaded Al and Ed to join him. He had, as was his wont, elaborated his own success and his living conditions. It was not long after they took up residence with Theo that Al discovered his affair with the landlady; and it took but a few weeks for the brothers, after pounding the pavements in St. Louis, to discover that work was unobtainable. They decided to leave and return to Chicago. It had been an effort made on the strength of brotherly love. They truly wanted to live together and to share one another's lives, but it was not feasible.

Shortly after they departed, Theo again severed his liaison with his landlady (becoming unreasonably jealous when he discovered she shared her affections with another boarder) and took up a new residence. He had not been able to forget the Miss White he had met on the trip to Chicago. He wrote to her, and she replied telling him she would be in St. Louis when the school term commenced in mid-September.

It is not surprising that Theodore Dreiser was attracted to Sara Osborne White when he met her, for she possessed a unique, delicate beauty that continued to attract men throughout her life. In her subdued, graceful manner, she projected a romantic etheral beauty that was made even more enticing by her natural reticence. Her great feature was her abundance of rich auburn hair which she wore in massive braids that served as an exquisite frame for her small oval face and caused Theo to write: "When your hair is down about your face and ears, you always look so meek, just like one of Rossetti's maidens, and that when your face belies your nature. You're not meek, not sorrowful, though I defy anyone to produce a better imitation." This halo of lustrous hair was the source of Sara White's rustic nickname, "Jug"–a name quite incongruous with her stately appearance. The name had been bestowed upon her by one of her brothers who, upon seeing her with her hair uncoiled from braids, commented, "When Sara lets her hair down, she looks like a little brown jug." The name, a term of endearment, stuck long after the adult woman had taken control and she was known as "Jug" by all who knew her.

Theo's courtship of Jug was such as to bring forth comments from the neighbors that he was a "big silly" and that "he was always going about gawking and mooning." He bought clothes for himself to impress her with his sartorial elegance and to overcome what he thought was his homeliness. He laid siege with roses, took her to the theater, and wrote to her every free moment he had. Despite all of his attentions, he could not penetrate the virginal armor she wore and an occasional kiss was the only reward for his attentions. Finally he capitulated and proposed marriage. He spent his last dollar on a diamond engagement ring and Jug gave him a photograph of herself in a silver frame which he kept in his room and stared at hungrily. Even the betrothal did not give him further privileges and he was obviously too poor to marry.

At this time Paul Dresser made a professional visit to St. Louis and the two brothers met again. Paul was the epitome of success and even though he was appearing in a ridiculous vehicle his singing of "The Bowery" was a decided hit. Paul had a strong affinity for Theo, even though he did not understand him, nor the complexities that were disturbing him. He had always felt there was an undeveloped genius in this brother who in so many physical ways bore no resemblance to himself or any of the other Dreisers. He urged Theo to come to New York where he had an interest in a music publishing firm and could possibly get him a job. Paul pointed out that Emma was now living in New York and would probably be delighted to have Theo with her. He painted a bright picture. Theo took Jug to meet Paul and the meeting was somewhat confusing. Paul found her "charming" but he did not feel that Theodore should get married, certainly not at this stage of his career.

Paul's visit was acutely disturbing. Theo was dissatisfied—for even though he had an interesting job, his pay was not increasing—sexually frustrated, restless, and although he was intrigued by Paul's suggestion of his coming to New York, he was inwardly afraid to tackle the "Big City." He was twenty-two years of age, deeply in love, and floundering when a young reporter friend on the *Republic* persuaded him to join him in a small-town newspaper venture in Ohio. His employers tried to dissuade him, but he departed, throwing over a promising career for a figment of his imagination. Probably at no time in his career did the congenital influence of his mother manifest itself more succinctly. In the middle of a nationwide depression, he went in search of a shadowy future in an unknown small town. He deluded himself with visions of becoming a great country editor—one of those men who had made names for themselves in politics—but when he saw the paper and the village and realized the prospects, he had to admit to his folly. He left and went to nearby Toledo, seeking employment. The editor of the *Toledo Blade,* young Arthur Henry, took a liking to him and gave him an assignment although he told him in advance that no permanent position was open and that the only assignment he could offer was a dangerous one covering a streetcar strike. Theodore took the stint and did an excellent unprejudiced reporting job, even though his sympathies were with the strikers. Despite the publisher's desire to have him remain, Theo could not afford the waiting time until another piece

Teresa

Emma

Claire

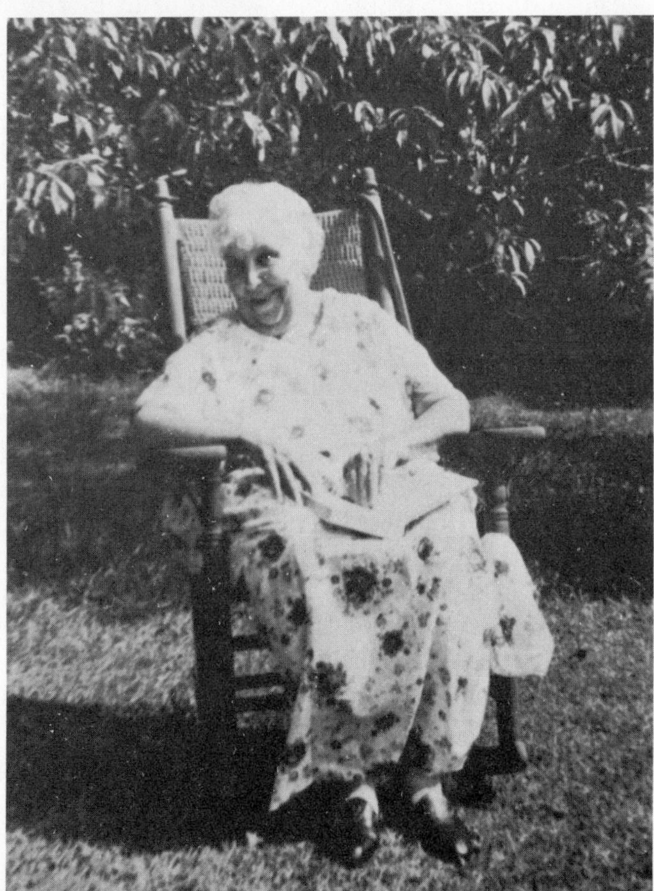
Mame

of work turned up. He wandered on to Cleveland where he did a couple of Sunday features until his money got so low that he moved on to Buffalo. Here he grew discouraged in a very short time and transported himself to Pittsburgh where he got a nibble at the *Pittsburgh Dispatch.* At the same time he received a telegram from Arthur Henry offering employment and he used the telegram to persuade the Pittsburgh editor to hire him.

In his writing in later years, the environmental effect of his residence in Pittsburgh cannot be overstressed. Here was crystallized the class struggle, the conflict between capital and labor, the incompatibility between the rich and the poor. At the time when Theodore Dreiser went there, the city was a study in contrasts. The rich were very, very rich–they were Carnegie, Phipps, Frick, and their lesser satellites. The poor were very, very poor, and were nameless. The rich lived in mansions, palaces protected by high iron gates and guards; the poor existed in river-flat slums. In Pittsburgh, Theo discovered Balzac–in the abundantly endowed Carnegie library. For years he had been told to read Balzac, but it was in Pittsburgh that he devoured Balzac, and Balzac devoured him. In the steel city, with its contrasts, he began to dream of writing the same type of literature that Balzac had created.

He was lonely and missed Jug. He wrote lengthy letters and finally he demanded a short vacation and went to visit her. He was overcome at seeing her in her own setting. Her family was one of the "best families" and it represented everything Theo had missed in his own upbringing–stability and family integrity. In the pastoral setting, Jug's beauty was even more overwhelming than it had been earlier and he desired a more intimate relationship. Jug, too, was passionately responsive, but the restrictions of the social order of her world simply forbade sexual intercourse before marriage. Theodore controlled himself and responded to a wire from Paul urging him to come to New York. He did.

Paul met him in Jersey City and took him by ferry to Manhattan where they went to the home of Emma, who had now married L. A. Hopkins, the man with whom she had eloped, the man who had stolen thirty-five hundred dollars from his employers in order to woo Emma (a sum which he subsequently returned). Everywhere on his visit, Theo saw evidences of material splendor. Even Emma had a maid (provided by Paul) to tend her two children, and although her husband was beginning his decline from his more affluent days in Chicago, they lived in a superior manner to any of the other Dreisers. Paul took Theo on a grand tour of the city, visiting Delmonico's, the Metropole, and some of the more famous brothels. In all of these establishments, Paul was well known and apparently greatly admired. Paul urged him to find employment on one of the newspapers but Theodore was intimidated.

Ironically, it was probably Paul's aura of success, his life style which frightened Theodore. How could be compete, he asked himself. What could he ever be in life except Paul Dresser's brother? His own sense of inferiority was actually intensified by the New York visit which his well-meaning brother had thought would inspire him to pick up his roots and move to the city while he was still young, ambitious, and not tied by bonds of marriage. Paul remembered the "charming" Jug and in his own way was trying to challenge romance with success.

Theodore returned to Pittsburgh and lived meagerly, shunning all entertainment. He read avidly and saved all of his money until he felt that he had a sufficient stake to give up his job and move to New York where he would seek employment on his own—without the help of his now famous brother. With two hundred and forty dollars saved by penny-pinching and half-starving himself, he set forth in November, 1894, to find his own place in the sun.

5

The Paul Dresser Story

"As with a finger in water, the aspirations, the dreams, and the achievements of men"

While Uncle Theodore was clinging to his mother's skirts and lamenting with her their plight in life, there occurred many events which affected his life and career and which must be intertwined to create the complete Dreiser story.

Of all of these happenings the most important was unquestionably the rise to fame of my other uncle, John Paul Dreiser, Jr., who became known to the world by his professional name, Paul Dresser. His success also encompassed the career of a young lady named Louise Kerlin, born in 1878 in Evansville, Indiana, who was later adopted by Paul and became known professionally as Louise Dresser, and whom I knew always as "Aunt" Louise.

Then there was the emotional involvement of Emma Dreiser (the favorite sister of the uncles—Theo, Paul, and Ed) with a married man, L. A. Hopkins, who, in order to procure her love embezzled a large sum of money (which he later replaced) and eloped with her to New York. The story appeared in the *Chicago Mail* and *Chicago Tribune* in February, 1886.

Another event was the birth in 1869, two years before that of Theodore, of Sara Osborne White who was known by her familiar name of "Jug" and who was the considerably misunderstood and misrepresented wife of Theodore.

And finally, the birth in 1880 in New York, one year before Paul Dresser made his professional debut there, of Mai V. Skelly who was to marry the youngest Dreiser, Ed, and subsequently became my mother.

It was the career of Paul Dresser which was the control for the other Dreiser careers, and next to his parents Paul probably had the greatest familial impact upon Theodore.

At the age of fifteen, John Paul Dreiser, Jr., went, without too many misgivings, to St. Meinrad's Seminary to study for the priesthood, according to his eldest sister, Mame. In later years, Mame was the official family biographer, but for reasons of vanity, she often tampered with many dates and ages and even altered the family Bible. Paul went mainly because he had experienced two encounters with the law and was sent away as a sort of probationary treatment for adolescent antisocial behavior. Actually no one in the family ever recalled the alleged pressure his father is supposed to have put upon him to get him to the seminary. It seems to have been an act of expediency. Rome, Mame, and Sylvia all recalled at different times hearing him say, "Life should be lived merrily, and money made plentifully. There must be a way." Certainly this secular philosophy was hardly in accord with the stringent life of a religious order. Like all of the children he adored his mother and had been overheard saying to her that he never wanted to marry because he could not be true to one woman and could not bear to break a woman's heart. At any rate, his brush with religious study lasted only a year and in 1875 he ran away to join a medicine show. He had a "genius for the kind of gaiety, poetry and romance which may, and no doubt must, be looked upon as exceedingly middle class but which nonetheless had as much charm as anything in the world could have." ("My Brother Paul.") He was outgoing, warm, and tender with an innate taste for simple beauty. Before he was seventeen he began writing songs which he was advised to collect in a volume. He changed his name because of the difficulty people had in pronouncing and spelling "Dreiser" correctly. Since it was very often pronounced Dresser, he decided to drop the letter "I" and substitute another "S," feeling that the change would produce a better moniker for a budding actor and songster. He also dropped the first name, John, and the junior and became known to his new coterie of friends as Paul Dresser.

Before the name was to become one of renown the one-time

Mai Skelly Dreiser

novitiate for the priesthood was a singer and entertainer with a perambulating cure-all troupe or wagon, Hamlin's Wizard Oil, traveling throughout Indiana, Ohio, and Illinois; both end and middle man with as many as three different minstrel companies of repute; the editor and originator of a "funny" column in a Midwestern newspaper; the author of a hundred or more songs; a blackface monologue artist; a whiteface monologist at Tony Pastor's, Niblo's, and Miner's; a comic lead; co-star and star in such melodramas as *The Danger Signal, The Two Johns, A Tin Soldier, The Midnight Bell,* and *A Green Goods Man* (a farce which he himself wrote).

Whatever Uncle Paul's relationship with his mother was as a child, he certainly loved and sentimentalized her in song. There is scarcely one without the word "mother" appearing once. He never failed to send money home to his mother who seemed to be the fountainhead of most of his genuine happiness. Some of his characteristics were similar to hers. He was clever, eager, cheerful, emotional, and totally lacking in business skill. He was generous to a point of destruction–his own. He had an ability to achieve success and a willingness to share it. His charm gave him a tremendous force and he accumulated many influential friends who recognized his ability to accomplish the tenderest results in the simplest way. As a consequence, his generosity was accepted without question, and the idea of repayment never occurred to the recipients of his many favors.

In 1885 he wrote a song little known today, but one which amassed a fortune, according to the publisher's records (Edward Dreiser), "The Blue and the Gray." His second big hit followed soon after and was titled "Just Tell Them That You Saw Me." Next came "I Believe It For My Mother Told Me So." It was shortly after this that Sarah Dreiser died and Paul quit Chicago permanently and went to New York where the publishing firm of Howley, Haviland and Dresser was formed to handle his outpouring of hits. It was in 1894 at the peak of Paul's success that Uncle Theodore came to New York and took up residence with Emma who was living with Hopkins as his wife. This was the year Emma's daughter, Gertrude, was born. Paul was on the road in a comedy, and the depression, now in full stride, meant a constant echo of "Sorry, no vacancies" to Theo's search for employment. He was later to admit that the "great city scared me stiff." Finally he did manage to summon enough courage to push aside two office boy lackeys and get into the office of one of the *World* editors, Arthur Brisbane, then also a young man, ambitious in his career.

"I want a job!" were his angry words and Brisbane, impressed with the young man's determination, took him to see the city editor who hired him. His career on what was then America's greatest newspaper was short-lived, due to a series of complications. And Uncle Theodore, despite his reportorial eye, within himself must have recognized his true creative talent lay in the realm of fiction. *Harper's* and *Atlantic Monthly* were good sources of income for such writers as William Dean Howells and Mrs. Humphrey Ward, while the type of feature writing he was doing was rare and paid very little and he was not a good "legman" reporter. Before he could be fired, he quit, and tried his hand at writing fiction with little or no success because he attempted to imitate the most popular authors—stories in which virtue was rewarded—and these efforts were rejected because of their unreality, their affectations. Uncle Theo was writing of a life he did not know, and of values he did not understand. He himself was living in a world quite different from the orderly, circumspect world of William Dean Howells.

Despite Paul's eminence and success, Uncle Theo's life as a resident in Emma's home was hardly one of serenity or security. The *grande passion* of the ill-fated lovers, Hopkins and Emma, had degenerated in an atmosphere of sordidness. Emma, whose story had been dramatic, even sensational, was lost in her predicament, and Hopkins, under the pressure of trying to find a suitable place for himself in society, was collapsing, morally and physically. It was hard to believe that the lovers who had captured the readers of the *Chicago Mail* in 1886 with such headline stories as HE CLEANED OUT THE SAFE!" (One of Chapin & Gore's Clerks Disappears with $3,500 and Some Jewelry); A WOMAN IN THE CASE! (Chapin & Gore's Embezzling Employee Said to Have Left with a Fair Companion); A DASHING BLONDE! (Embezzler Hopkins Had a Fair Companion When He Skipped for Canada; The Crooked Clerk Proved False to His Marriage Vows, and Made His Home Miserable) were the wrangling, disillusioned couple with whom he was living. Finally Theodore swallowed his pride and went to the office of Howley, Haviland and Dresser with a proposition for Paul who had returned. The firm had a smash hit in "The Sidewalks of New York" and Uncle Theodore persuaded them to let him publish a monthly magazine to compete with the periodical put out by a rival company. The partners agreed and Theo was hired to edit *Ev'ry Month* (as the magazine was called). The first thing he did when he was established was to help Emma separate from Hopkins, and to send for his brother Ed, who had been living with Al in Chicago.

In New York, the three brothers—Paul, aged thirty-six, Theodore, twenty-four, and Ed, twenty-two—tried living together in the Hotel Martinique. For a while it was a prolonged party. Paul "shone like a star when there was only one in the sky." The elaborate suite was filled with Paul's many acquaintances: "Bat" Masterson, the Western and Broadway "bad" man; Muldoon, the famous wrestler; Tod Sloane, the jockey; "Battling" Nelson, James J. Corbett, Kid McCoy—prizefighters all; Tammany district leaders including Richard Croker; Eddie Foy; George M. Cohan; George Ade; George Primrose; Teddy Roosevelt; Lillian Russell; Richard Harding Davis; Clyde Fitch; "Diamond" Jim Brady. For the Dreisers it was great, but it was doomed not to last. "It was wonderful, the loud clothes, the bright straw hats, the canes, the diamonds, the 'hot' socks, the air of security and well-being" in the "pretty, petty world of make-believe." Paul was in his element. "It was 'Paul' here and 'Paul' there—'Why, hello, Dresser, you're just in time! Come on in . . . what'll you have?" There followed more drinks, cigars, tales—magnificent tales of successes made, "great shows" given, fights, deaths, marvelous winnings at cards, trickeries in racing, prizefighting, the "dogs" some people were, the magnificent, magnanimous "God's own salt that others were." It went on ad infinitum.

But the housing arrangement did not last very long. Theo was frankly shocked at Paul's fascination with women and the shameless daring of the women in relation to Paul. He wondered about the "stabilizing morality" of the world. Paul was a sensuous, virile jokester who would arise each morning and accentuate his masculinity by hanging a towel on his erect penis while parading naked around the room. My father said Uncle Theo would become ill and rush to the bathroom and vomit in disgust. Finally he could no longer stand the bawdy atmosphere and moved out.

By 1896 *Ev'ry Month* was a success (Uncle Theodore had the good taste to publish a story by Stephen Crane and one by Brete Harte, and it is significant that he recognized realism and quality in writing and dared to publish it in a magazine which was read almost entirely by conventional, light-hearted women), and my father, Ed, was making a name for himself on the stage appearing in *Shenandoah.*

It was at this time that Theodore's friend Arthur Henry undertook to pay a visit to New York, and he found Theo most disconsolate, despite his vastly improved financial status. Uncle Theodore had been an ardent admirer of William Jennings Bryan and a supporter of the Populist Movement which had been defeated. But Theodore Dreiser's political naivete had been born, and until the day he died he would present an enigma as a man with a driving ambition for money and success and conviction which prompted him to sponsor movements of diametrically opposed motives. However, that Christmas saw the Dreiser family gathered together in a sort of reunion. John Paul Dreiser, now seventy-five, was present with Mame and Austin Brennan; Claire was there with Harry V. Gormely; Teresa, the beauty, with her husband, Ed Davis; Al–all visiting from Chicago. Paul, Theodore, Ed, Sylvia, and Emma were the New York hosts. Excepting Rome, who was, as usual, God alone knew where, all assembled for the final Christmas as a family unit. There can be no doubt that the ghost of Sarah hovered over the group–the woman who had prompted her son Paul to declare the word "mother" to be "the most beautiful of any language in the world!"

Uncle Theodore had made a visit to Missouri to see Jug, and he returned to New York more frustrated and more deeply in love than he had ever before been. He dreamed of establishing her in a handsome Fifth Avenue townhouse such as the friends of Paul occupied. As he slaved away on the little magazine (which the owners used primarily to promote songs) he grew more and more envious of Paul. Their relationship was becoming increasingly hostile as Theodore grew jealous of the successful brother whose works did not greatly impress Theodore, and whose life style rankled the unhappy Theo.

Of late there has been a great deal of controversy over who wrote the lyrics of "On the Banks of the Wabash." I choose to believe my father's version as all three brothers were in Paul's office.

> Theodore said casually, "Say Paul, why don't you write a song about a river? How about the Wabash?" Paul was delighted and said, "Theo, you draft out some words." He wrote out

LEWIS HARRISON AND PAUL DRESSER, IN "LOST, STRAYED OR STOLEN."

Here is presented the delicate humor of three gentlemen, in search of a lost infant, inquiring in the wrong home. A jealous Cuban lover's sudden return causes them to assume strange roles and mirthfully smash furniture in imitation of laborers. Uproarious applause.

Paul Dresser—very few people today know that he wrote plays and acted in them

> words for the first verse and gave it to Paul. Paul changed some of it, polished it, wrote the second verse, the chorus, and music. So there can be no argument about who wrote the song. Theo himself never wanted, and even resented being given any credit for it. (Ed Dreiser)

The song was an instant success and was later adopted as the official state song of Indiana.

The "Banks of the Wabash" doubled Paul Dresser's fame and fortune overnight. Everyone was singing it. Paul hired Max Dreyfus (who was later president of Chappell Music Company) as a song plugger and office boy, but he badly needed a singer–preferably a pretty girl. About this time a serious little note of admiration arrived from a girl named Mai Skelly, my mother, who had been studying music as long as she was big enough to sit at a piano. When the famous Paul Dresser answered her letter and arranged to see her, she was ecstatic! Mai's mother was unaware of her daughter's correspondence until Paul suggested that Mai and her mother join him for luncheon at Sherry's. At first Mrs. Skelly rebelled, as she was not prone to favor "show people," but willful Mai threatened to go alone if her mother refused. At the correct time, they took a Hansom cab up Fifth Avenue to Sherry's where Mai immediately recognized Paul from his news pictures. He was in his customary attire of beige flannel, Prince Albert coat with the mink collar, silk hat, and walking stick. Mai noticed that he wore spats and he looked to her every inch the celebrity he was. To Mai's surprise her mother was overwhelmed with Paul's charm, hospitality, and graciousness. After finishing a sumptuous lunch, they retired to Paul's suite of offices where Mai sang "On the Banks of the Wabash" for him. She had learned it well and Paul was delighted with her rendition, the quality of her voice, and her blonde beauty but he was afraid that because of her inexperience she would require considerable coaching.

During this period of further study for her singing debut, Mai Skelly was seen everywhere on Paul Dresser's arm. She led the Grand March with him at the White Rats Ball and was the envy of all the women who adored Paul. During this period Mai's mother behaved with the proper matronly dignity of a character from a Jane Austen novel. Mai was totally chaperoned until Mrs. Skelly became convinced that Paul was an honorable gentleman who was as proud of Mai as if she had been his own daughter and treated her accordingly.

It was not a difficult thing for Paul Dresser, lover of feminine beauty, to be delighted with my mother. She was petite—five foot two—with a tiny waist and trim delicate ankles which she displayed coyly beneath her fashionable skirts. Her hair was the color of honey in an era where there was little aid to hair coloring beyond a lemon rinse or a bit of camomile tea used after washing to highlight one's natural shade. Her enormous eyes were like two pieces of lapis lazuli set in her high forehead.

One day when she was rehearsing, Theodore was in the office working on the magazine. He could not keep his eyes off her and she was uneasy in his presence. He neither smiled nor spoke—he simply stared, and there was something in his stare that made her uncomfortable until Paul entered and they were formally introduced. Mai could not believe they were brothers, they were so different in appearance, in manners. She was much too young and unsophisticated to realize that Theodore was completely entrapped in his own feelings of inferiority and silenced by his shyness. They met again and Theo tried but the meeting did not augur well for friendly relations. In today's vernacular there were "bad vibes" between Mai Skelly and Theodore Dreiser and they lasted almost to the very end. In conversation, Mai learned that Theo was engaged to a girl in the Midwest. She was delighted with her name, "Jug," little knowing that in the ensuing years she and this girl would become and remain best friends.

One night Clyde Fitch, who was residing at 113 West 40th Street, was giving a large party for many notables, among whom were Ethel Barrymore and Richard Harding Davis. Paul arranged for Mai to be present and sing "On the Banks of the Wabash" and for his younger brother Ed to also attend the party on the speculation that Ed might procure a role in the forthcoming Davis play, *Soldiers of Fortune.*

For Mai and Ed it was a propitious night. They fell in love, as characters in the storybooks do, at first sight! He persuaded her to let him escort her home. Politely she asked Paul if he would mind. Ed, who was much younger than Paul, was, in Mai's eyes, more handsome, more sincere, and much more desirable as a husband.

Max Dreyfus wrote to me, "Of the three—Paul, Theodore and your father, Ed—my preference was Ed. Theodore was aloof, Paul was my boss."[1]

By the end of the evening Ed had been promised a role in Davis's play, and Mai had set eyes on her future mate. Mai decided

Sheet music for "In the Baggage Coach Ahead," a real teer-jerker

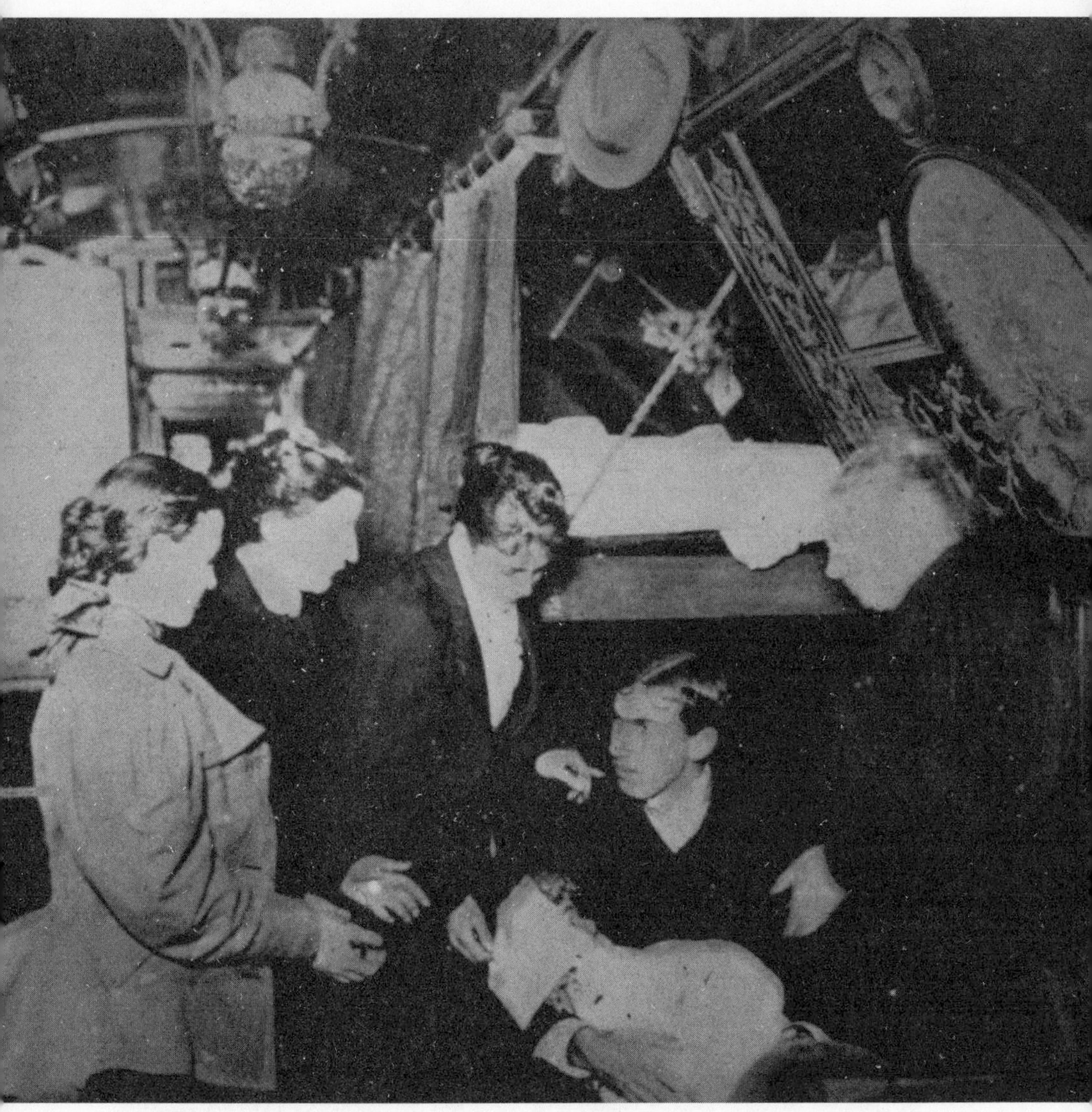

The song slide for "In the Baggage Car Ahead" showing Ed holding the motherless baby

Paul at the peak of his career

to forget her career–if Paul would forgive her!–and make her life work that of being the wife of Ed Dreiser. Ed was willing, and Paul with his typical generosity gave them his blessing and arranged for them to be married at the main altar of St. Patrick's Cathedral on June 1, 1899.

All of this hustle and bustle of romance in the glamorous setting of old Broadway amidst the white lights that shone on the famous was a part of the magic that brought about a change in the life of a young girl who was but two years older than Mai Skelly and who bore such a close resemblance to her that they were often taken for sisters. She had been on the stage for two years when Mai Skelly gave up her career to marry Ed Dreiser, and Paul needed a new girl singer. The girl was Louise Kerlin and I am including her own story of her encounter with Paul Dresser.

6

"Aunt" Louise Dresser's Story

"God is Shining My Shoes"

This was inscribed to me:

To my dear niece Vera,
In case anyone wants to know—this is how it was.
Love always,
Aunt Louise
Glendale, May 11, 1963

William S. Kerlin, of Evansville, Indiana, my father, was for many years an engineer of the E. T. & T. H. Railroad, running between Evansville and Terre Haute, Indiana. Paul Dresser at one time in his life had been a "candy butcher" on Bill Kerlin's train, and that's how the engineer and the boy became friends.

In 1899, I had been "on the stage" for a little over two years and was at that time the wife of Jack Norworth. I then went to the professional department of Howley, Haviland and Dresser Music Company in Chicago to learn some new songs. Later that same year I became Louise Dresser.

Raymond Hubbell, who has since become most prominent in the music world, was the piano player in the professional department of the music house. It was his job to teach singers all the new songs, and it came about that on the day Louise Kerlin learned "Take Me Back to New York Town" and "There's Where My Heart Is Tonight," Mr. Hubbell asked her and her husband to come and meet the author, Paul Dresser.

Of course I knew that Paul Dresser had written the "Wabash" and another song I had been singing, "You'se Jes A Little Nigger But You'se Mine All Mine." I also knew he was at that time considered the greatest songwriter of his day. Naturally, I was a little nervous. When we went to the office Paul was sitting at his desk and I remember thinking at the time that I had never seen such a fat man.

Ray Hubbell said, "Paul, I want you to meet a young lady who has been singing some of your songs and has just learned two more. Miss Kerlin, this is Paul Dresser." I said, "How do you do," but Paul just sat staring at me, and finally said, "What did Ray say your name was?" And Ray answered, "Louise Kerlin." The following conversation is verbatim.

PAUL Where were you born?
LOUISE Evansville, Indiana.
PAUL Any relation to Billy Kerlin, who ran an engine on the E. & T. H. Railroad?
LOUISE He was my father.
PAUL *Was* your father? Is he dead?
LOUISE Yes sir.
PAUL When and how?
LOUISE He was killed in a railroad accident on the C. H. V. & T. in Ohio in 1893.
PAUL Mother living?
LOUISE Yes sir.
PAUL How long have you been away from home?
LOUISE Over two years.
PAUL Married?
LOUISE Yes, this is my husband. [And Ray introduced Mr. Norworth.]
PAUL I see. Ray says you sing. Will you sing for me? Will you sing the "Wabash?"

So with Ray Hubbell playing the accompaniment, I sang the "Wabash" and the two new songs I had just learned.

They were lovely songs and I loved singing them. When I finished, Paul's face was wet with tears and he got out of his chair, crossed over to the piano, and took me in his arms. Before I knew it, I was crying too, and both Mr. Hubbell and Mr. Norworth had tears in their eyes. I don't think any of us realized it or could have told you why.

Paul asked a million questions: What had I done, what had I in mind to do–more questions than I had ever been asked in all my life, more interest than I had ever had shown in me.

Suddenly he wheeled around in his chair and called a number on the telephone. It was the *Chicago Tribune,* I think, and this is what he said to the friend he had called: "I just want you to know that my kid sister, Louise Dresser, is here in Chicago and is opening on the 'Masonic Roof' in a few weeks. I didn't want her to go on the stage, but she went anyway. She's been calling herself Louise Kerlin, but from now on she is Louise Dresser."

Then he called the Masonic Roof Garden, at that time the finest vaudeville theater in Chicago, owned and managed by John J. Murdock, one of Paul's best friends. He told Mr. Murdock he wanted an opening for his "sister"–and he got it.

Then he turned back to me. "Your father was an idol of mine when I was a boy. If there is anything I can do for his girl to help her make a name for herself, it's done right now."

He hadn't asked my consent, how I felt about it, and the two men in the room were completely ignored. It was his idea, his way of thanking my father and none of us had anything to do with it.

Do I have to tell you that we were speechless and couldn't have spoken anyway?

All I could think of was, "What would mother say?" I had completely forgotten I had a husband in the room.

We were all terribly excited. I don't mind saying that had I realized the tremendous obligation Paul was passing to me I know I would have hesitated, but I was young and never for one moment grasped the tremendous import that situation held.

We were all sworn to secrecy. Paul's younger brother Edward was at that time playing with Lottie Gilson at one of the combination houses in Chicago. He was called in, told what Paul intended doing, and he evidently approved, for he was most friendly, although I think he thought it would only be a good story for a few days, good publicity for Paul and his songs and then go the way of all good press stories.

We all had to tell many white lies, but they were harmless, and in less than six months Paul Dresser's sister Louise was definitely and firmly established in vaudeville. I opened at the Masonic Roof Garden and later on was booked for a tour of the Orpheum circuit, the goal of all good vaudevillians. I was using Paul's songs, but at the end of the act I introduced two pickaninnies who sang in German, as well as their own darky melodies, accompanying themselves with guitar and mandolin. We finished the act with a rollicking song, one boy playing a cornet, the other a tuba horn, the orchestra, of course, playing with us.

The act was always a very big hit. I always used Paul's ballads to open the act and sang three of them before bringing on the boys. The songs always were a hit and as I look back on those days I marvel at their beautiful simplicity and sentimentality. Oh, thank God, I have known people with sentiment bubbling out of all their pores; thank God I have sung to and pleased people who loved "heart ballads" and "home songs" with gestures.

Paul was proud of the success I was making, and although we seldom met, we corresponded with one another regularly.

In 1902 the Orpheum Road Show was formed, ten all-star acts, and Louise Dresser was one of them—and was I proud. We toured the regular vaudeville circuit and then special engagements through the South and West in the legitimate theaters in town where there was no regular vaudeville house. It was a grand tour and I realized I was climbing rapidly into the top ranks of vaudeville favorite. At least the act was. I did have sense enough to realize that while Paul's songs were going over beautifuly, the "picks" and our brass band finish was what made the act sensational—and the "picks" knew it also. Toward the end of the season they began to get very hard to handle, and by the time we reached Washington, D.C. they were completely out of hand. Seems they had been doing all sorts of things along the line that had been kept from me, and Mr. Norworth, who was also with the company (and also a big hit), had made up his mind that the next outbreak would be the last.

It also seems that he was thinking out another plan for me and was only waiting for a chance to put that plan into effect. In Washington he got his chance. Before one matinee I caught the boys "shooting craps" in the alley entrance to the theater (stage entrances are usually up an alley), and reproved them. The big boy turned on me, and Mr. Norworth fired them instantly. He packed their clothes, wired their mother, and put them on the train for home, all in about two hours' time. I was petrified! What would I do? What about the act, where and how could I break in two more boys? What would Martin Beck say? Who would go on in my place on the bill on such short notice?

I could see my entire "career" ruined and me back in my old number two spot on the bill. But that isn't what happened at all! I went on in my usual spot, sang Paul's songs as I usually did, only I added another one, and while I was not the "knockout" the finish of the act had been before, I did take two encores and in the vernacular of vaudeville "a couple of bows." That was what Jack Norworth had been planning for a long time, to make me stand firmly on my own two feet, and here I was doing it—and oh! how good it felt!

I began to improve in every way and developed my own little way of delivering a song, a way that sent me into the headline class before I left vaudeville and commanding a salary of $1,750 a week, a lot of money in those days (a lot of money any day.)

I loved singing simple songs, Paul's songs. Occasionally I sang songs of other writers, but not unless I liked the song, not unless I could feel it and know what it would do to an audience—unless I could feel a tear or pull a heartstring, I wouldn't touch it.

About 1904 or 1905, I was playing Keith's Union Square down on 14th Street in New York City and my act was going exceptionally well. In the repertoire of songs I was using one of Vincent Bryan's called "That's How I Love You Mame," a great song written by a great songwriter. Paul was in New York then, the firm having their publishing house on 28th Street. He sent for me to come to the office; he had just finished a song the night before, wanted me to hear it, learn it, and sing it the next matinee. It was then about five o'clock on Tuesday afternoon. My act was running so smoothly and going so well, I did hate to disturb it, especially at the Union Square where everyone came to see you, but I also hated to refuse Paul. I hesitated, and that hesitation was fatal; it was the nearest Paul and I ever came to an argument. He insisted the new song go into the place of "That's How I Love You Mame." I said "Mame" was the biggest hit of any song in my act and I thought it selfish of him to ask me to take it out. Never will I forget the look that came into his big blue eyes. For a minute they were like steel, then sarcastic, then hurt, and finally determined. "You're going to sing this song, Louise, whether you like it or not." And that settled it.

Paul was not a great musician; he strummed a few cords and melodies on a little white organ he had carried about with him for years. He had no great voice–no more had I–but oh! how he could sing!

Well, he sat down and played and sang that little song for me, had me learn it fairly well, and back I went to the theater. After the show I went back to the office, rehearsed until I was nearly dead, because I promised I would take out "Mame" and sing the new song at the matinee next day. It was a simple song, a simple melody, and although I learn songs very rapidly, you must remember I was doing something dead against my own inclinations and it was a tough job. About midnight I stopped and said, "Now, Paul, I'm going to try out this song for you, I'm going to do it the very best I can, but on one condition–you must stay away from the theater. I'll be nervous enough, and if I fail I am not going to do it with you looking at me, and if you do come to the theater, I'll go all to pieces." Finally he promised, gave me his word of honor, he would wait until I got easy in the song. Never before or since have I been more nervous opening in play, picture, or doing a new song than I was that day. In the first place, everyone around the theater was dead against my making a change in my act, "Mame" was such a big hit. Well, the time came for me to go on. I sang my first two songs, and then, just as I was about to start the new number, my eyes were drawn to a corner in one of the boxes and there, fairly stuffed into one of the chairs, trying to hug the wall so I wouldn't see him, sat Paul Dresser. I knew the orchestra was waiting for me to begin, but to save my life I couldn't think of the words. Finally, they came, but oh! so badly. I fairly stumbled through the song, fishing for both melody and words, knowing what a flop it was going to be–and it was. I ran off the stage into my dressing room and was crying my heart out when the door opened and in walked Paul. Was he sorry–did he apologize for breaking his word–did he appreciate how awful I felt? Not a bit of it. He gave me hell for being so weak-kneed and such a quitter. I called myself a performer–I could sing songs–I wanted to be a somebody in the theater–Well, I wasn't and never would be! All that he said, and more. So much, in fact, that Elmer Rogers, who managed the theater, came in and said it wasn't fair, that I had learned the song in a hurry, no orchestra rehearsal, the fault was not all mine. What Mr. Rogers didn't know was that seeing Paul had knocked everything out of my head. Finally Paul saw where he had been a bit hard on me, leaned over and kissed me, said I was a good kid and he hadn't meant a word he said and he was wrong to come to the theater. Then I said, "Now get out, all of you. I'm going to rehearse with 'Katzy' after the matinee" [Katzenstein was one of the great vaudeville orchestra leaders], and I'll sing that song tonight if it kills me." I did sing it, and have been singing it ever since. "My Gal Sal" was the biggest song hit I ever had and has come down through the years as one of the greatest heart ballads ever written.

When I got back to my dressing room after my act that night, there stood that great soul, Paul, his arms full and overflowing with violets he had bought from a flower vendor who always stood in front of the theater–he bought all the boy had. Dear Paul, dear, dear great-hearted person, what a wonderful old world this would be if there were more men like you in it.

And so Louise ended her story, telling it how it was.

It was my misfortune to never know my Uncle Paul in real life. However, he was a most important "ghost" in our household. Scarcely a day passed that his name did not crop up in association with some personality of the stage to whom he had given impetus. "Aunt" Louise Dresser, for example, during her singing days after the death of Uncle Paul, had as her piano accompanist none other than the now famous George Gershwin; and Gus Edwards, who was renowned for his vaudeville act composed of talented youngsters, had been given his first bit of encouragement when Uncle Paul published Edwards' successful "School Days." I have in my possession many of his unpublished songs, including one entitled "The People Marching By"–a protest song which makes one wonder if the lyrics were inspired by Uncle Theodore.

The people, the people are marching by,
The cry of the down trodden far and nigh,
Is heard in the homes where the weary sigh,
For the people, the people are marching by.

"The Banks of the Wabash" had been so successful that Uncle Paul wrote another river song entitled "The Voice of the Hudson," but it never obtained much popularity.

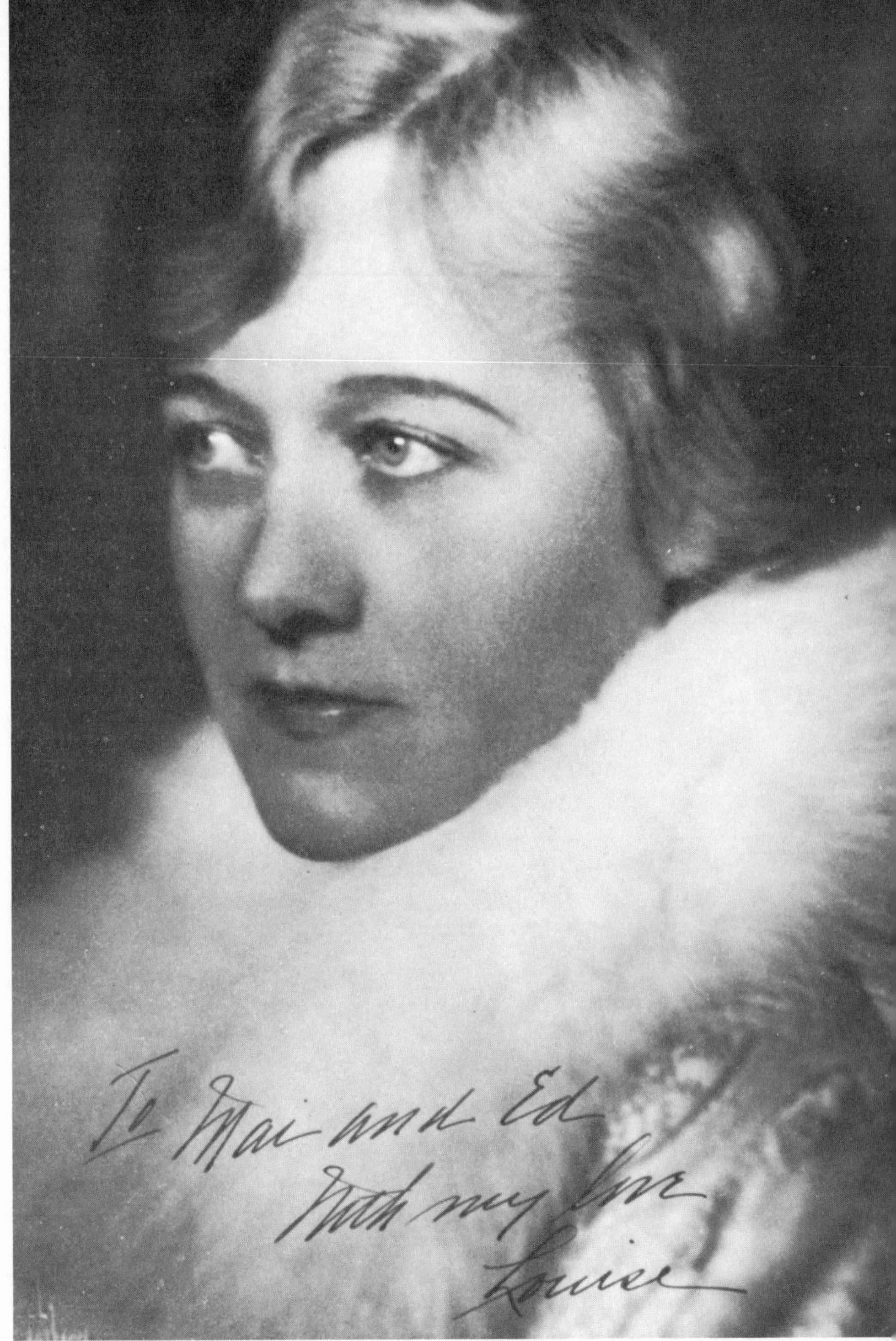
To Mai and Ed
With my love
Louise

Louise Dresser

As a man he was greatly beloved by people in all walks of life, and before he died he was urged to return to Indiana and run for the senate, but he declined.

In the 1950s I went to visit Mabel (Mrs. Fred Haviland) the widow of the Howley and Haviland Publishing Company who originally bought Uncle Paul's songs. She remembered him as always being jolly and full of fun. He was always a gentleman, she said, treating all people alike, black or white, rich or poor. Men seemed to like him as well as women and among his avid admirers were Mrs. Haviland's two maids, who vied for serving honors whenever he dined with the Havilands. Mrs. Haviland recalled that Paul worried about each song, wondering if it would be a hit. She remembered my father working at the firm when he was very young, tall and thin and "very handsome." She also recalled Uncle Theodore working at the firm but her remembrance of him was that he was "not very friendly." The relationship between Uncle Paul and the Havilands was of such importance that they named their daughter Pauline in his honor. It it had been a boy, Mrs. Haviland told me, she and her husband had planned on naming the child Paul Dresser Haviland, in memory of a man whom they truly loved and admired. Before I departed she confessed that of Paul's songs her favorite was "Just Tell Them That You Saw Me." She shook her head sadly, observing that the song made a "lot of money" but somehow they just were never able to hold on to any.

In the 1920s Uncle Theo first got interested in the Paul Dresser Estate and wanted due credit given to Paul's memory.

118 West 11th St.
N.Y.C.

Feb. 11, 1924.

Dear Ed:

You know, of course, that some years ago the state of Indiana made On the Banks of the Wabash the official state song of that state. More recently, as you may or may not know, a committee known as The Paul Dresser Memorial Committee was organized at Terre Haute, the purpose of which was to commemorate the memory of Paul in various ways. One of these is or was, for a part of this purpose has already been accomplished, to buy the old house in Third

Street, Terre Haute in which Paul was born, remove it to the banks of the Wabash, place a small park around it, plant a grove of sycamores about the house and on the grounds somewhere prepare a tomb in which Pauls ashes are to be placed after being brought down from Chicago. As you may or may not know, I was instrumental in having Pauls grave in St. Boniface, Chicago properly marked with a large boulder brought from the Wabash and a bronze plate. I pulled the string which caused the Chicago Indiana society to do that.

In regard to the purposes of the Terre Haute Committee it has already done this much. The old house has been bought by it and plans are now afoot to get the money to move it, prepare the park and the like. Quite recently this committee wrote me and asked if I would not trouble to get together copies of every one of Pauls songs with a view to having them preserved in this house. As you may or may not know, I have Pauls old piano and am going to place it in this house when it is ready. Also, a year ago I presented the Elks Club of Terre Haute with a very large framed portrait of Paul that will be transferred to this house when it is ready. What I want now is some little help in getting together everything that Paul ever wrote with a view to having them preserved in this old home. I think, also, that photos of mother and father should be preserved there.

However, just now, I want to get together as many of Pauls songs as possible. If there are any unpublished manuscripts I want those to. Have you any,—any of the very old ones, I mean, The Letter That Never Came, say, or Mother Told Me So. If you haven't any at all do you know where there are any. I have already been to see Mr. Marks and he has given me all that he has,—only a few. Paul wrote about seventy-five. I have been to see Haviland. He merely sent me to a man named Glassmaker at Ditsons. I have written him but have not, as yet, heard anything. Would Louise Dresser have any. And do you know her well enough to ask her for them. Is there any person or friend of Pauls who would be likely to have a few,—here in N.Y. I mean. How about that cousin or something of Pauls from the west who once worked for you and Paul,—Myrtle something. Would she have any of the old ones. And do you know her well enough to write her and urge her to surrender them.

Along with the rest of us this should interest not only you but your wife for it will certainly tend to cast a little honor on your daughter and she will appreciate it in due time. For the memorial is to be very beautiful. And Paul and it will be discussed for many a year.

What, if anything can you do for me in this respect.

[Theodore]

My mother's ludicrous reply to him was not only insulting but abusive and fraught with enough emotion to be suspicious. My father never knew of this until we came across a copy in her own handwriting much later. I never re-read it without laughing and meditating over the aspect of his character that made him come back again and again.[1]

Feb. 24, 1924

T. Dreiser

Put you mind at ease please, for the wife and daughter of Edw. M. Dresser will never look for honor nor glory from you nor yours.

The honored name Skelly and Kelly is the one respected name we shall depend on. No one ever can cast a slur of dishonesty nor filth on those names.

Thousands of honest dollars have been made with the honored name

Mrs. Margaret Skelly
and
Miss Annie Kelly

also by yours truly Mai V. Skelly Dresser
My husband should answer your letter as you did his –"Go to Hell"

Thats where your heading for.

Ed wanted you to do an honorable act by paying half of your brothers funeral Expenses and you told him to "Go to Hell" Write on a marble slab for the death house of Paul that his youngest brother, the baby of the family, started Paul in business when everyone else turned him down, and lost

$9,000* nine thousand dollars–and again when everyone turned their back on him–gave him a decent burial and paid for his funeral–all he got from you was "go to Hell"

Mai V. Skelly Dresser

This body was stolen from our beautiful grave by forging my mother's name to the order–forged by your sister Mary Brennan

7

The Courtship of Theo and Jug

"The little flowers of love and wonder that peep and dream, and quickly die"

Uncle Theodore's personal neurosis finally reached a stage where at one time, seated at his desk, he was actually overcome with the thought that he could not walk and was temporarily paralyzed. These seizures of panic were, undoubtedly, attributable to Sarah's constant threats of leaving when he was a child. Now that she was actually gone, these attacks would occur whenever he would feel inadequate or depressed. In the atmosphere of Paul's success, Theodore finally reached such a stage of despondency that he left the company and attempted to survive by free-lance writing—or "hack" writing as he termed it. In addition to his own problems all was not "good news" in the Dreiser family either. Teresa was struck by a train in Chicago and instantly killed. Claire wrote from Phoenix that she hated to "think that I am consumptive and doomed to end my days in that slow, miserable way. . . . " On the credit side of the ledger were the facts that Sylvia had married Hide Kishima, a Japanese-born photographer, and now lived happily in Newark, New Jersey, and Emma had finally left L. A. Hopkins, who had returned to his wife in Chicago, and she was again married.

In spite of his depression Uncle Theo managed to turn out a considerable amount of work for *Leslie's, Munsey's,* and *Cosmopolitan* magazines. On one of these assignments he took time off to once again see Jug. Their meeting had the same effect as all the others. He was madly in love with her, but he was terrified at the idea of a marriage ceremony. In his heart he wanted the pleasures of a loving wife, well trained in the arts of housekeeping (which Jug was), but he also wanted the freedom that accompanied the life of a writer, artist, philosopher. He wandered on to Chicago where he interviewed the giants of the now rich, rich city–Phillip Armour, Marshall Field, and Robert Lincoln, the son of the "Great Emancipator" who was president of the Pullman Company. While doing his writing chores, he also searched fruitlessly for Al.

It was during his travels as a wandering journalist that Uncle Theodore decided upon marriage. The lady of his choice was, of course, Sara Osborne White–Jug. Their courtship had been long and frenetic with constant lover's quarrels and reconciliations achieved via the U.S. mails. Uncle Theodore's letters to Sara Osborne White were always addressed to Miss S. Jug White, or Miss S. J. White. Only when he was irritated with her did he address her as Miss S. O. White. After one of their lover's quarrels, when he had addressed her as Miss S. O. White, he wrote to her, "I had to laugh at the request not to sign the papers S. O. White, but rather S. J. I didn't imagine it would make much difference on the papers, although I intended to use S. O. to indicate less familiarity. If you do not approve of me, I should not want to discontinue all marks of that order, because they might prove distasteful. Of course you saw it. Your great eyes see everything."

Jug had waited a long time–five years–building her hope chest while her other friends married and had children. Even when she was finally married, Jug was denied all the joys a romantic girl of her social set would have desired. The wedding took place outside the church, without any friends or relatives attending. Only Jug's sister Rose was present. It was years later with a forgetful and cruel pen that Uncle Theodore wrote: "After the first flare of love had thinned down to the pale flame of duty. . ."[1] the marriage was consummated. During their courtship their passions had reached such a peak that the denial of sexual fulfillment became a theme upon which Uncle Theo dwelt years after the marriage had been dissolved. His comments are classic:

> Love should act in its heat, not when the bank account is heavy. The chemical formula which works to reproduce the

Sara Osborne White, known to all as "Jug," was Theo's lovely first wife

> species, and the most vital examples at that, is not concerned with the petty local and social restraints which govern all this. Life, if it wants anything, wants children, and healthy ones, and the weighing and binding rules which govern their coming and training may easily become too restrictive. Nature's way is correct, her impulses sound. The delight of possessing my fiancee would have repaid her for her fears and me for the ruthlessness if I had taken her. A clearer and better grasp of life would have been hers and mine. The coward sips little of life, the strong man drinks deep. Old prejudices must always fall, and life must always change. It is the law.[2]

Those readers of Dreiser's *Newspaper Days* should realize that he was fifty-one when the book was published and was faced with the need to fortify his own masculine identity and was not likely to recall a dismal failure in the arena of love with either clarity or objectivity. Few of us have escaped the need to reshape our past in terms of the needs of the present—the more demanding the exigencies of today become, the more necessary it becomes for us to define yesterday in our own terms.

Uncle Theo's needs in his masculine identity pattern were very great indeed, and his marriage to Aunt Jug became one of the sacrifices of the past. I have no doubt that when he married her in 1898, he thought he loved her deeply; likewise I am inclined to believe that she represented the ideal in womanhood to him throughout his lifetime struggle for a meaningful love relationship. The length of their courtship was not unusual for the pattern of courtship in the Gay Nineties; his letters during this period do not indicate that their five-year courtship resulted in his becoming bored with their relationship. He appears to have accepted the custom of the era that an ambitious young man should attempt to establish himself professionally before accepting the financial and social obligations inherent in a marriage. In *Newspaper Days* he shows genuine concern for this matter when he states, "No girl of real beauty and force would have anything to do with a man who was not a success; and so there I was a complete failure to begin with."

He frequently expressed regret that he was unable to share her life because of the demands of his work as editor of *Ev'ry Month.* He reminded her by letter that he needed money to afford their marriage.

> If I had a fortune I would not need to banish these thoughts of Sara that consume my time and me when I give way to them. . . . As it is, desire for success invites, and each new point gained urges me on until I fairly lose myself in running forward. It isn't possible to go on alone and loveless. I need you and would gladly take you, but for the conditions involved. It won't be long tho' and you can afford to wait that time, which is nearer than ever.

Another letter speaks of his fear of losing her before he had established himself in a career.

> Mine is a wretched condition that calls me away from where inclination would lead me to rest. It is one of the misfortunes that overtake ambitious young men who have not inherited a competence. I left you that I might eventually draw you inseparably to me and it would be another fine irony of my fate if my venture should prove my loss of you. I would not be surprised—nothing in life can surprise me now.

Because of his concern with proving himself before marriage, there is a ring of genuine pride in his pronouncement to his bride-to-be in a letter dated February 23, 1898.

> As for clothes, I have no comment to make. You know I want to dress you according to your own good taste and shall as long as ever I am able. I am perfectly free as to time now. All my work is purely literary and my relations are with magazines exclusively. There is no more uncertainty about my income.

Theodore Dreiser's reputation as a confident Don Juan disregards the reluctance and bewilderment that marred his sexual identity. Sara evidently attempted to help him allay his fears of the marriage ceremony by making a list of everything he would need to do in preparation for the event. However, his real fears were not of the ceremony but of human demands that existed beyond the ritualistic formalities—physical demands that nauseated him. To Sara he wrote:

> We have exactly the same opinion about publicity of affection. I could not kiss you before a crowd—nor friends, nor relatives . . . people who make public display of affection sicken me.

At another time, a few months before their marriage, he returns to this fear of public display of their love; as the day of their marriage neared, his apprehensions turned to agony.

> Went and read an article on "all that relates to the marriage ceremonies and, oh dear, I almost gasped in agony. I can't, I can't do all these things. I shall be a dismal failure . . . I can't tell you, Jug, what a nervous horror I have of doing before others what seems a private matter of ours. I wish there were houses already furnished for lovers and a book to buy which would tell husband and wife what to do. The need of preparation will unstring me wholly. Write me Baby, and do help me to secure you without nervous, distressing forms.

These are not delay tactics of a deceptive Don Juan, but the indications of a deep-seated psychoneurosis. Most frightening of all to him was the sexual responsibility of marriage to a beautiful woman. In his letters, Sara could remain idolized and idealized as his source of spiritual inspiration—his "red-headed Venus" existing nymphlike in the sylvan beauty of a natural paradise. From the comfortable distance of his New York editorial office, he rhapsodizes about the possibility of sharing the splendors of nature with her as he visualizes her in her rustic Missouri setting.

> I would rather lounge under the trees there, Baby, than to be prince here. There, it seems, life means so much more, especially to me who dwells so much within myself. I would give all if I might come and always have such pleasures as that—resting beside you and enjoying nature's wide simplicity. I am not happy anymore, anywhere, except beside you.

In reality he became more and more concerned about the consequences of delaying their relationship. On the one hand, he feared that he was incapable of establishing a satisfying love relationship with any woman, least of all with one whom he had idealized. On the other hand, he was haunted by the fear of losing her, thus fortifying his suspicions of his inadequacy and casting himself into the depths of psychological despair. He was trapped in the throes of a psychological dilemma.

Sara made the sacrifice of a wedding ceremony to save Theo the personal agony of a family marriage ceremony. It was the first of many sacrifices she was to make as his wife, causing her to be described by Theodore's friend Arthur Henry as "the best wife I know." When she became Mrs. Theodore Dreiser, Sara Osborne White became involved in the entangled personality of her husband.

The marriage was doomed from the beginning, no matter how hard they struggled to make it a success. Their mating was an attraction of opposites. When Theodore recalled their ill-fated meeting, he commented, "Sometimes. I have grieved that she ever met me, or that I so little understood myself as to have sought her out."[3]

As a product of an improverished childhood he knew only change and adaptation. Born outside the comforts and traditions of middle-class America, he placed no value on her desire for constancy. When they were married Theo was still emotionally attached to a mother who had dwarfed his capacity to love, leaving him forever in a state of arrested emotional development. Consequently, he transferred to his young wife Sara the latent hostilities that rightly belonged to his mother–a woman whose death eight years earlier had served only to deepen his psychoneurosis.

Many of their mutual friends noted Jug's patience and her constant attempts to provide the right kind of environment wherein his troubled spirit might find tranquility. Theodore even recognized her efforts and told Arthur Henry: "She makes me so comfortable in a thousand ways that I'm lost now when I must take care of myself or where my personal surroundings are not just so."

Perhaps Uncle Theo's most poignant tribute to Aunt Jug's efforts was delivered the weekend he spent with my family in Far Rockaway in 1944, two years after her death. Leaning on the porch rail and looking out into the world that had always evoked his private thoughts, he asked me in a melancholic voice, "Did your Aunt Jug ever talk about me?"

There was no doubt that Sara Osborne White was the ideal

Theo and Jug in the early years of their marriage

woman embedded in the psyche of Theodore Dreiser—the one identified with the joys and bounties of nature, the pastoral beauty and the power of human goodness. In his imagination he linked the beauty and grace of Sara Osborne White with Emily Brontë and the English Romantics. Conversely, it was the theatrical Helen Richardson who appealed to the more sensuous nature that made him the literary kin of Zola and Balzac. Both women were equally important in his life, and it was his perpetual struggle between these antipodal aspects of his nature which created the towering enigma that was my uncle, Theodore Dreiser.

My own experiences with my Aunt Jug were the greatest moments of joy in my childhood. Following her separation from Uncle Theo in 1910, she spent many weekends with my family at our Far Rockaway home. Her visits were always special occasions for me as well as my mother who loved her as much as I did. Often we would play lawn games—especially croquet—but more characteristically, she would read to me or tell me stories as she was an imaginative storyteller who might have had a career of her own as a writer of children's fiction. Her voice, although soft, was resonant and projected a silken smoothness which enhanced every story and suggested a spiritual essence which was arresting. She was the only "grown-up" I knew who was captivating enough to entice me to desert my young playmates.

Always she remembered the event I looked forward to most during these visits—our climb up the ancient, gnarled apple tree which dominated the view of our spacious backyard. Donning a pair of walking shoes, which were battered but comfortable and a staple in her weekend valise, she, the eternal spirit of a free spirit, a wood-nymph, would climb with me to our leaf-fringed hideaway where I once again became the spellbound listener to one of the world's greatest, but unrecognized, storytellers. Often, Aunt Jug would pack a delectable lunch of tempting delicacies which we would share in our tree world. In retrospect, it is difficult for me to believe that she was in her mid-forties at the time of these joyous weekend visits; she had the vitality and appearance of a much younger woman. Undoubtedly, this enigmatic youthful quality may be explained not only by her enthusiasm for life—a trait which she retained in spite of numerous difficulties—but also by her striking physical beauty which she never lost, even as she grew older. For many years after she was separated from Uncle

Vera and her Aunt Jug

Theo, she was courted by a number of well-bred, urbane men who recognized her cultivation and beauty—one was an editor of *The New York Times;* another was a high-ranking naval officer. She always referred to these interesting men as her beaux, but she apparently never considered the risk of another marriage. She chose always to live alone, but she remained socially active.

Complementing Aunt Jug's physical beauty was her exquisite taste in matters of dress. Never an advocate of the décolletage, she accented her slim, supple figure with well-designed clothes in a classic vein. Most of these expensive-looking costumes were of her own creation for she was a meticulous seamstress with the imagination of a first-rate couturiere. Her ability to recognize superior quality in medium-priced fabrics, to match fabric textures to dress design, to choose the correct design for her particular figure, and to accent her pale complexion with well-chosen colors were much admired traits which undoubtedly accounted for my mother's initial enthusiastic acceptance of her into the family circle.

I remember that she often wore brown outfits because she felt that earth shades blended best with her skin and hair coloring. One of her most stunning outfits, and one that I can recall vividly, was a coat and hat she wore during the mid-thirties. The natural camel's hair coat featured a fitted bodice, a wide cinched belt, and a flared skirt boasting a wide border of brown sable at the hemline. The deep, luxuriant cuffs of brown sable extended almost to her elbow. The pillbox, her favorite hat style after her hair had been shortened, was also of matching brown sable with a jaunty pom-pom in the crown. The contrasting elements of elegant fabric and simple design produced a dramatic and appealing ensemble, but the fact that the costume was well-suited to Aunt Jug's personality and lithe figure made it even more memorable. It was the kind of outfit that every woman longs to own but seldom finds—one that expresses the inner self that she visualizes but cannot often express in her wardrobe choices. Aunt Jug was more capable than most women in expressing herself in her manner of dress, but this particular ensemble was an especially effective blending of fashion design and individual temperament.

Similarly, the basic black dress was never more in harmony with female beauty than it was with Aunt Jug—she knew well the kind of magic that black velvet worked for her. She chose simple designs with long, fitted sleeves; possibly her sleeve choice was dictated by her tender skin which freckled easily. To soften the elegance of the dark velvet, she added a carefully chosen lace collar of a good quality. In the decade following her separation from Uncle Theo, her wardrobe budget must have suffered immeasurably for her income during this period was quite limited and irregular. Her older sister, Ida White—a generous woman whom my family and I called "Aunt Handy"—worked for a magazine company; it is quite possible that she contributed to Aunt Jug's support during these financially difficult years. Even during the sparse years, Aunt Jug somehow managed to dress well; her outfits, however simple, always evidenced the good taste and imagination that were her fashion hallmarks.

Biographers and literary historians have portrayed Aunt Jug as the old-fashioned school marm with limited social poise—this depiction is such a distortion of fact that one wonders if it is ever possible for history to be recorded accurately. Although trained as a teacher, she never worked in this capacity during the thirty-four years that I knew her, nor did she ever speak to me about her teaching experiences before she married Uncle Theo. She certainly did not possess any of the stereotyped mannerisms or appearance of the turn-of-the-century school marm; on the contrary, she displayed that combination of social poise and personal charm which puts many woman at the top of envied guest lists. Always quiet in manner, she could be engulfed in laughter to the point that tears rolled down her cheeks; yet, her laughter could not be heard a few feet away. My mother, who liked to entertain in a lavish manner with large dinner parties, always counted on her confidante, Jug, to keep the party alive and interesting. These many years later, I can recall a typical party scene at the Ed Dreiser residence. Aunt Jug, dressed in a favorite outfit—a fitted black velvet jacket with wide peplum and a matching, slim, floor-length skirt, and wearing a tiny black velvet cloche with ermine trim matching the Peter Pan collar of her jacket—confident and poised, circulating among the guests and introducing herself with a charming smile, "I'm Aunt Jug, everyone calls me that so you may too if you like. . . ."

During the years of her marriage to Uncle Theo, she did not encourage social drinking at her own elegant dinner parties; in this respect, she must have fit perfectly into the image of the American housewife which Uncle Theo was uncharacteristically attempting to create as the editor of *The Delineator,* a woman's magazine to which he ascribed the highest ideals of womanhood:

> *The Delineator's* message is human betterment. Its appeal is to the one great humanizing force of humanity—womanhood. To sustain it, to broaden it, to refine it, to inspire it, is our aim.... This, then, is *The Delineator's* broadened purpose—to help every woman in this land to live better by teaching her practical home-craft . . . by strengthening her in her mortal fight for righteousness in this world.

In these years, Aunt Jug retained the stringent codes of the Missouri household in which she was reared; she was also undoubtedly frightened by the drinking behavior of some of Uncle Theo's liberal friends. In later years, she found social drinking more acceptable. I can remember seeing her standing amid small groups of admirers with a cocktail poised deftly in her right hand. However, I am sure that her opposition to drinking during the years of her marriage has been exaggerated; she was much too tolerant and understanding to have been the narrow-minded moralist. Arthur Henry, their journalist friend who encouraged the writing of *Sister Carrie,* described Aunt Jug in this difficult period of her life in terms which I find more compatible with my memory of her:

> She was not a philosopher, but just a complex combination of child and woman, a being of affectionate fidelity, devoted to the comfort of her husband, and managing, in some mysterious fashion, to reconcile her traditional beliefs with his unorthodox thoughts and ways.

Her parents demanded adherence to strict behavorial codes, but they taught their children to adapt to the world outside of their small Missouri village. Aunt Jug's family did not remain isolated in Montgomery City; one of her brothers became a Navy commander while another joined the diplomatic service and worked abroad.

Uncle Theo's letters to her, written between their initial meeting on a train trip to the Chicago World's Fair in 1893 and their marriage on December 28, 1898, indicate that she traveled a great deal in the years of their courtship. During this period she waited patiently for him to establish his career and gain the courage he needed to face marriage, a relationship he feared not because of her restraining nature, as has been claimed, but because of his own problems of self-identity.

> Do you really understand how consuming my love for you is? Do you ever dream how you walk before me, the very air and spirit of all things fair and good. Why the very essence of charm which settles like a twilight of peace about my weary heart is that which reminds me of you, my own precious love! You are here, you are everywhere, though I sigh that I cannot make you real, and I am happy, for all my longing.
>
> Lovingly,
>
> Your Theo

His letters often mention her travels, not only around the state of Missouri but also to points in the West. For example, in June, 1896, he writes, "No doubt you have left Danville by this time and are on your way West. I thought you had gone before (until your letters corrected me) but I believe you really are on your way not—or rather it's all over now, for you are in Colorado." In another letter he writes, "You're back in Montgomery now as your letter indicates. . . ." Still another opens, "A little note came from Mexico this morning and it wasn't any too soon for I was just beginning to wonder what had happened to my love—no letter in six days. . . ." Occasionally, upset by her failure to correspond regularly or fearing that she may have fallen in love with a fellow tourist, he warns her of the dangers of permitting the beauty of the landscape to unleash her passionate nature:

> I ought to tell you that—you love me, that I know you love me, but—I doubt, I doubt—because you are long silent and because I know the influence of outing life and beautiful scenery. It evokes sentiment, and in such a nature as yours, a perfect storm of sentiment. Everything in such soft and languorous climates appeals to you and in such a moment of

supersensitiveness, of wistful tenderness, almost anything appeals. In such a time there might come another, and then where would be I.

Many years later Aunt Jug became a world traveler. When one of her nieces, the daughter of her sister Rose, was graduated from high school, Aunt Jug took a group around the world to celebrate the graduation. With her usual thoughtfulness, she asked me to accompany them since I was also graduating from Wadleigh High School in New York City; but my mother, with her usual fear of permitting me a glimpse of the outside world, declined the invitation for me.

Of course it was impossible for me to grow up in the Dreiser family without becoming aware, at an early age, of the break-up between Aunt Jug and Uncle Theo. My mother, who frankly disliked Uncle Theo and felt that he constantly disgraced the Dreiser name, sheltered me from as many details of the separation as was possible. But, like most children, I was curious and took advantage of every opportunity to eavesdrop. When Aunt Jug came for weekend visits at Far Rockaway, she often brought a sewing project so that she and my mother could share their common interest. Mother's sewing room was located on the second floor near my bedroom; consequently, it was possible for me to hear some of their private conversations. Aunt Jug would relate incidents involving Uncle Theo's artist friends, many of whom she admired, or events such as the dinner parties at their elegant Riverside Drive apartment, or travels they had shared—much of her conversation tinged with nostalgia because it centered on happy times. Sometimes, following the remembrance of an emotion-packet incident, there would be silence. Most puzzling to me were the moments when Aunt Jug would erupt in tears, and Mother would begin another tirade on the subject of Uncle Theo—his wayward life, his lack of love for his family, his inability to feel shame. My father never responded to her diatribes against his famous brother; nor did he encourage Aunt Jug to reminisce. He admired Aunt Jug for her domestic talents, but he was never enthusiastic about her weekend visits; he complained that "she talked too much." His complaint was really his way of saying that when Aunt Jug was around he did not receive Mother's doting attention to which he had long become accustomed. My mother could equal Aunt Jug in her ability to spoil a husband with too many domestic comforts.

Some of Theo's letters would interest literary historians since they indicate that in his youth America's greatest naturalistic novelist showed much potential in the tradition of the English Romantic writers. At times, his desire for spiritual union with Sara White is redolent of the passionate relationship between Catherine Earnshaw and Heathcliff, Emily Brontë's immortal characters whose love dominates *Wuthering Heights,* a novel that Uncle Theo admired. On May 10, 1896, he writes to Sara:

> . . . you must think of me some evening when you are sitting on the old stoop and the moonlight is silvering the trees and blending the shadows, you know I love such scenes. They fill my heart to fullness and make me sad. I do not know why, other than that when all is so fair I feel as tho my soul were alone and that would be better were it dissolved and blended with yours. I would be you, my darling, if I could have my choice of heavenly gifts—just the deep look that rests in your eyes or the beauty that seems to dwell in the soft tresses about your forehead. I would be the feeling in you that makes you so gentle to touch, so wistful, sometimes. Oh, I'm bound my love by my own miserable personality. I pray that my regard may be that I shall be part of you. Then, surely, I shall have peace.

Likewise, his letters manifest the interest of the Romantics in their desire to grasp the ideals of man. Attempting to explain his restless nature to Sara, he writes:

> I am always moving, seeking to be nearer and more in touch with my ideals. You are one of them, quite the most dominant tho but still one. I could not rest long away from you. If I did, it would be as now, at the bitter expense of my own heart.

A recurring pattern in the love relationship as it manifests itself in the letters is the struggle between the real and the ideal aspects of his love, about the real world that placed financial, social, and physical demands on his love. Theodore would at times write about practical matters:

> What you say about St. Louis applies equally well to New York. There is a fashionable section here (or used to be) which is very small and exclusive within which any kind of quarters

> rent at $150.00 per month, but only millionaires occupy it. . . . We could get a nice four or five room flat for $95.00 here and even less. Outside of Fifth Avenue, where prices are exclusive, the average price of six and seven room flats in New York is $35.00. Some acquaintances of mine have a lovely little flat in West 21st Street, over-looking a Seminary campus–5 rooms I think–for which they pay $25.00 on the 2nd floor.

Often he demonstrates his penchant for graphic description, a writing trait which was to become an important part of his naturalistic method as a novelist; thus, he comments, "Houses here are only 22 feet wide (frontage, they call it) and the flat rooms are usually very small. You will be astonished when you come to look, but several million people seem to exist in them."

Possibly recalling the Chicago furniture dealer who twelve years earlier had repossessed the family's furniture at the railroad platform as they moved from Chicago to Warsaw, Theodore discussed the alternatives for furnishing the flat:

> I thought that we would get married, and on coming back to New York stay at a hotel or take a large room in one of the private houses for awhile. Then we would talk over the flat idea and carry it out at our leisure. I know furniture costs a great deal if you fit up a flat and settle for it–spot cash. I am not inclined to venture that until I know more, but my friend Gray advises me to have the place fitted up on credit–and should it work all right, settle for it. If not, there would be no loss, whatsoever. Or I can rent a furnished flat which is about the same thing, except that you pay all to a landlord, where in the other case you pay both landlord and furniture dealer.

More representative of Theodore's letters are those in which he transforms the reality of the moment to include an ideal existence with Sara whose absence produces a melancholy longing in him. More and more, parting from Sara becomes painful for him; he explains the torment of separation as the result of their growing interdependency, "We have grown together as things are wont to do," he writes, "and it was simply tearing physical fibre to separate."

In June, 1898, he visited Sara in her rural Missouri home. Returning to New York, he writes longingly:

> . . . I must lose myself in these poor written words since I cannot do as I would and whisper them in your ear. I have been wretched since the moment you left me and I shall be so, I know, until I see you again. I loved you before I saw you this last–but now there is but one woman in all the world for me and you are she. I love you, I want you. There is no beauty under high heaven, no merciful God, no peace, where you are out of my sight. . . . I am yours, wholly, unquestioning, until death, and I hope forever. I am yours, because in giving myself wholly to you, I realize how small a gift it is. . . . I would dwell in a shaded pathway, even though I walked the open street, and would always be somewhere, where you are, though everything about me denied it. . . . I am more than ever yours, and to be happy only need to have you near. God keep my Jug. I have learned to love. Theodore

This letter also includes a long passage in which he describes the sense of despair which engulfed him when he left Sara at the railroad station. The section is reminiscent of an 1896 letter in which he assured her that love is believed to produce only pleasure, but he has found that it also entails suffering: "But love, oh yes, love too is suffering. I have learned that also tho' once I dreamed it was endless delight. But it is pain, bitter suffering which one only too gladly endures, like He who took his cross and kissed it. . . . " In still another letter, he writes, "If Heaven is earned by suffering, surely I may claim it, tho I would willingly exchange all hope for a score of years with such love as yours ever filling the blissful moments of my days."

To the student of literature–at least those who have read *Sister Carrie*–the most interesting section of this June, 1898, letter is his recounting of the train trip from Missouri to New York. He describes the transforming effect of the sounds of the train as it sped through dark space–a sense of motion that permitted his mind to move freely in time and space, and thereby return him mentally to the loved one he has left behind:

> . . . the flying wheels and in their rhythmic beat find some thoughts which my brain would frame. I sped onward in body,

> but it was with objection and rebellion, and as the hurrying engine sped onward, marking each new village with a long cry of steam, and each farther main-road with four lonely shrieks, I sped ever backward through the far night to my Jug. Shadow was nothing, distance nothing, for I sat with my love in one dear remembered place and would not leave. . . .

One year later, in describing Carrie Meeber's momentous train ride with Hurstwood as he forces her to accompany him to Montreal, Dreiser would recall the tranquilizing effect which the motion and the sound of the train had produced in him. Of this fictional ride he comments:

> The progress of the train was having a great deal to do with the solution of the difficult situation. The speeding wheels and disappearing country put Chicago farther and farther behind. Carrie could feel that she was being borne a long distance off....

In both the fictional and the actual experience, the movement of the train placates and soothes the troubled mind, much as the motion of a rocking chair would do for Dreiser throughout his life, and provides the individual with much needed mental equilibrium.

Over and over, these letters repudiate the popular view of their relationship as an exhausting struggle between the aging, puritanical old maid and the deceptive, erotic young artist—the king of distortion which Dreiser himself would help to create by his treatment of the affair in *The Genius,* a novel that reveals wish-fulfillment more than it does fact. The feeling that dominates his letters is an intense desire to express his youthful, passionate nature in the hope of retaining the love object that inspires him—one that, at times, he fears he will inevitably lose. Caught up in the excitement of a vast, changing urban world, he seeks to share this sensually charged environment with one whose love he hopes is unchanging.

> Tuesday night . . . I walked about the outer confines of Madison Square Park. It was so beautiful that evening. A little while before it had rained, but the cloud had parted and drifted away and the yellow light in the low west made the sky . . . serene, not quite blue and not quite violet. And as I

walked along the Eastern edge of the park, I looked beneath the leaves of the thick trees which were all the more soft and odourous because they were wet, and over the carpet of close grass, and there on the west walk were lined the brilliantly lighted windows of Delmonico's, the Hoffman House, the Fifth Avenue Hotel, and all the many bright shops of flowers, candies, and knick-knacks that make Madison Square a blaze of fire by night, whose lights glimmered like floral patches of fire, most exquisite because framed in emerald of grass and leaves. Beyond still glowed the yellow sky and overhead was the soft blue, and I said, "Oh if I might walk here with Jug, or sit with her by one of these windows of the mansions that look out upon it all, and just hold her hand, how complete it would be."

The loneliness of separation appears periodically; her letters tempt him to visualize how she would have spoken the sentiment had he been present:

I take your few letters that have come since we parted—and read and reread them, because they are the only things about me that fully revive your memory to me. I try to realize how the words would sound if you spoke them, how your lips would form and your eyes soften, and then, well then some times even they become too much for me and I am compelled to turn away and let the misery of your complete absence undeceive my heightened fancy. . . . The misery of it is that I cannot materialize you and make these moonbeam fancies substantial flesh.

In his lonely moments he sometimes muses on the joys of his boyhood days, but even these moments of reverie darken to include thoughts of death. Such is the case of a response to Sara's letter from Colorado in which she praises the majesty and beauty of rapid mountain streams. As would not be surprising to those who have read his novels, Uncle Theo's preference was for quiet waters. Recalling the youthful pleasures of his Indiana boyhood, he concludes his remembrance of things past in a manner that suggests a latent death wish:

When a very young boy, I used to lie beside the banks of the

> Tippecanoe in Indiana and watch the little fishes hurrying here and there, after their own eccentric fashion. . . . The long green blades of water grass stretching one with the current and waving as the water changed its flow from side to side, always impressed me. . . . I always imagined that should some overwhelming sorrow take from life its natural delight, I would love to seek that quiet nook and lie down to rest in that crystal sepulchre and pillow my head upon the grass and shining sand. There would be peace at last, for the flesh, there would be quiet and beauty unmarred by sorrow and wearisome longing. Even now, sometimes, I fancy such a nook would prove a haven of rest indeed.

In the spring of 1898 he writes in an especially nostalgic mood–his lonely state of mind causes him to reflect on the earlier years of their relationship–the winter of 1893–94 in St. Louis–when their love was filled with a sense of joyous expectation:

> All evening a strain of remembrance has revived the nights when I used to "call" in St. Louis, and somehow I have lived over to myself the lightness of heart that swayed me when you were coming, the tremblings of joy I experienced when I knew you were really come, and were waiting for me. And I have said to myself that nothing since has been at all so good or so delightful as the nights that I spent with you who loved me.

Further, in paying tribute to the depth and endurance of her love for him through the five years of their courtship, he added: "Such a wealth of love no man deserves, and much less I–I know you would lay down your very life for me. I know that your love, even for your own peace, will not die, and yet I am not worthy to kiss your feet."

Perhaps the real tragedy of the marriage of Uncle Theodore and Jug–especially for Aunt Jug–was the lack of children. Like the wives of many creative artists Aunt Jug had to suppress her own desire for children. Her husband and his works of art have to satisfy the woman's normal procreative urge–both become the children of the genius. Aunt Jug could not have been blissfully happy in her unfilled role as a woman, and she must have been wounded by much of Uncle Theo's attitude toward her and their marriage. Nevertheless, she struggled on with sincere devotion. She called him "Honeybugs" and he called her "Kitten," and in these pet names one can sense the immature and flimsy structure of their marital relationship.

It was eight months after marriage that Theodore's good friend Arthur Henry came to their rescue by inviting them to come and visit with him and his energetic wife, Maude Wood Henry (who was one of the first career women, a female publicist, handling publicity for the Theodore Thomas orchestra). The Henry home was a handsome old fourteen-room riverfront structure. Here, the Dreisers and the Henrys had a happy sojourn. Jug, an excellent cook, presided over the kitchen while Maude Henry supervised the housework. The men wrote together in the wood-paneled, basement study which had an open fireplace and a good rocking chair for Uncle Theo. Nearby was a little river where the men could take a morning plunge. The nights were occupied with the men and their wives sitting on the back porch, talking and singing, while the wooded world glittered with the lights of fireflies and their happy voices were accompanied by the croaking bullfrogs. It was an idyllic setting. Arthur Henry greatly admired his friend Theodore and urged him to write fiction. Even then the name Theodore Dreiser was indeed impressive. He was already listed in *Who's Who* as an editor, poet, and author. Henry was insistent and Uncle Theodore later said, "Finally, I took out a piece of yellow paper and to please him wrote down a title at random–*Sister Carrie.* My mind was a blank except for the name. I had no idea who or what she was to be. I have often thought there was something mystic about it, as if I were being used, like a medium." In September, the Dreisers returned to New York to an apartment at 6 West 102nd Street and during the winter of 1899 Theodore Dreiser wrote the novel which was to change the course of American literature and which with its publication in 1900 was to alter the lives of Theo and Jug. In a single work the destiny of my Uncle Theodore was finally shaped. He had unknowingly created a revolutionary work of art. "I thought it was rotten," he later recalled, but his friend Henry persuaded him to forge ahead. Without the restrictions he had suffered while writing for editors he found that his pen was like a magic wand. He wrote easily, and with an appalling honesty told the story of his own sister, Emma, as he had seen her drama unfold. He wrote with a compassion for human suffering and a tolerance for transgression against the existing codes of morality. He had taken his stand on the side of the "sinner," the "immoral ones." He shot a straight arrow at the heart of the hypocrisy which garbed the world about him. Once it had hit, there was no walking away from the corpse for Theodore Dreiser.

During the writing, Jug helped him with copy reading and grammatical corrections, Arthur Henry assisted in "cutting." When Uncle Theo suffered from insomnia and paced the floor, Aunt Jug trotted behind him like a faithful puppy. In order to survive while he was writing *Carrie* Theodore also had to turn out magazine articles, but he, nevertheless, completed the manuscript in seven month's time and had it ready for a publisher.

The year *Sister Carrie* was completed and published, John Paul Dreiser, Sr., died at the home of Mame and Austin Brennan where he had lived quietly, enjoying himself tending the flowers in the garden and making himself useful doing chores around the house. Mai and Ed were there too. Before he died he had the satisfaction of being offered the salary of twelve thousand dollars a year to manage the mills of the American Woolen Company of Massachusetts. At the time he was no longer physically able to handle the responsibility but it was a boost to his ego to know that his ability in his field of work had not gone unrecognized by those in a position to know his true worth. Years later his daughter Mame, who had been one of his more rebellious daughters in her youth, wrote to his granddaughter the following letter in reply to Gertrude Hopkins' query as to what he was really like. Since the letter was written after his death, and the tone is tempered with the passing of time and the cooling of flaming passions, it might be regarded as sentimental nostalgia, but Mame was not made of such an emotional woof.

THE HOME OF MY EARLY CHILDHOOD

My Dear Gertrude

You have always wanted to know something of my girlhood and I am trying to recall what I remember. Was born in Indiana in a small hamlet and up to the age of nine was very happy in a little home amid large trees, flowers of every description, dear little brothers and sisters for playmates, a pet pig much loved and bathed every day, likewise a big dog loved by all.

Darling Mother (may God bless her) one of the best that ever lived, ever patient and fearless lived to make everyone happy. In the summer we had an immence swing and every Sunday, Father would give us a treat.

I love to recall those days . . . Father and Mother always happy with their brood about them. Father was an expert woolen man with a good business making blankets and woolen cloths, was a generous provider. When he passed from this life no money was left nor any collection of things material, but what was left could not be measured by any material standards . . . a man of stability whose word was his bond . . . Father lived his Christianity seven days a week. Never uttering a blasphemeous word or relating an obscene story. In my mind's eye again I see the little home and the little white church down the street in Sullivan. It brings a picture of Father's sincerity and the true value of his daily life, very precious to me now. Since learning more of the spiritual truths and the great secret of prayer recalling particularly the morning and evening prayers when all would gather around hearing again the earnest voice raised and noting the spiritual glow in his face as he would state with conviction Grosser Got Were Zobendech.

For years he asked God's blessing for the day and the night. We were a large family and I am sure He was asking God's protection. I like to think that wherever He is the prayers are still ascending for us all. I am sure things would be better in this dear good Earth of ours would all families unite with their children for prayers night and morning teaching them to express gratitude for the blessings received.

Sincerely
Mary Frances Brennan (Mame)

(Original lent by Gertrude Hopkins [now deceased] and returned at her request.)

8

The Delineator Days of "The Genius"

"To walk a lonely, cold road with one's own lonely, cold, desperate soul"

When *Sister Carrie* was presented to Doubleday, Page, it was first read by Frank Norris, author of *McTeague*, who said, "It is a wonder!" What happened to the novel has become a segment of American literary legend–its suppression by the publisher (a fact brought about because of Mrs. Doubleday's aversion to the book) and the critics' apathy to the work or condemnation of its "immorality," dreariness, and overall philosophy of despair. Dreiser was ahead of his time. Not a single American critic recognized that the novel was so surpassing in its realism and humanity that it bypassed all existing forms of literary criticism.

The treatment *Sister Carrie* received was a terrible blow to Uncle Theo and to his self-belief which had never been absolutely secure. The world of *Sister Carrie* was a world which he knew firsthand and had written about in his earlier pieces of journalism and hack writing–a world of factories where men and women worked long hours for little pay, of tenements, railroad yards, of Tin Pan Alley and Broadway, of music and lights, of breadlines and poverty, of elegant restaurants and luxurious hotels as well as cheap rooming houses and cutthroat saloons. The novel was not only the story of his sister Emma and L. A. Hopkins, but it is also the story of Theodore Dreiser coming to grips with himself. He was beginning to make up his mind about the meaning of family, of the city, of moral conventions, and he, in the writing, reached certain conclusions which dominated his life thinking. It is a story of longing and desire, of struggle and ambition, of weakness and strength. Money is the prime motive for his characters and money was to be the prime motive in all of his succeeding books. In *Carrie,* Theodore first expressed his belief in blind and insignificant man continually struggling for fulfillment in the face of death. Through his reading of Spencer and his involvement with that philosopher's work, Theo had made his final break with formal religious rituals. In *Carrie* he created an amoral world in which there was no relationship between the virtuous life and earthly reward. The literary world's inability to accept this theme merely intensified the emotional problems which had beset him from early childhood.

His hurt was of such a nature that it can be comprehended only by someone who has suffered a similar rejection. And it was magnified by the death on Christmas day, one month after *Carrie's* publication, of his father, a man whom he had never understood and who had inspired in him an ambivalence that controlled much of his behavior. At the death of his mother, Dreiser had felt deep sorrow, but also relief; at the death of his father he was haunted by puzzling questions and inner torments of guilt.

The unfavorable reaction to *Carrie,* however, sparked Dreiser's belief in his ability as a writer and he refused to return to hack writing. He then started a second novel, *Jennie Gerhardt,* and wrote several short stories. But his psychoneurosis had commenced to manifest itself. He suffered from pains in his fingers and brooding thoughts of suicide. In September, 1901, *Sister Carrie* was acclaimed in England. It was compared with Zola's *Nana* and its author was hailed as "an author of exceptional merit." But even this news could not lift him from his oncoming depression. He moved from place to place, he fought with his good friend and collaborator Arthur Henry, and he was at odds with Jug, whose morality offended him. He felt a need for the admiration of women to supplant the admiration the world was denying him. In sexual activity, he found stimulus and beauty. He wrote, "The whole matter of the sexes, their contacts, the sense of beauty and color and romance that surrounds the physical lure each has for the other, is to me more beautiful than I can say, the quintessence of beauty." As is customary during the process of a nervous breakdown, the person closest to the object becomes the most maligned. Aunt Jug was the hapless victim. In their pursuit of his comfort Theo and Jug left New York and went to Bedford, Virginia, a quiet town near Roanoke. There were mountains nearby and for a time he seemed better, but the effect of the change was shortlived. His depression returned and deepened. He and Jug made a trip to the White farm in Missouri which instead of helping him activated the nervous condition, apparent even to Jug's parents. They felt he needed "a rest." Actually, he needed to feel confident in his work, and he needed money to offset his chronic worry about poverty. Like the sick and despondent man he was, he was in constant flight from himself. He tried the curative springs, walking which had always previously helped him, visits to the beach, all to no avail. By June he was a "basket case." He was convinced he was going "crazy." He brooded over *Carrie* and he was unable to proceed with *Jennie.* He and Jug were in Philadelphia when Uncle Theo decided she would have to return to her family, and he would have to fight his own battle for his sanity.

At the end of six months he left Philadelphia and returned to New York in search of a job—any job. His living conditions were horrible. He suffered from insomnia and when he slept he was tortured by nightmares. He was now in the throes of a severe emotional disorder. That he had family, places to go for help, never entered his mind and he lived on a ten-cent-a-day food allowance and $1.25 room rent. Finally he swallowed his pride and went to the Imperial Hotel where Paul Dresser and Pat Howley, richly attired, happened to step out of the door as he was standing debating with himself whether to enter or not.

Paul was shocked at Theo's appearance. "For God's sake," he begged, "don't let your pride stand between us." He was further alarmed by Theo's determination to go to work for the railroads as a simple day laborer for he was convinced his muse had deserted him. He was filled with self-pity and self-degradation. Paul stopped him in the midst of his senseless speech and said, "You'll do nothing of the sort—why you're not able to work!" Paul decided to send him to Muldoon's—"a repair shop" as Muldoon called it—an estate in Westchester maintained mostly for wealthy alcoholics to dry out and make a reentry into the world of the living. It was an ordeal for Uncle Theo, who was physically not up to the strenuous program, but somehow he managed to survive and Muldoon's harsh criticism brought him to his senses and made him realize that he had to get his mind off himself, repair his badly neglected body, and make a fight for actual survival. When he left he got a job piling lumber at fifteen cents an hour at a lumber yard in Kingsbridge and was eventually joined by Jug. He spent three years working for the railroad, all the while in deep despair, but Christmas Eve, 1903, he resigned from the railroad and was able to write. "After a long battle I am once more the possessor of health. . . . I have fought a battle for the right to live and for the present, musing with stilled nerves and a serene gaze, I seem the victor." He got a job as an assistant feature editor of Frank Munsey's *New York Daily News* and he and Jug made an attempt to pick up the pieces of a badly shattered marriage. He was bitter over the loss of three years from his life and his work and when he was not busy writing he was studying, educating himself in history and philosophy. In the meanwhile, he made friends with Charles Agnew MacLean and was eventually made editor of a new journal, *Smith's Magazine.*

While Uncle Theodore's fortunes had been at an all-time low, Paul wrote "My Gal Sal." Although it later made a small fortune it was only a moderate hit when written. Paul and Pat Howley had bought out Fred Haviland and continued in business as the Howley-Dresser Company. They fared poorly and when the firm failed, my father, Ed, left the stage, as a result of an accident which temporarily blinded him, and established the Paul Dresser Publishing Company on West 28th Street. In business, Paul was so notoriously inept that he was actually barred from exercising any authority but was paid twenty-five dollars a week for the use of his name. But the venture was not a success, although Ed did make his debut as a songwriter with his initial song, "The Girl in the Gingham Gown," published by Charles E. Harris Co. The loss of prestige and money was too much for Paul Dresser. He began to decline in health as rapidly as he declined in wealth and, in time, he admitted defeat by leaving his Broadway residence and moving in with Emma at 203 West 106th Street where he tried futilely to knock off some new tunes on his big rosewood piano. His mood was no longer jovial and he had a strange presentiment of his death. Just before he died he completed his final song entitled "The Judgment Is at Hand."

Theo was very concerned and took time to visit with Paul and buoy his fading spirits, but he sensed he was coping with the impossible. Without his boisterous companions, his life on the

Great White Way, his free-spending, generous giving, Paul was already dead in spirit. He had taken to his bed and only seemed alive when Theo would come and the brothers would reminisce. At times Paul would momentarily be his old self, "full of ridiculous stories, quips, and slight *mots.*" Then, one evening in November 1906, Uncle Theo got a call from Emma. Paul had died at five in the afternoon, a blood vessel bursting in his head. When Theo arrived, Paul was already cold in death, "his soft hands folded over his chest, his face turned to one side on the pillow, that indescribable sweetness of expression about the eyes and mouth–the empty shell of the beetle."[1]

Since Paul was ostensibly a Catholic, and his sister-in-law Mai a Catholic, arrangements were made for a solemn high requiem mass at the church of one of his favorite priests. All Broadway was there and flowers, flowers, flowers! The family was shocked to discover that Paul had died penniless. Mai and Ed paid the funeral expenses and he was buried in the family plot.

The later removal of Uncle Paul's body from my Grandmother Skelly's plot in Calvary Cemetery became a tall tale, to be told and re-told in the Dreiser family lore. When it occurred it caused a great deal of consternation and not a small number of problems. In retrospect it has assumed the diabolical aspects of humor which often accompany death. The playwright has ofttimes relieved the pressure of death with a moment of comedy (witness the confrontation of Hamlet with the Grave Digger). And death in the emotional and volatile Dreiser family, as we have already noted in the incident of Sarah's death and burial, assumed a colossal structure of high drama.

After Paul had been buried in the Skelly family plot, my parents, who were responsible for the upkeep of the grave, were not a little bit disconcerted when the cemetery custodian notified them that the body had been removed!

When, where–and by whom? And, with whose permission?

After considerable effort, my mother discovered the body had been taken from its resting place by Mrs. Austin Brennan who signed the necessary papers. Years later, doubting my mother's accusations of forgery by the Dreisers, I decided to check the matter out with the trustees of Calvary Cemetery. Their reply indicated that my mother was indeed correct, as my grandmother's name had been forged!

Calvary Cemetery
L.I. City 1, New York
STillwell 6-8000

Gate of Heaven Cemetery
Hawthorne, New York
Pleasantville 2-3672

TRUSTEES OFFICE
29 East 50th Street, New York 22, New York
PLaza 3-4883

April 7,1960

Miss Vera Dreiser,
225 West 86th Street,
New York 24 NY.

Re: 16-22-A-11/15

Dear Miss Dreiser:

In reply to your communication I wish to advise you that the records of Calvary Cemetery indicate that the remains of Paul Dresser were interred in the above mentioned graveholding on February 6, 1902.* Under date of March 19, 1906 the remains were removed on written authorization of Mrs. Austin D. Brennan and Maggie Skelly.

Trusting the above information will be of service to you.

Yours very truly,

V. Rev. Msgr. Henry A. Cauley
Managing Director

*Typographical error. Paul died in 1906.

Mame?. . . But it had been a forgery, as the papers permitting removal of the corpse were signed by a Maggie Skelly–*heavens!* My grandmother was Margaret Skelly, never Maggie.

When the tumult and the shouting died it was learned that Mame had brooded about Paul's being buried in the Skelly plot instead of where she felt he should rest—by the side of his beloved mother in Chicago, where, along with his father, he now lies, I hope, in peace. The hassle over full payment of the burial brought forth a letter from the funeral director to my mother telling her that he told Mr. Brennan and others a few things that "I would not mention to a lady which I found you to be" and that "I like your feeling in the matter and hope at some future time you would throw a funeral my way to make up some of the losses I have sustained." I thought this was too priceless to omit.

Uncle Paul's beloved piano was given to Theo and he had it converted into a desk. It was the one possession he treasured all of his life, and carried with him as a cornerstone wherever he lived. When Theo finished his short story "My Brother Paul," H. L. Mencken wrote him to say, "You missed a fine chance when you didn't write a book about your brother Paul. . . . Why not a full length book on a genuine American original?" But the sibling rivalry was too overwhelming, as it rested largely on the personality factor Theo lacked—self-assurance. He envied Paul this asset all of his life and although he made many overtures to see that Paul had his due recognition, the gestures were made after Paul was long since deceased and no longer a threat to Theo's ego. Later, a memorial was erected to him in Terre Haute, the site of his birth. Paul Dresser received a love and acclaim from all of Hoosierdom that was never afforded Theo.

After Paul's death, Theo's career took an upturn, again based on that trick word—chance—upon which he leaned heavily in his fictional plots. If there is one consistent theme in Theodore Dreiser's work it is that society tries to make man into something he is not. Underneath the respectable surface of social conventions there is a realm of life—vital, forceful, chemical, and crude—something which most civilized minds cannot and will not tolerate. Chance experiences surface all of the elements and the ensuing action of the individual is ascertained by the whims of chance. It was a chance encounter with Flora Mai Holly, one of the first New York literary agents who undertook to find a publisher brave and daring enough to republish *Carrie* (the plates which Theodore now owned), that was the necessary chance turn of the screw in his career. His growing paranoia and distrust of publishers made him very skeptical and he would not enter into an agreement with the publisher Miss Holly found until he was convinced that *Carrie* would get the proper attention and critical reviews. He put five thousand dollars into the firm so that he could guide the launching of the reborn *Carrie*. The money was from Paul's music royalties, which he handled. The result was spectacular. *Carrie* was hailed as a "work of genius." Dreiser was a name of fame. He was interviewed and praised. This time his goal was money and he let it be known in literary circles that he desired an important job. It came in the form of editor of the Butterick "trio" *(The Delineator, Designer,* and *New Ideas for Women)* at a starting salary of five thousand dollars with a percentage as circulation increased. He had finally arrived, but he was torn in his ambitions—in his search for financial security, his rags-to-riches philosophy which clashed with his belief in a higher reality that negated man-made laws and material goals. The personality split was in the open when he assumed his role as editor of *The Delineator* and announced his goal: A BIGGER DELINEATOR.

The man who assumed the editor's role at *The Delineator* bore little resemblance to the struggling, frustrated writer who had endured one of the most incredible persecutions in literary history. The suffering had taken its toll and added to the many psychic injuries of childhood, adolescence, and early manhood. His outward behavior was indicative of the personality problems. The Theodore Dreiser who came into office with every department of the organization under his control was determined to succeed—no matter what sacrifices had to be made. If he could not be recognized as an artist, he was determined to get the recognition he needed as a successful man of business. He had not been able to complete *Jennie Gerhardt* so he undertook to pay off the advance he had received and put the novel aside while he carved a new career for himself. His reputation was that of a tough, at times cruel editor who drove himself and his staff to the breaking point. There were times when he would revert to the sweet side of his nature and be kind and considerate, but his gift for sarcasm was renowned in the publishing circles of New York. All of his behavior was promoted by the fact that he had concluded that life was a struggle and one was either a winner or a loser. To date, he had been a loser. His fear of being a total loser like his father (who once had attained considerable recognition, but had been defeated) had become an obsession, and his bout

Theo, no longer the "ugly duckling"

with poverty had left scars which would never totally be healed even after he had attained recognition and wealth.

When he came to *The Delineator,* he was to experience two new emotions. The first was the feeling of *power,* which he acquired through the authority vested in him. He discovered many doors were open because of his position on the magazine and many people were willing to work on his behalf for the ideas he presented. Granted that these schemes were for promotional purposes, he, nevertheless, managed to corral the energies of such women as Mrs. Edith Rockefeller McCormick, Mrs. Frederick Dent Grant, and Mrs. William Jennings Bryan on a campaign sponsored by *The Delineator,* the Child Rescue Campaign, "for the child that needs a home and the home that needs a child." The campaign lasted for three years and Theodore devoted many hours to the cause (it was extremely useful in subscription results). (Here again is an example of the contradictions in Theo's personality. He loved children in the abstract, that is, so long as they were not under his feet. He genuinely did not want to see children homeless and deprived, yet he forbade Jug, who was a frustrated mother, the privilege of having children.) All of these promotions sponsored by *The Delineator* not only contributed to the growing mailing list, and to Dreiser's personal income, but put his name before the American public, before men and women who had never heard of the author of *Sister Carrie* which was now well accepted in intellectual circles as a masterpiece.

The second emotion he was experiencing–alienation–resulted from his final removal from family intimacy. The death of his father had brought about a fight with Mame and Austin Brennan over the burial expenses; Paul's death had relieved him of any emotional or financial responsibility; and his relations with his brother Ed had been strained ever since Ed had married Mai Skelly with whom Theo constantly disagreed. After the publication of *Sister Carrie* Mai had little but contempt for Theo and as his treatment of Jug worsened with his success, she sided with Jug who had been a bridesmaid in her wedding and of whom she was genuinely very fond. In time, Mai estranged herself and her husband from Theo. Mai was disgusted with Theo's book despite the acclaim it had finally received because she felt it disgraceful that he had capitalized on the unsavory career of Emma who was now married to George Nelson but was still unhappy. After Paul died, her son ran away because he could not tolerate his stepfather. Years later,

Emma, who was the frailest in spirit and mind, entered into an early senility and her only plea in life was for "Peace." To be away form the bickering, the daily problems, the emptiness of life when youth was gone, away from the forces which eventually destroyed her. Yet, ironically, both of her children made successful careers–George becoming the manager of the Ambassador Hotel in New York City, and Gertrude, after an unsuccessful try at concert and theater, becoming educational representative for Con Edison in New York. Rome was, as usual, in transit; and Al, long lost and forgotten, existed only to haunt Theo in his writings. Claire was ailing.

And Theo had begun the quarrels with his friends which lasted throughout his career. That he had great charm, and great ability to attract people is evident, but he lacked that quality which made it possible for him to retain a relationship over a long period of time whether it was with man or woman. He quarreled usually over matters of money, and his increasing paranoia made him suspect his best friends and become convinced they were either trying to cheat him or turning against him. The first of his good friends to fall by the wayside was Arthur Henry when his book *An Island Cabin* was published and Dreiser was portrayed as Tom, the hypocritical Thoreau worshipper who found nothing but things to complain about in his visit to the idyllic cottage in the woods, by the sea. Actually, Theo had resented his friend's interest in Anna, the girl Henry later married, and felt "left out." With Henry lost as a friend, Theo found a new one in H. L. Mencken. The friendship came about under a somewhat amusing set of circumstances in view of the facts known about each man's life. Theo was editing a magazine which specialized in dainty stories for dainty women and Mencken was ghostwriting for Dr. Leonard Hirschberg a series on "The Care and Feeding of Babies." The two men became fast friends, although they often argued over literary matters. Mencken had just written a book on the philosophy of Frederick Nietzsche and he tried unsuccessfully to convince Theodore that Nietzsche was an important thinker. Theo wrote Mencken: "I can't say I greatly admire him. He seems to be Schopenhauer confused and warmed over."

There is some humor in the idea of these two literary giants concerned with the literary requirements of ladies, but as yet there was no place for either of their efforts. However, it should be noted that while Theo was editor of *Delineator* and was in a financial position to pursue his writing he did nothing except promote his career as an editor. His recognition as a crusader came after a visit to the president of the United States, Theodore Roosevelt. Theo persuaded the president to take an interest in his campaign on behalf of orphans. His visit ultimately resulted in the founding of the National Child Rescue League.

The association with Mencken also helped Theodore make the final break with organized religion. He had become a recognized churchhater, but he had begun his search for a different form of religion. He wrote to Mencken in criticism of Mencken's *Decay of the Churches:* "Isn't seeking knowledge (scientific) a form of prayer? Aren't scientists and philosophers at bottom truly reverential and don't they wish ardently for more knowledge. . . the truth is men are not less religious–they are religious in a different way–and that's a fact."

That Uncle Theo had the world in the palm of his hands at the period of his editorship at *The Delineator* is evidenced by letters to be found in the Manuscript Department, Lilly Library, Indiana University, Bloomington, Indiana. In these letters from the president of the American Civil Alliance, Uncle Theo was asked to be a guest of honor along with such dignitaries as President-elect Taft, J. Pierpont Morgan, Andrew Carnegie, Admiral Dewey, and other such eminent citizens. Later he was to be made secretary of this organization whose purpose was "To establish a great national CENTRE of reliable political knowledge." (Quote from constitution of the American Civil Alliance, Dreiser Manuscripts, Indiana University.) Along with such men as Charles Eliot of Harvard, representing education, former presidents of the United States, statesmanship, Luther Burbank and Thomas Edison, science, Theodore Dreiser was to represent American letters.

In addition to this honor, Judge Ben Lindsay recommended Uncle Theo to attend the National Congress on Home Education held in Brussels. He was recommended as a result of his "splendid work" in bringing about the White House Conference on Dependent Children, called by President Theodore Roosevelt.

Uncle Theo used his power as editor of *The Delineator* to foster child care–especially the placing of orphans in desirable homes. He was highly commended by such organizations as the State Charities Aid Society, of which Joseph Choate was president, and the Russell Sage Foundation. Correspondence attesting to his industry and help are on file at Indiana University.

While his interests were primarily humanitarian and

sociological he also exhibited a strong interest in all of the arts, as is evidenced by correspondence between him and the curator of the Metropolitan Museum of Art which approved his recommendation for a circulating system of art exhibits making it possible for the people residing in other cities and small communities to have the opportunity to see the same masterpieces the people of the great metropolitan centers were privileged to enjoy.

All of these civic projects are mentioned to illustrate the enormous scope of Theodore Dreiser's genius, and also to point out the depths of his insecurities which made him throw over a life which would have been more than satisfying to the most ambitious of men—in order to satisfy a mere romantic whim, an insatiable, frustrated passion for a girl young enough to be his daughter.

There is little doubt that Theodore Dreiser could have continued as editor of *The Delineator* as he was indeed a success in every sense of the word. He was highly regarded by his co-workers, even if occasionally there were personality rifts, he had vastly increased the circulation of the magazine, and he had even elevated its standards of literary production. He, himself, was famous and prosperous. Even though his life with Jug did not come up to his expectations, it was not unpleasant and the one who suffered from Theo's negligence was Jug who tried to compensate with an interest in Christian Science and an attempt at a good social life. All might have continued smoothly if one Thelma Cudlipp had not appeared on the scene.

Thelma was the daughter of one of the assistant editors, Mrs. Annie Cudlipp. She was seventeen, beautiful, and talented, and was enrolled in the Art Student's League. The mother and daughter were frequent guests at the literary soirees which Jug supervised, and Jug and Theo went to parties at Mrs. Cudlipp's apartment along with Homer Croy and Fritz Krog, both protégés of Theodore. Without any forewarning Theo fell madly, hopelessly in love with a girl less than half his age. He threw all discretion to the wind. Before long the entire staff knew of his infatuation, and when Mrs. Cudlipp went to the owners, Theo was fired with the face-saving announcement that he was taking a year's leave of absence. The dismissal did not deter Theodore in his passionate pursuit. He left Jug and went to live in the Park Avenue Hotel, but later moved to the Riverside Drive apartment of his friend, Elias

Rosenthal. Mrs. Cudlipp was so terrified by Theo's infatuation for her daughter that she literally kidnapped the girl, taking her to England. Theo was not given her address, nor allowed to communicate with her for one year. "I am so lonely . . . I love you, love, you, love you. . . ." he had written her. His nickname for Thelma was "Honeypot." Six months before he deserted Jug he had commissioned an article, "How To Keep Your Wife's Love."

In every form of analysis, Theodore Dreiser was a romantic. The romantic is constantly in flight, believing in the flux of experience that some kind of chance occurrence will result in his total self-realization. Theo always felt "I was destined for a great end," and "that certain lives are predestined."

At the very hour of his denouement as editor of *The Delineator,* he responded to the question of his young secretary, William Lengel (who was to be a lifetime friend), as to how so young a man could have possessed such a knowledge of life, such pity and understanding to have written *Sister Carrie,* with the simple reply, "Genius, I suppose."

It was not conceit, it was just Theodore Dreiser's acceptance of a destiny awarded him by powers over which he had no control, by an accident of nature for which he was not responsible.

In an era of big business, Theodore Dreiser created a complex type of Horatio Alger hero whose problems were money, success, and sex. He had come to believe that if one desired something long enough and hard enough one obtained it and in most instances this was what happened to him. The women he desired eventually came to him, as if drawn by a magnet, some force beyond their control. It was when he was confronted with opposition, as he was in the case of Thelma Cudlipp, that he became frustrated and behaved as if some other person had taken control of his mind and body. He was prostrated to find himself the center of a melee of gossip, enmities, embarrassments, and sexual longing. He began to collapse physically as he found himself defeated at every turn. He had lost his position, his income, and his home—and he had not obtained the love of his life. In his despair he turned to his writing. He picked up the unfinished manuscript of *Jennie Gerhardt.* A chance force had once again compelled Theodore to write full time. He finally became convinced it was his destiny.

If "chance" were the element that impelled Uncle Theo to resume his literary career with the writing of *Jennie Gerhardt,* it was also the element responsible for increasing the paranoia he was subject to from childhood. It created a period in his life in which he became convinced that "the world"—certainly the literary world of which he longed to be a part—was decidedly against him. For there is scarcely an author who suffered the trials and tribulations he did during the years of his career which are generally described as the "Bohemia span." He was harassed by publisher and public alike—proclaimed on the one hand as a genius, and denounced on the other as a writer of pornography, a sex pervert whose private life was more evil, more wicked, and more sexually outrageous than any of the writing he was doing in the name of "literature."

During the years when he was struggling to reestablish himself as an author (while he was constantly being torn between the free-lance writing which provided a meager existence and seeking reemployment in a position such as he had enjoyed at Butterick with money and prestige) my family had little contact with him. My father was beginning his business career with Mallinson Silks and my mother was involved with her home and baby daughter. Any contacts my father had with my Uncle Theodore during this period must have been casual. It is possible that my mother, with her great concern for "respectability," would have been too offended by Uncle Theo's life in the Village, and his fights with John Sumner, the replacement for Anthony Comstock, and the moralists who had assailed him and his work ever since the publication of *Sister Carrie.*

That Uncle Theodore was good copy cannot be denied for stories about him were legend and newspapers wrote more about him as a man than as an author. Had he been encouraged, instead of badgered and beset with financial worries, his private life and his monumental writings might have taken a different course.

Following the affair with Thelma Cudlipp which had cost him job, income, and prestige, and which, in addition, had put him in the ridiculous position of being "no fool, like an old fool"—an older man losing his head over a girl young enough to be his daughter—he and Aunt Jug for a few years had a "working arrangement"—due to meager financial resources—in which they continued to live under the same roof. Uncle Theo pursued his career with Aunt Jug assisting as copy-editor, good cook, and typist (Uncle Theo wrote all of his manuscripts in longhand, a delicate, almost feminine script which was very neat and precise and, to a handwriting expert, a penmanship which was indicative of his dual personality). To understand the role she was willing to assume following Uncle Theo's disastrous affair with Miss Cudlipp, one must realize that at this stage of her marriage Aunt Jug had learned to make compromises and to "weather the storm" in the manner most women of her generation did. She simply felt that this affair, although it had been more catastrophic than the others, would, in time, be relegated to the past. This in fact was what finally happened. Perhaps Aunt Jug had come to recognize that Uncle Theo was a man who accepted marriage for its comforts; perhaps she was blinded by her never-ending love for him and hoped that time would chill his errant passions and improve his talent. She stood by for three years. It was she who took a copy of the original manuscript with her on a trip to England when Uncle Theo began the writing of *The Genius*—the book which probably officially ended the marriage, although the publication was put aside by his publisher who encouraged him to write *The Financier* and allow the publication of this manuscript before that of *The Genius.*

During this period Uncle Theodore became acquainted with Grant Richards, an English publisher whom he admired for his style of living and his belief in Theodore Dreiser, the author. Uncle Theodore outlined his plan to write a book based upon the life of Charles Tyson Yerkes. Uncle Theo felt it urgent that he travel abroad and follow the life of Yerkes in order to be able to write factually about Yerkes' life experiences. Grant Richards subsidized the excursion which has been described as Europe on "the worry basis." During this period, the problem of insecurity, of lack of self-assurance, which was a large part of Uncle Theo's neurosis, took over and managed to make his behavior such that what commenced as a fine friendship ended in disaster. It was only due to a recommendation of Grant Richards that when Uncle Theo was returning to America he did not travel on the newly constructed *Titanic* but took the less expensive liner, the *Kroonland,* and survived to write. But quarrels between the two men over money and petty situations ensued. Years later, Uncle Theo, in one of his wistful moods, regretted his behavior. "I would have given anything not to have quarreled with him, and over money too! I owe him so much; that trip to Europe! It was like a tonic that lasted me for years . . . ."

His work on the "Trilogy of Desire" about the life of Yerkes returned him briefly to Chicago where he expressed his observation that the will-to-power was the motivation of America. "I am certain that the mind of the great merchant is conscious of the poetry in his work. . . ." He did not feel that the hero of his trilogy was unscrupulous. He defended Cowperwood; "Nature is not because of, but in spite of, her pieties and her moralities. . . ." suffering caused, and the fittest survive. . . Today, America is great not because of, but in spite of, her pieties and her moralities. . . ."

During this period Uncle Theodore established certain rules and regulations for social behavior and the consequences. He had come to the conclusion that the masses and their leaders are likely to be wrong and that the nonconformists and the individuals who have the courage to flaunt unconventionality and defy orthodox laws are in all probability right! Here again Uncle Theo was expressing the conflict that had existed between Sarah and John Paul, his parents—the mother was unconventional but protective and the father followed the letter of the law and was ineffective. The parental schism had left its permanent scars on the most talented son, the genius, who was torn between his yearning for success and financial security and his inability to compromise artistically and produce manuscripts that could be published or if published attain popularity and proper remuneration.

The evidence that Uncle Theodore was aware of his personal shortcomings at this period is borne out in the declaration issued to a range of people which extended from Grant Richards to any lady love: "There is something strange in my make-up. I quarrel with my friends. . . . I am too suspicious!"

Uncle Theo lived in Greenwich Village during a period when it was a residential area that extended from Washington Square to the North River (now called Hudson). It was inhabited by many artists, writers, actors, and anarchists—people in open rebellion against convention. Most of the people probably lived there for the same reason Uncle Theo did—the low rents. But it has become romanticized as a locale where creative and rebellious people such as Uncle Theodore mingled with the wealthy patrons of the "new art" who sponsored free love, birth-control, and free verse, such women as Mabel Dodge whose salon was frequented by many now-famous personalities. Amazingly, Uncle Theodore was not among those present. He was not too fond of heiresses like Mabel Dodge who used their inherited wealth to pick the brains of such people as himself. However, Uncle Theo belonged in the Village as much as he belonged in any atmosphere where individualism was striving for expression. Although he was criticized by his friend Mencken for his association with the "crack-pots" of the Village he wrote to Mencken, "You make a mistake in regard to my supposed interest in the red-ink fraternity. . . . I hold no brief for the parlor radical. . . ."

It was during this period that Uncle Theo made the kind of trip later used by Thomas Wolfe in titling his own work: *You Can't Go Home Again.* He returned to Indiana to write *A Hoosier Holiday* and to revisit the scenes of his childhood and boyhood days. His first sponsor, May Calvert (Baker), was his hostess. Although she did not approve of Uncle Theodore's life style nor the realism he was transcribing, she was impressed with her protégé and, I presume, secretly delighted with the fame her investment had brought. Uncle Theo was totally charming to her in spite of the fact that she represented all of the social structures he was opposing—organized religion, puritanism—and she, like many, many other women could not resist mothering this huge, sad, doomed man of genius, and Uncle Theodore, in return, loved to be mothered. It was while he was on this visit that he decided to have Uncle Paul's body moved again—this time to Indiana. It was a "bad trip" for Uncle Theo, this return journey to Indiana where he had faced rejection from people who adored the memory of Uncle Paul. Had they not made "On the Banks of the Wabash" the state song? And had they not named the place of his birth "Dresser"? But to the author of *Sister Carrie, Jennie Gerhardt* (stories of his sisters reared in Indiana), the people were more than cool—the atmosphere was frigid.

By any psychological analysis, to have expected *A Hoosier Holiday* to have been a chamber of commerce travel book on the glories of that state would be preposterous. With few exceptions Uncle Theodore found that his visit was merely the reawakening from a nightmare he had spent years trying to obliterate. If rejection is necessary in order to be whole—*it was* certainly heaped on him in his revisit to the place of his birth. For an individual in whom paranoia had been established in his formative years, certainly the painful years of rehabilitating himself after "the fall," the years of fighting for the cause of an author's rights, the confusion of lack of money (although he was writing more than one can imagine any author doing under the same set of circumstances), the lack of a "roof over his head," forcing him to relive his early years of similar instability, are of interest only to prove that the "genius," Theodore Dreiser, survived in spite of himself, and in spite of the barriers he placed between himself and other human beings, and despite all of the placebos he indulged in—enacting the role of a Don Juan, minor attempts at using stimulating drugs (which were totally ineffectual), interests in psychic phenomena, etc. In spite of himself and because of himself Uncle Theo survived and will, insofar as the world is concerned, continue to survive—as a man of genius. Incredible, unfathomable, controversial—the artist as a functioning schizophrenic. And, in the creative world, he is not alone.

9

The Long-Suffering Helen

"But, O, I have not love."

In 1919 my father had a visitor—a young, attractive woman named Helen Patges Richardson, a divorcée—who came announcing that she was a cousin on his mother's side and she was interested in locating the other brother, Theodore, the author, whose work she greatly admired. My father, who normally was the most considerate and compassionate of men, took an immediate and intense dislike to her. One can never explain such reactions, but they do occur. Almost reluctantly he gave her Uncle Theo's address, for, after all, she was a legitimate, if distant relative (her grandmother having been a sister of Ed and Theo's mother, Sarah).

The result was the birth of a relationship that was to endure until the end of Theo's life. It was to be the most extended, passionate, complex female affiliation of his existence. Helen was stagestruck as a young girl living on a farm in Oregon and at sixteen she had married an actor, Frank Richardson, and left home. Their career was not very successful and eventually they separated. Helen came to New York, studied to be a secretary, and found employment in the firm of William E. Woodward, an executive of the Industrial Finance Company. Helen was nothing, if not theatrical—especially in appearance. She was tall, with a beautiful body which reeked of sex appeal. She had a wide smile which indicated her basic genial nature and she possessed the gold-chestnut hair Theo so admired in women. Upon reading *The Genius* she became determined to meet him. She told her employer, who was also an admirer of Theodore Dreiser's writing, that she was a distant relative and he urged her to contact Dreiser. Acting upon her boss's advice, Helen was able to locate my father who gave her Theo's address–165 West 10th Street. In mid-September, 1919, Helen Richardson took a walk to the home of Theodore Dreiser.

Theodore Dreiser rarely answered an unannounced call at his door, but that day he did. When the bell rang, he grabbed a Chinese smock (inside out) and opened the door to see a good-looking, young woman standing there. She asked, "Are you Ed Dreiser's brother?" When Uncle Theo answered, "Yes," he became acutely aware that he had his robe on with the wrong side out and with his yen for the superstitious this became a sign of a "most drastic and inescapable and invariable sign of change." Helen then announced, "I'm his cousin." Obviously, if this were true, she was also his and he invited her in "for tea."

If there was a sexual chemistry at work upon their meeting, there were also forces of "chance." One "chance" factor was that Helen fell into the category of many women who were attracted to Theo during his lifetime–she was "fame-struck" and unconsciously, perhaps, determined to hitch her wagon to a star, regardless of the price she would have to pay. (It was possibly this condition my father recognized and in his mind categorized as characteristic of an "adventuress.") The second factor was that she was a member of the younger generation of women who were in search of "freedom" and a career of glamour which could be most easily obtained–or so they thought–by a sexual relationship with a prominent man (to them such a liaison spelled liberation, although in reality it was a lifetime of sadomasochistic slavery). On his part, Theo was in the right state of mind so that a chance opening of the door to his apartment could lead to an entanglement. He was on the rebound from a recent love affair which had curdled; he was fighting with Boni and Liveright; he was financially strapped and he was suffering from a creative "dry spell" which to a writer is a curse worse than menopause to a child-bearing woman. In Helen, he saw a new grasp on life. She was twenty years younger than he, she was ambitious, and she became almost overnight slavishly devoted to him. It was a very special ego trip and bound to appear choice. Helen wanted to go to

Hollywood and become a screen actress. Theo saw possibilities of selling some of his material to the films and he thought that Helen with her looks might make it in Hollywood as a movie actress. She was endowed with the then-current Hollywood front and style, flashy and melodramatic. It required very little persuasion to convince Uncle Theo that their mutual destiny lay in Hollywood. Soon after meeting, they left New York and went to Los Angeles where they lived for three years in six different residences, keeping their real address a secret from everyone. "P. O. Box 181 is all you get."

That such a grande passion would develop never occurred to my father or my mother that fateful afternoon when Helen first appeared at our home saying she was a relative and wished to become acquainted with "her family." She was friendly and upon being invited to remain for dinner she took me walking in Central Park. During dinner she talked of her desire to pursue her career which she had already started on the West Coast before coming East. When she left with Uncle Theo's address, no one realized what the consequence would be.

When they retreated to California, Helen obtained extra work in the movies and Liveright came through with a sizeable advance for Uncle Theo to pursue his work on *The Bulwark.* Helen proved to be extremely shrewd in financial matters and her investments in Los Angeles real estate supplemented Theo's income. But their personal relationship became more emotionally disastrous than any of Theo's previous amours. They were developing a dependence upon one another which was extremely unhealthy and would prove, in the final analysis, that even though Helen won over her other adversaries, she won by default and gained very little—by any set of standards. She endured years of torture, and knew only a brief period of identity as Theo's wife and widow before she suffered a stroke which crippled her and left her to eke out a miserable existence until her death. Nevertheless, from the moment of encounter they were like Siamese twins joined at the hip.

With the advance money Theo received for *The Bulwark,* he undertook a new work, one which was to be his major creation and a novel which would become, in the eyes of many critics, the most important piece of writing in America: *An American Tragedy.* But before he commenced the actual writing he satisfied his Boni and Liveright commitment with *A Book About Myself.*

Horace Liveright, his publisher, was disappointed. Even Lengel, his personal Boswell, thought it "not only careless, but extremely slovenly." It was filled with errors, and was apparently a book to tide over a period in which he was stymied with *The Bulwark* and dreaming of a far greater work whose theme had obsessed him.

For years Theo had been fascinated with a type of murder that made headlines in American newspapers. It was a crime in which the killer was less motivated by hatred and revenge than by a passion to rise in society and wealth. In Theo's eyes this was an indictment of the false standards that manacled most Americans. In each of the murders he had noted illicit sex was involved and, in each case he studied, the pregnancy of the ill-fated girl sealed the fate of the girl and boy involved. The case that captured his imagination was that of Chester Gillette, a poor relation straw boss in his wealthy uncle's shirt factory in Cortland, New York, who seduced a pretty millhand, Grace Brown. Gillette then became enamored of a wealthy society girl who encouraged his suit and sponsored his dream of becoming rich and a member of the upper set. But pregnant Grace presented a formidable menace so Chester took her to Big Moose Lake in the Adirondacks, pretending that he would marry her. Instead he took her boating, hit her over the head with his tennis racket, overturned the boat, and abandoned her to drown while he swam safely to shore.

Like the other cases Theo had read about, the protagonist did not appear murderous by nature but driven to homicide by ignorance and a weakness for the American yearning for money and social prestige. It is possible that the theme rang the familiar note of identifying with the underdog. At any rate, it was this theme that obsessed him and caused him to write his masterpiece.

He found California a bad atmosphere for his writing. His friends in the East feared he was "going to seed" and he himself disliked Los Angeles, a city he dubbed "the city of folded hands." He determined to return East for he felt his publishing problems were unsolvable from Los Angeles. And his affair with Helen was becoming increasingly difficult. There was no reason why he should not return, except that Helen's career was at stake. She had appeared in a couple of films, and although stardom did not beckon she was able to make a living. There was really no logic in Helen's accompanying him on his return trip for there was only the remotest possibility that he would divorce Aunt Jug to marry her. Her rationale for giving up her chances for a movie career to follow Uncle Theo back to New York are best explained in her own words: "I longed to develop spiritually. Where, I thought, could I do better than at the side of so great a man as Dreiser?"[1]

The die was cast, and they sold the house they had bought, stored the Maxwell car in which they had toured the California countryside, and took a train for New York.

When they reached New York, Theo took up residence at 16 St. Luke's Place while Helen resided in a flat on West 50th Street where she took voice lessons and entered into the second phase of her long career of suffering for the sake of Theodore Dreiser.

The fact that Theodore Dreiser had not published a novel for seven years was of great concern, not only to his publishers but to his admirers. H. L. Mencken had written him in California, "I believe it would be a good time for you to show up again in New York. You are so damned securely buried that thousands of boobs are growing up who have never heard of you."

Even Theo felt he was dying on the vine, although he was not actually pinched financially, as he was selling articles and had a healthy advance from Horace Liveright (Boni had resigned from the firm) who never ceased to believe in him. But Theo was a man who required many projects for stimulus, jumping from one to another as his constantly varying moods changed. He did not like to be contained within one chore. And as prolific as he was, he was not as yet truly self-disciplined. He refused to grind away on a book which eluded him; he loathed the slave aspect of writing when he did not have complete control of his subject. His constant wrangling with himself over *The Bulwark* is an example of the way his mind functioned as a creative writer. However, when he gained control of his subject, words poured onto the paper endlessly. More was usually cut from the finished work than was published.

Upon his return to New York he once again felt free. Helen was always available but not underfoot, nagging him about divorcing Jug and marrying her. His letter to Mencken, once he was settled, is indicative of his satanic humor: "I hear that Theodore Dreiser is at large in New York and that he has already pulled several crooked deals."

Although he and Helen lived apart, she wrote in her book, "However, he kept in close touch with me. We dined together often, and sometimes I could not resist following him to what he called 'home.' Possibly the next day the other woman would be there with him, and it seemed more than I could bear."[2]

Why did she? She was still young, attractive to other men. When she was cognizant of the fact that she no longer appealed to him sexually, why did she insist upon answering his every beck and call? It is an almost perfect case history of feminine masochism, unless one accepts my father's insistence that she was an "adventuress" determined to cling to Uncle Theo until she obtained her desire to be his legal wife and to carve for herself a niche in history.

Theo found New York considerably altered and he was disturbed by the crass commercialism which he saw all about him.

At that period in his life he became sexually involved with a young woman, Sally Kussell, who applied for a job as secretary-editor. The hiring of Sally Kussell must have been a blow to Helen, who was a good typist, for it severed another link between her and Theo, indicating that he did not trust her editorial ability. (In contrast, he approved of Jug's typing and editing, and to a critical eye, some of the succinct realism of *Sister Carrie* could be attributed to Jug's literary ability.) Sally Kussell qualified and he set her to work on *An American Tragedy*.

At this moment Helen sent for the Maxwell and in June Uncle Theo asked her if she would like to tour the countryside where the Gillette murder had taken place. Theo's "reader-identification" with the locale was so intense that Helen became concerned for her own safety and wrote, "Maybe Teddy will become completely hypnotized by this idea and repeat it, here and now."[3]

But no such "tragedy" occurred. Uncle Theo rented a house in Monticello and occasionally my mother and I, while visiting her friend, Mrs. Cora Stratton, would catch a glimpse of Helen shopping in the village.

It was while they were in Monticello and Theo was writing daily to Sally Kussell ("My Little Yankee Zulu") that Helen opened a bundle of letters from Sally to him. She has written, "Ordinarily I would not have touched them but at that moment I could not overcome the feeling that they concerned me in some way and I should read them. After reading a few I had seen enough to know this was a more serious triangle than I had supposed. I was jealous, fiercely so."

When Theo returned to the cabin, Helen told him she was

leaving—"for good." They drove to New York and she moved her things out of his apartment, but did not leave New York as she threatened. True to form, she stayed on at 50th Street. In September Uncle Theo moved to 118 West 11th Street, into a two-room apartment in the old grillwork-fronted Rhinelander Gardens. Mame and Austin Brennan lived next door and were the rental agents for the property.

Uncle Theo had never really liked Austin Brennan, whom he had predicted would die of an early death from overindulgence. But Austin was still alive, hale and hearty. It is unfair to accept Theo's opinion of the Brennans and their way of life. Actually, they lived extremely well in Rochester where they had a beautiful home and were highly thought of in the social community. My mother and father visited them and were well acquainted with the life style they enjoyed, and my mother, who excelled in the art of entertaining and was quite conscious of material attributes, would never have credited any of the Dreisers with social attainments that were not legitimate. At the time Mame was sixty-two years of age, big and outgoing, a creature of great sympathies, enormous charm, enthusiasm, and subject to occasional outbursts of temper, similar to those of Theo. Perhaps it was their similarities that often separated them. Certainly Mame's dictatorial mannerisms annoyed Theo, but time had mellowed her to a large degree and at this time they were able to give a reasonable appearance of compatibility. Like Theo, Mame wavered in her emotional judgments regarding Jug and Helen.

The New Year—1925—did not bring a miraculous turn of events for Helen, and in March, she wearied of her humiliating role and left for Portland. To obtain her end, her means were justified. Uncle Theo missed her and wrote to her daily. He was at his best, as a romantic lover *in absentia.* When he was writing to Helen, she was his "Babu," his "Golden Girl," his "April and December Girl." He could not live without her and he even broached the dreaded subject of marriage. Helen, who nourished ideas of thought transference, attributed his words in which he described his physical longing to hold her in his arms to their mutual chemistry which caused her to experience the same vacuum at the exact same hour. Theo rationalized his impotency by writing that her physical beauty was too overwhelming and rendered him incapable of sexual coition. Helen's own ego was stimulated by such statements. Her descent into the maelstrom of unreality is quite understandable. Her sexual frustration (and boredom) caused her to leave Portland after three weeks and return to Hollywood where she was able to tease Uncle Theo with tabulated records of her "dates" with Hollywood stars and producers. Naturally, in his own inability to satisfy her, he was driven to imaginative jealousy of her affairs with truly virile men. As is customary in impotent sexual relations, Helen and Theo thrived upon imaginary sexual indulgences enjoyed with other partners.

While she was away, Theo had black fits of depression and one of the few people he turned to for diversion was my father. They used to meet and walk and talk. They discussed practical affairs, and reminisced over their boyhood experiences. It was possibly during these walks and talks that the practical side of Theo emerged. He knew that Helen had been an excellent money partner. Her profitable land speculations in California had represented much freedon from financial worry for him, and with the urge to finish *An American Tragedy* foremost in his mind, he finally asked Helen to return. Her departure had been too big a blow to his ego, despite the fact that during her absence he had lived an extremely active social life and was a frequent guest of the Powys brothers, Carl Van Vechten, Zoe Atkins, Ernest and Madeline Boyd, Alexander Woollcott, and other literary notables. One of his acquaintances of this period was Dr. A. A. Brill, the noted psychiatrist.

It is well known that Uncle Theo had some compulsive rituals he indulged in regularly to relieve tension and anxiety. His folding and unfolding of his handkerchief when he was uncomfortable in the presence of certain people is a matter of record. The fact is, he did not merely fold and unfold it, as has been described, but he made a "mouse" out of it! This fact is not common knowledge.

At one time just prior to his collapse, Uncle Theo became a hypochondriac. These indications of nervous tension would indicate to a trained therapist that the origin lay in early childhood; there is usually some lack of acceptance and love. Apparently the two men were fascinated with one another. Dr. Brill saw sexual symbolism in Theo's constant handkerchief-folding, and Theo probed Brill for hidden psychological motivations for his fictional characters. Yet never was there any discussion of a doctor-patient relationship although it is difficult to believe–as a therapist–that Dr. Brill was not fully aware of the deep emotional childhood hangovers that riddled Theodore Dreiser the man.

The announcement that Helen was scheduled to return was most upsetting to Mame who was in the process of starting a restaurant, The Green Witch. The brother and sister, now neighbors, were constantly weeping on each other's shoulders and airing their miseries. Mame was having troubles with her partner, and Theo was having his usual difficulties with his publishers. Their nerves were ragged and Theo wrote, "Mame is a nuisance. I am warning her today though that this has to be cut out, or I move . . . I am in no mood to be annoyed now."

Helen returned. Once again Theo had his living doll, and once again they could revel in hours of baby talk, offsetting hours of bickering and mutual ennui. She did not return to live in his apartment, but moved into the Albert Hotel on 10th Street and contented herself with his promise that they would soon establish a single residence.

Certainly when Helen returned she was fully cognizant of the role expected of her–if she wanted to share Theodore Dreiser's life. She later wrote: "He expected his complete freedom in which he could indulge to the fullest, at the same time expecting my undivided devotion to him."[4] She returned despite the admonitions of her mother and many of her friends. Her explanation is in her words: "I would picture him ill or depressed so that he could not work, and this disturbed and troubled me. . . . Perhaps I should be with him, good or bad. . . ." In January, 1925, Theo and Helen took a sixty-dollar-a-month apartment at 1799 Bedford Avenue in Brooklyn. This time he allowed Helen to do the typing of *An American Tragedy,* but he left the editing of the manuscript to two other women, Sally Kussell and Louise Campbell.

Uncle Theo must have written a million words in the original manuscript of *An American Tragedy* since Miss Kussell and Mrs. Campbell have left records of the many words they edited out. Theo was very concerned that the manuscript be authentic and he managed to persuade H. L. Mencken to get him permission to visit death row in Sing Sing as a representative of *The World.* A misunderstanding ensued, as *The World* thought Dreiser would, in exchange for the opportunity to spend the last hours with a condemned prisoner, write an account for the newspaper. He refused unless he was paid five hundred dollars, and a rift occurred between him and Mencken. It was not completely repaired when Theo and Helen visited Mencken en route to Florida. After they departed Mencken was extremely upset that Theo had not inquired as to the state of health of his mother, who was dying. (She died the following day.) Mencken was as devoted to his mother (and remained unmarried until her death) as Theo had been to his, and the apparent lack of interest on the part of Theo disturbed him. This possibly caused his later critical and even, at times, abusive treatment of Theo.

Helen and Theo drove the trusty Maxwell to Florida where they lived penuriously and quarrelled constantly. *An American Tragedy* was finally published and Theo assiduously avoided reading any reviews. He and Helen spent their time together looking at real estate and making some speculative purchases which were to be proved disastrous. In his diary he recorded: "Wretched days with someone I don't really care to be with." In January, 1926, the wandering lovers shipped the Maxwell back to New York and sailed up the coast on the same ship on which Theo had returned from Europe in 1912 when he barely escaped being a passenger on the *Titanic*.

When they returned to New York they both awoke to the fact that Theodore Dreiser was now a literary sensation. Helen had received her reward to be recognized as *the* woman who had devoted herself entirely to a man whose genius she had never questioned. For the time she was content to be his mistress and share the spotlight of fame, even if her role was socially considered somewhat infamous. Joseph Wood Krutch, in *The Nation*, called *An American Tragedy* "the greatest American novel of our generation." H. G. Wells observed that "Dreiser is, in the extreme sense of the word, a genius." All of the literary world, both at home and abroad, seemed to be ready to accept Theo as the greatest—all except H. L. Mencken who had previously defended Theo when the world had found him offensive. His review was scathing and overly critical. The end result was that the eighteen-year friendship was ended.

An American Tragedy changed the lives of Theo and Helen. Under the supervision of Horace Liveright it was made into a play and opened on Broadway, with Glenn Hunter playing Clyde Griffiths and June Walker, Roberta. Following this, negotiations were made for a film for which Theo was to receive $100,000. For once in his life he was rich, famous. The world was truly his oyster. The news of his movie sale was in all the papers. His own enthusiasm is best evidenced in his exuberance when he rushed into the studio of his dear friend John Cowper Powys, and shouted, "I am opulent! Opulent! What can I give you?"

His success created many personal problems for him. One was the necessity that he make some adjustment toward Aunt Jug, who was still his legal wife. It was at this time that he could have divorced Jug, made a final financial settlement, and freed himself to marry Helen. But he did not choose this route. Instead he made arrangements to pay Jug a modest sum for life and retain her as the legal Mrs. Theodore Dreiser. For himself he set up a trust fund so he would be free to pursue his literary interest without financial strain. And then he and Helen gave a party to celebrate his success. Helen wore "an evening gown bought especially for the occasion, shimmering with red spangles like circus riders." Following the party they sailed as Mr. and Mrs. on the *Frederick VIII* for Oslo where Theo wished to do research for the third book of the *Trilogy of Desire (The Stoic),* sightsee, talk with his European publishers, and meet with the literary great of Europe—meet, this time, on his own terms.

From Helen's point of view, Uncle Theo's decision to give Jug a monetary settlement, instead of demanding a divorce and a total financial agreement, must have been a blow from which she never fully recovered. Obviously, Helen was too fearful of him to insist upon marriage. If she had not been able to bring him to this decision in the salad days of their romance it was hardly possible now that wilt had withered Theo's passion. His need for her was minimal in the midst of the glamour, glory, fame, and wealth *An American Tragedy* had produced. At this stage Helen was tarnished merchandise, yesterday's gardenia, no longer quite so young and so beautiful as she had been when many of Dreiser's acquaintances envied him the bed partnership of his delectable "Babu." His treatment of her was such that it is almost impossible to comprehend why she endured it. In public he was indifferent toward her, often ignoring her presence. He ridiculed her attempts at intellectualism and was quite contemptuous of her comments and observations. Some of the people who knew the two of them wondered if their private fights and arguments attained the pitch of physical violence. There is no evidence that such a stage was reached although Helen did record that once he slapped her face while they were walking down Fifth Avenue, causing passersby to stop and stare. Whatever the motive, the fact remains that Helen was willing to accept a trip abroad, basking in the light of her lover's fame and fortune, in return for a wedding ring and a public avowal of love and fidelity. She set about to acquire the atmosphere and adulation she desired and required.

Helen Patjes Richardson

Upon their return to the United States, when Helen discovered the money was rolling in, she decided that the addresses they had previously occupied were beneath the dignity of one of the world's most renowned geniuses. "It soon became apparent," she wrote, "that a larger and more suitable place in which to live was absolutely necessary to cope with our increasing social and professional obligations."[5] She decided upon an elaborate apartment building—the Rodin Studios at 200 West 57th Street. Helen hired an interior decorator and soon Uncle Theo and she were residents in a duplex on the thirteenth and fourteenth floors that included an impressive foyer and a huge double height living room with indirect lighting and stained glass windows facing north on 57th.

Helen acquired an elaborate wardrobe, as did Uncle Theo., whose sartorial taste was exciting and colorful—pastel shirts, beautiful bow ties, and a malaca cane.

A Russian wolfhound, Nick, was the third member of the household.

That year Uncle Theo began sending out letters on his stationery which became his trademark—a thick gray paper with his name engraved in blue. On this paper he sent invitations to informal Thursday evenings—at home—where the great and the near-great of the literary, art, and social worlds of Manhattan convened.

That the elaborate and gaudy apartment was more Helen's idea than Uncle Theo's has been conceded—even by his enemies. The role he was enacting was so out of character that most commented upon it. Fannie Hurst, for example, refused to believe that the host was *really* Theodore Dreiser. Perhaps he indulged Helen as a token payment, and perhaps she convinced him that she was providing him with the accoutrements of success. However, the famous Thursdays must have satisfied in Theo his endless yearning to grow, learn, and associate with intellectuals in all fields. Both Helen and Theo had their portraits painted and Theo was photographed and sculpted. The artist Ralph Fabri, who painted Helen with Nick, became a member of a type of ménage à trois—in which he was cast in the unfortunate role of an observer of the stormy antics of Helen and Theo. He customarily sided with Helen as it was usually her version of the situation he heard.

During this period Theo and my father became extremely close. They had a regular weekly ritual—long private walks together in Central Park during which they would discuss current events, as well as reminisce about boyhood days. I learned much about the Dreiser boys, and gleaned some contemporary facts about the lives of Theo and Helen, when my father would return while still in a nostalgic mood. Every Sunday Ed Dreiser would walk to 57th Street, enter the lobby, and call Theo on the phone to say he was downstairs. One Sunday when he called Helen answered and said Theo wasn't in. Ed returned home, not seeing anything particularly meaningful about his brother's absence. However, on the following two Sundays the same thing happened—Ed called from the lobby only to be told Theo was not in. Ed, feeling Theo did not wish to continue their walks, did not go back the following week. He was convinced something was amiss.

My mother, Mai, who had never become reconciled to Theo and who thoroughly disapproved of his life style, used this apparent rudeness on Theo's part as a new excuse to drive a permanent wedge between the brothers. (In a purely objective analysis, I must not overlook the fact that Mai possibly might have been unconsciously resentful of the Thursdays to which she was not invited, but the fact remains that had she been invited she would not have accepted, and Theo well knew this.)

Several weeks later, Theo and Ed accidentally met on the street and my father, seeing the obvious sincere warmth of Theo's greeting, asked him point-blank why he had treated him as he did. Theo was shocked. *He had thought Ed had caused the interruption in their walks!* He swore to Ed he never got any of the messages Ed left. The brothers put their "noggins" together and soon figured out that both Helen and Mai in their own "inimitable ways" had tried to estrange them. They agreed that *nothing* or *no one* would ever succeed in alienating them.

One of the tidbits of family gossip was the fact that Helen had a Steinway and was studying piano and voice—piano with a young Hungarian musician named Kovacs, who had been given permission to practice on the Steinway in lieu of owning an inferior instrument unfit for him to practice on for his forthcoming concert. Helen was very impressed with Kovacs and he, apparently, fell in love with her. At the time, Theo was imposing more and more of his illicit relations upon her and she was in a most confused state. She was undoubtedly sexually frustrated and afraid to make a move for fear of losing what little she was procuring from the hectic relationship. Finally, in accord with the times, she asked Theo if he would object to her having a liaison which might help her to endure the periods when he left her alone, while he was in the company of another woman. Despite all of the writing Theo had done on the subject of sexual freedom, he was enraged and announced that Helen could do as she pleased, but "when you do, I'm out!"

What was sauce for the goose was not sauce for the gander and Helen lacked the facilities to cope with this affront to her self-respect. She dismissed Kovacs, but when Theo discovered who her partner in her "constructive emotional attachment" was, he rendered a treatment which was completely imitative of that of his dead mother. He went on a silent retreat. "For days," Helen wrote, "he came and went without speaking a word. . . . If I thought I had been neglected and lonely in times past, I was to learn what spiritual isolation meant . . . he seemed to be trying to kill me by degrees with neglect and indifference. Day after day he spent most of his time away from the apartment. . . . And yet, I never gave up in my attempt to draw close to him again. While he was shaving or dressing, I would try to talk with him. This usually led to abusively cruel words on his part, with a final sarcastic remark on his part as he went out the door."[6]

These episodes had an effect which Uncle Theo could not have anticipated. They opened the door for Helen to become intimate with many of the women whom Theo had also used, and many women who, although they admired his genius, disliked his attitude toward women and abhorred his promiscuous sex life. My mother was one of these. My mother had seen Aunt Jug turn to Christian Science in her bout with arthritis—some of which she undoubtedly thought was aggravated by Theo's passion for Thelma Cudlipp at the peak of his early success—and now she heard of Helen's interest in yoga and her daily visits to the roof of the Rodin building where she practiced controlled breathing until she was able to record: "I had the distinct sensation of expanding consciousness."

It soon became apparent to Helen that she was trying in vain to gain control of a formidable giant, an individualist who was as impregnable to her assults, threats, dog-like devotion, and physical charms as an inanimate structure of granite and stone. She began to take a new tack, one which, eventually, was to bring her the allies she needed—members of the Dreiser family. And the person who eventually became a co-conspirator was, at the beginning, her most unlikely candidate–Mai, my mother!

At this period Uncle Theo was invited–with all expenses paid–to be a guest of the Russian government. He had great curiosity about the collective farms, the engineering and mechanical feats, but he gave no promise that he would like what he saw or that he would write favorably about this impressive twentieth-century political enterprise. It was the tenth anniversary of the revolution and Theo set off with a group of other American officials, artists, and celebrities, including Diego Rivera, Morris Ernst, Dorothy Thompson, and Sinclair Lewis.

The opening lines of Chapter One, page nine of *Dreiser Looks at Russia* read:

> While it is known that I am an incorrigible individualist–therefore opposed to Communism–the Soviet Government invited me to visit Russia to investigate conditions there; and I accepted the invitation on the following terms:
>
> 1. That I be free to choose my itinerary and make any inquiries I desired to make.
> 2. That I be provided with a secretary-interpreter wherever I went.
> 3. That I would not be considered rude to my government host if my study of Russia should result in an expression of unfavorable conclusions.
> 4. That I would be under no obligation to publish any report of my trip, favorable or unfavorable, if I did not feel so inclined.
>
> These terms were graciously accepted by cable, and I sailed from New York, October 19, 1927.

Despite the fact that forty-eight years have passed since that trip was made, and forty-seven years since the book was written, many things that were said or predicted in it are coming to pass. For instance: "It is possible that Russia will become one of the mightiest economic forces the world has known." He praised their educational system, although it was embryonic at that period. (Anyone who thinks and evaluates today knows we have one of the poorest educational systems going. Our children leaving school cannot spell or speak proper grammar. Yet in some countries in Europe children not only speak their own tongue but have mastered a second.) Dreiser very candidly pointed out the things he liked and disliked, but I guess it would have suited him better had he disliked it all. He admired the legal and political emancipation of women in Russia at that time. His comments on their tacky taste regarding furnishings, color, and clothes interested me as well as his commentary on their sluggishness, lack of personal cleanliness, and indifference to hurry. The group of Russians who settled in Manhattan, all with royal or artistic backgrounds, displayed some of these characteristics so vividly one could not miss them. The temperament is well described in *August 1914.* So to say that Dreiser was ambivalent in his mental vagaries is plain stupid. To say that six months before he died in 1945, some thirty years ago, his gesture toward the American Communist party is contradictory, is admitting to a complete lack of understanding of his life's work. He was still the *incorrigible individualist,* who could not have tolerated anything akin to McCarthyism.

Parts and fragments of his comments have been taken out of context and reprinted by some biographers and parroted by others. The result gives the reader a lopsided idea of what Dreiser intended to convey.

One of the examples of Theo's mischievous humor is recounted in his listing of tips—overly generous—which had to be refunded by the anticapitalist state which had invited him for the "grand tour." "They think I'm a millionaire," he wrote. "Am I not an American?"

On the trip he suffered a severe attack of bronchitis, and what appeared to be a heart attack. As he had always behaved in a siege of illness, he became childlike and frightened. He missed Helen, as before her he had missed Jug when he was incapacitated, and before that, his mother when he was a sickly child. Before the trip was over, he sent for Helen. When they met in Paris, his opinion of Russia was completely bourgeois. His thoughts were not even newsworthy in Russia.

When they returned, they began the construction of their one famous home, "Iroki" (the Japanese word for "beauty"), in Mt. Kisco, New York. The architecture of the house was as confusing as its owner. Fabri, the artist, told Theo, "Most houses are built from the foundation up. This is the first I have seen built from the roof down." But it was built and became the scene of many strange gatherings, and more visits from the immediate members of the Dreiser family. Since the death of Austin Brennan, Helen was courting the family through Mame by paying visits and offering consolation. When we were invited to Theo's Mt. Kisco home Helen had to leave, in deference to Mai's respectability.

Following the visit to Russia, Helen and Theo made a cross-country tour, during which Theo became more of a public figure than a man of letters. He openly said what he thought—at the moment—on any subject with which he was confronted.

During this period with him, Helen's life, by any set of standards, must have been nightmarish. That she chose her role was a part of her personal sickness. She made her existence bearable by her private beliefs in astrology, numerology, tea leaves, the power of mind over matter, and any new philosophical cult that was popular at the moment. Ironically, while Theo could not possibly have seriously considered any of Helen's interests, they must have reminded him of his own mother's similar beliefs and he tolerated her idiosyncracies. In these unscientific philosophies, Helen must have found some sort of premise which made it possible for her to endure an existence with a man with whom she had not had sexual relations for several years although he openly indulged in sundry affairs with other women, occasionally under her own roof. In addition, she was not allowed an established income such as that allotted to a housekeeper, but was dependent upon whatever occasional gift he chose to bestow—like a bone thrown to a hungry dog. That she resorted to the faith of fakirs and often assumed certain theatrical and rather pathetic poses—such as when she appeared after Theo's Russian trip wearing a dress of white homespun fashioned after a Cossack coat and a striking white Russian hat, with the white Russian wolfhound "Nick" on a leash at her side—are quite understandable, an effort to patch a badly damaged ego.

The cross-country trip not only included a return visit to Hollywood, with deliberations about the filming of *An American Tragedy*, but an encounter with Helen's mother and sister and the picking up of Rome, the long-lost brother. It also incorporated a visit to the Mayo Brothers Clinic where the physical diagnosis of Theodore Dreiser was excellent—with the exception of a chronic form of bronchitis and an enlarged prostate gland.

Rome and Mame lived in one of the two cottages at Iroki. When Theo built his "retreat" we were invited to visit. As we drove up the driveway a convertible just left, and the driver and sole occupant was Helen. My mother got talked into inspecting the house and my father and I sat talking with Theo, acting the lord of the manor, comfortably seated with his wolfhound, Nick, at his feet. He joked, "This creature is much nicer to me than Mai is." I recall the incident because of the recorded experience of a tenant in the Rodin apartments who claimed to have seen Theodore Dreiser upon several occasions kick the animal. This is completely inconsistent with Uncle Theo's behavior toward animals throughout his life. In addition, in spite of his outbursts of temper, the only recorded acts of violence are the famous slap which he administered to Sinclair Lewis and the throwing of the glass of wine in the face of Horace Liveright. Both acts were childish, petty, and highly indicative of a deeply disturbed personality. Theo has been described as a study in "suppressed violence," which is reasonably accurate. Fortunately his violence was never channeled into acts of crime, but merely displayed in his relations with people whom he alternately loved and despised.

During that winter when Mame and Rome lived at Iroki, Theo's autobiography was published. It appeared on May 8, 1931, the anniversary of the birth of Sarah Dreiser, and was called *Dawn,* What a fracas! All hell broke loose in the Dreiser family. Critics and public alike were shocked at Theo's frank revelations about his masturbation, his sister's exercises in sexual promiscuity which amounted almost to prostitution, his libido, and his family tensions. The entire family was up in arms. They had accepted his novels, *Sister Carrie, Jennie Gerhardt,* and *The Genius,* because these were fiction, and in their innocence, I presume, it never occurred to them that future biographers of one of the most important literary figures in America, even the world, would, in time, detect his sources of inspiration and reveal them to students of literature.

One of the more serious things Theo had done was to give his readers a saintly image of his mother and an unfavorable and prejudiced portrait of his father without any attempt to understand him. The truth about his parents lay somewhere between the two polar facets he had established. But the family was not concerned about this part of Theo's book. The "girls" were upset because he had maligned their reputations unto the third and fourth generation! Rome, on the other hand, was disturbed because, according to Theo's book, he was dead. He was thought to have died an alcoholic death at the time Theo originally wrote the book, and even though Rome was living at his home, Theo had never bothered to make corrections in the galleys before the book was published.

It is interesting that the same events recorded in the book which created such a torturous childhood for my Uncle Theo, apparently did not injure my father who was only eighteen months younger and was subjected to all of the same traumas. Until I read *Dawn* I had no concept of the miserable childhood they both endured as described by Uncle Theo. Although I knew they were nearly always impoverished, the impression I gained from my father of his parents was much more generous, understanding of their frailties, and even more realistic. He told tales and sang songs he had learned from his father as a child and recounted many happy childhood experiences. As for the lack of shoes and the wearing of hand-me-down clothes, he accepted it as something familiar to most kids in Indiana who were brought up at that time. As for the amoral behavior of his sister, my father never condemned nor approved; he remained forever aloof, loving, and empathetic.

On August 27, 1931, Uncle Theo was sixty years old. Helen was in her early forties. The world was suffering from a great depression and the style of life which they had enjoyed for many years was impossible to maintain. His fame now was that of a public figure and it was based upon his love of grievance and his urge to defend the unpopular cause. He had spent his early days fighting censorship and prudery and now his target was organized capital as the enemy of the common man. He and Helen separated and he moved from Iroki to the Hotel Ansonia, also giving up the apartment in the Rodin building. Although he lived apart from Helen, whom he saw only on the occasions when she came to New York, he knew she would never remove herself from his life. After he moved from Iroki I did not see him for several years although he and my father often walked and talked together and my father indicated that there was an exchange of opinion as to Helen, her devotion, and her motives. My father was convinced that she was willing to play the eternal martyr, as it was now her only chance in life to procure for herself fame and money. Whatever Theo's opinion was, he never said, but Theo told Louise Campbell, "Don't worry, she'll be there at the end to close my eyes."

Once in 1933, Mother, Dad, and I met Helen and Theo at the Century of Progress Fair in Chicago. Mother was amazingly cordial, but my father was indifferent and ready to be on his way. He repeated his opinion of Helen: "She is nothing but an adventuress."

Certainly her life as the adventuress companion of Theodore Dreiser gave her an existence which, while not a joyous or happy one, was more exciting than anything she could have originated for herself. From the sidelines she watched him act his role in the Kentucky coal miners' strike, in which his importance was overshadowed by his reputed liaison with his secretary which resulted in his being summoned to appear on a charge of adultery, a charge to which he answered with his admittance of sexual impotency. Helen was constantly involved as a voyeur with his many projects and his involvements with many other women. In response to a letter from her asking if he was going to leave her, Theo responded, "I scarcely know what to say. If I only knew or could believe that we could go on in some helpful or constructive way. But I can't help feeling it is likely to come to nothing."

But it did come to a reunion in Los Angeles. Helen was still optimistic about a career for herself and Theo was there primarily to sell his wares. He sold *Sister Carrie* to the films and again saw a financial future for himself in the movie industry. They bought a home on North Kings Road and became figures in the movie colony. It was at this time that Helen became a sort of legal representative for Theo and his family. Much interest had been stimulated about Paul and there was interest in a movie to be called *My Gal Sal* based upon Theo's story "My Brother Paul," using the song as the theme for the musical. Helen became the agent in the project. Since Paul had died penniless and my parents had assumed all of the financial responsibility of his debts and burial, the rights legally belonged to them. Helen had no problem with Ed, but Mai presented a stumbling block. I argued with my parents that Paul's material was worthless in its present state and there might be a possibility that there could be some remuneration from the movie. They agreed, and Helen wrote, "Teddy said that if this goes through it will be because of Vera."

The following letter written to Helen Dreiser by my mother, Mai, before the marriage had taken place, is one of the many which illustrates the lingering impact my mother had on Uncle Theo. He unconsciously honored her inbred devotion to "respectability" throughout his lifetime. Eventually he acceded to her urgings by marrying Helen. A final letter from Helen came after the ceremony, thanking my mother for her role and saying, "Teddy says it makes good sense!"

Dear Helen

Many people have a ceremony performed to celebrate a 24th or 25th anniversary–why not you–One needn't announce particulars, just that you would like to celebrate that way–We heard of some one the other day going through a 25th marriage ceremony in Church –

You are deserving of great happiness, as a reward for your faithful devotion

Love from all

Mai

THEODORE DREISER

1015 N. King's Rd.,
Hollywood, Calif.
March 22, 1941.

Dear Mame, Syl, and Ed:

It is necessary, on account of the expiration of my administration letters, to appoint someone else in this immediate situation to administer unadministered properties, such as future royalties, etc. on the songs of Paul. I cannot be reappointed without considerable delay, whereas a new person can be appointed immediately. It would help me greatly at this point if you would appoint Helen. She is here on the ground and can attend to everything, under my supervision. Naturally, I will dictate the policy right along, through her. It is quite a job and requires time and a certain business sense, and I think she is the right party at this time. She will naturally have to go under bond and everything must be accounted for anyway to the Government and to everyone else. She will not charge anything for her services in this matter. She says she is willing to do it if it is perfectly satisfactory to all concerned. Not otherwise.

If this is agreeable to you, Ed, Mame and Syl, it is to me. If so, please convey the acceptance by telephone immediately to Mr. Stanley Moffat of Moffat & Sanford, 342 Madison Avenue, New York City. He will then send you a form to sign. There should be no delay of any kind, for the whole matter should go forward at once out here. If she is not agreeable to you, then appoint someone else immediately. I cannot do it at this time. But if you appoint someone back there, it will make for delays, confusion, explanations, this and that, which will be very bad. Helen is here and she is taking care of many matters already in connection with this picture.

I will appreciate a quick decision on this matter.

Sincerely,

[signed] T.D. (Theodore Dreiser)

(Copy to Mame, Syl.)

P.S. For this appointment it is not necessary to secure the signatures of anyone other than Mame, Syl, Ed and myself.

During this period Helen corresponded with my mother and established some sort of a rapport which must have made it possible for my mother to plant in Uncle Theo's mind, the last time she saw him, the importance of marrying Helen—now that Aunt Jug was dead and there were no obstacles. Theo had come to New York without Helen because her mother was ill and she was with her in Portland and unable to accompany him. Once again he was aware of his need for her as age took its toll. Helen used every advantage she possessed to become Mrs. Theodore Dreiser.

10

Theodore, Ed, Mai, Mame, Rome, Sylvia, Helen, and Vera Together

"For a Moment the Wind Died."

I was born at the time my father was approaching his peak in the theater. One year after my birth he achieved it, playing the lead in the road company of *Paid in Full* in which he not only acted the leading role but was also the stage manager. The reviews spoke of him glowingly: "Shows future promise as a fine actor with good looks. . . ."

While I was an infant there were continued relations between my father and mother and Uncle Theo and Aunt Jug. In fact, Uncle Theo's secretary at Butterick, William Lengel, recalls a dinner party at Uncle Theo's apartment in which Lengel had to caution him to stop staring at my mother and attempting to flirt with her. That was the year 1910, and it was the year that Uncle Theo and Aunt Jug separated and the intimate relationship between the two families was terminated. In 1912 my father had a serious accident and was temporarily blinded. Dad and I were in the garage in back of our home, and for some reason, probably because he didn't have a flashlight with him, he lit a match. The engine hood of the car was up and suddenly there was a flash. He staggered out onto the lawn calling, "Mai, Mai." My mother came running out, saw what had happened, and started telephoning all the local doctors she knew. None of them could help her. My grandmother suggested one she knew in New York City who turned out to be none other than the well-known eye specialist, Dr. John W. Weeks. He immediately asked for the name of the car battery, and by the time Dad arrived at the hospital, Dr. Weeks knew the type of acid in the battery. When he examined Dad he said, "I can save the left eye, I am not sure about the right." Dr. Weeks did eventually save both eyes over a period of two years. All I remember was that horrible white film over both his eyes as he groped his way out of the garage. For two years he was incapable of working—he had eye surgery twice—and finally when he returned to the stage in *Within the Law* he knew his acting career had come to an end after the nerve shock he had sustained. He perspired so profusely during rehearsals that the cast nicknamed him "The Dripping Kid." Incidentally, at eighty-six he was able to read without glasses. So he ceased to be a matinee idol. With his tenacity and adaptability he had started on a career with Mallinson Silks as a business executive. He was no longer Edward M. Dresser, but Edward M. Dreiser, having never used the name "Dresser" except for stage purposes. My mother, however, always preferred to be known as Mrs. Edward M. Dresser, although my father never legally changed his name.

The change of life style between the two couples—in 1913 Aunt Jug and Uncle Theo were legally separated, while my parents resided in Far Rockaway, Long Island, and were intent upon their own family unit— widened the breach.

There was a long schism during which time Uncle Theo traveled between Chicago, Europe, and New York where he set himself up as a resident of Greenwich Village. It is possible that I might have encountered him before but my first recollection of him when I was eight years of age.

During this period Uncle Theo was living with an actress named Kirah Markham, whom he had met in Chicago in a little theater group. Kirah had an allowance from her father and was "liberated," free to enjoy the life Edna St. Vincent Millay was writing of: "My candle burns at both ends. . . ." That it would not last the night was obvious but the young group of "radicals" did not care. "But, ah, my foes, and, oh, my friends—/It gives a lovely light."[1] Their free-love nest address was #7, 165 West 10th Street.

I recall that my first encounter with my Uncle Theo was at a period when he was in one of his states of confusion. He was in trouble with the censors over *The Genius,* which was denounced as obscene. The publication must have been embarrassing to Aunt

Jug for she was easily identified as "Angela Blue," the wife. Although few of Uncle Theo's friends and admirers regarded this book in the same light that he did, they, nevertheless, came to his aid in fighting the suppression of the book.

This book, along with Uncle Theodore's manner of living, of which my mother totally disapproved, made him not more famous in her eyes but more infamous—"a degenerate"—to quote her favorite description of him. She could neither understand him, nor see any reason why she should tolerate him. Consequently, my first meeting left an indelible impression.

It was a hot, humid Sunday and we were on our way home from church. We lived in a large, rambling, comfortable home on Long Island. The house was surrounded with a porch, and as we approached it became apparent that there was a rather wilted, hot, and uncomfortable-looking man seated in one of the rockers. It was my Uncle Theodore, who had traveled all the way from Manhattan to be reunited with his favorite brother, Ed, my father. I can still recall the look of horror on my mother's face when she saw him. She was in a state of double jeopardy because she had invited his estranged wife, Jug, to visit and she was expected within the hour. My mother came forward in a manner completely lacking in tact or diplomacy by exclaiming as she walked up the porch stairs, "Jug will be here shortly and I should imagine you would rather leave than be uncomfortable." There was a silence, an awkward time space. The heat and the humidity were murderous, but the chill of my mother's icy words did not fail to penetrate, to blow a cold wind. Uncle Theo slowly rose, and lumbered rather forlornly down the porch steps. He looked to the left and the right in a sort of daze in search of the railroad station. The back of his coat was wrinkled and wet with perspiration. He looked old and tired as he walked down the street. My father went after him but what ensued between them was never related to me. I remember only that scene of my uncle with his jacket clinging to his angular body, departing—rejected, unwanted. It was the first time that day I felt the oppressive heat. Aunt Jug came and went. But for once I failed to remember what we did that Sunday. I think now of that torrid summer day as the beginning of my genuine understanding of my celebrated uncle. The forgiving, sympathetic, pitiable aspect of his complex, misunderstood personality blended for the first time with the selfish, despicable picture that my mother always painted of him. I never failed to be interested in him as a family figure after the fleeting incident of an unforgettable summer day.

In writing of Uncle Theo it is impossible for me not to draw a comparison between him and my father. While their features were much alike, there was no sadness in my father's face, while Uncle Theo's was a mask of tragedy. My father had a fine, sensitive face with a ready smile and eyes that twinkled beneath his animate brows. His eyes defied description, looking rather like those of a child who has just done something so funny that he has surprised himself. Ed was the most handsome of all of the family with a wealth of wavy chestnut hair complementing his hazel eyes. He carried himself with a characteristic natural ease that made it possible for me to identify him among the commuters when I was a small child going to the station to meet him returning from work. He was always relaxed and never hurried. I never saw him run and he moved with the true athlete's body grace, whether he was figure skating, on a tennis court, or waltzing on a ballroom floor. He taught me to do all of the things he did so well and I adore him. He recited poetry to me and enacted many of the roles he had performed on the stage for my special benefit. He wrote poetry, songs, and painted and drew sketches which were quite good. He was a perfectionist and anything he undertook to do he did well, conquering the task by himself in his quiet, unobtrusive way. He was very popular with women, and my mother was not always silent about her jealousy over the admiration incurred when he was a matinee idol. She was especially outspoken about the attention Jane Cowl showered upon him, and, I suspect, secretly happy when his stage career came to an end and he became a proper business executive. As I have matured and attempted to assume an adult, objective point of view about my father, I have never ceased to wonder how, with his charm, good looks, and abilities, he remained so loyal and faithful to one woman all of his life when this behavior pattern was not characteristic of any other member of his family. Of all the children he had the least contact with his parents, but he seemed to have assimilated the best to be offered by both. Certainly, he acted out to perfection the role of husband and father, never allowing his love for either me or my mother to come into open conflict.

During my adolescence Uncle Theo was living with Helen. Our contacts were somewhat restricted although we now lived in

Manhattan. Once Uncle Theo became very important in my own life in the role of a "shining knight." It was when I was attending high school and was not going to be allowed to graduate with my class as I had forged ahead but was not given credit for work I did outside of my prescribed classes. Uncle Theo, who did not heartily approve of America's educational system, came to my defense and called in his lawyer, no less a personage than Dudley Field Malone, to see that I got my diploma–which I did.

> May [1925] Going to night school to graduate earlier. Duke [my teacher and man I was engaged to but never married] knows about it. I have to tell them any day now in order to get on the graduation list. What a mess! It seems carrying day and evening classes is taboo. They said they would have to withhold my diploma because of disregard of rules! I'm scared, but excited . . . somehow I love a challenge like this. Duke says I'll make it. Told Mom and Dad and they are upset. Mom mad as–at the principal. I hope she does not decide to go up there. Dad decides to call uncle Theo who says our educational system is the worst in the world. Everywhere else in the world, he said, kids learn to speak English as well as their own language and here we don't even seem to learn to spell correctly! He is going to call on his friend Dudley Field Malone. The board is meeting tomorrow to decide my fate.
>
> They decided to let me graduate. I think they were influenced by the fact that I made it known that they were in for a hassle by my uncle Theodore Dreiser and Dudley Field Malone, if they didn't.
>
> I got in their hair again by wearing my beautiful maize colored dress with the hoop. We were required to wear straight dresses. O well![2]

It was shortly after graduation that Uncle Theo's *An American Tragedy,* which had been dramatized, opened at the Longacre Theatre on Broadway and we were there. It was one of the most exciting nights in my life. There were ovations for the author: "Bravo, Dreiser!" and the applause was deafening for the leading characters. Only my mother was shocked by the performance. She thought the book and the play disgraceful in subject matter.

> 1926. Mom is having a fit because she doesn't want me to read uncle Theo's *Tragedy.* What a marvelous book! Mom does

an about face when she gets a special invite to the play. Duke and I are going too. How exciting!

My gosh, was I embarrassed by Mom's remarks. She annoyed everyone around us. "Tsk, tsk, tsk . . . Filthy, etc!" She almost walked out on the bedroom scene, only Dad refused to let her.

Duke can't understand Mom's attitude. She told him tonight that she didn't know how anyone could write such filth. She said she was ashamed to know him![3]

Following the success of the book and the play Uncle Theo went to Russia and when he returned he and Helen built Iroki. When it was liveable they made a cross-country tour during which Uncle Theo found his brother Rome and brought him back to live with him and Aunt Mame whose husband, Austin Brennan, had died. I did not meet Uncle Rome until 1938 when he and Mame had left Iroki and were living in Mame's house where he stayed until he died in 1940. He was a tall and handsome man, despite his earlier riotous habits of living. I recognized him as a Dreiser the first moment I saw him when I drove up to Mame's house and he was seated on the front porch, rocking to and fro. When he met me, he took me in from head to foot and then drawled, "Ed's daughter . . . we–el!" And then after a few minutes of perusing me he commented, "I think you look like Ed." In his wanderings he never married, but I am certain his life must have been filled with many affairs for there was still evidence of the passionate, rebellious youth he had been—the embarrassment to his family with his uncontrollable alcoholism.

During my university days Uncle Theo was quite a public figure, very outspoken in his views on politics and science. After the publication of *Dawn* and the riot it caused in the family, Uncle Theo's relations with his family were again somewhat strained. During this time, whenever I was around him with my family, I felt that only my father was at ease. There was a definite strained atmosphere between Theo and my mother whenever they met. I really think *he was afraid of her!* Uncle Theo was a victim of a constant emotional war within himself and his inability to get along with people, and the inability to sustain human relationships was incomprehensible to my mother. His genius and his fame did little to alter her loathing of his private life or his public behavior.

She had little more tolerance for the now universally recognized GENIUS than she had once expressed for the uncouth young man she had met in Paul Dresser's studio.

When I was going to New York University I stayed with Mame during the week as the long drive home each day was too much to make. It was during this period I grew to know Mame and I came to realize the great power of Sarah Dreiser's charm as it was revealed through Mame who was in her eighties at that time.

Mame, Sylvia, and an old friend, Frank Thomas, shared a little house in Queens. The three–all past seventy-five–had evolved a workable system of communal living. Each had eminent domain over a portion of their home and all observed a simple but solemn ceremony in their use of the shared areas.

Sylvia was very retiring. She had long before lost her sparkling good looks and had taken to wearing a wig, and was inclined to be secretive and mysterious. She once made an appointment to see my mother and selected as a suitable spot for their meeting the "seventh maple to the east of the Schiller Memorial in Central Park." Mother didn't actually have to count the trees. She arrived a bit late but had no difficulty in spotting the black-cloaked, black-hooded figure standing motionless under a holm oak. Yet this was only the flamboyant exterior of a mysticism that had brought Sylvia great peace. She would remain in her room for days, perfectly content, and then would emerge suddenly full of some splendid plan of action. Once she burst out upon me carrying the words of a patriotic song she had written, which would match Paul's "The Blue and the Gray" and make our fortune. She had me write the melody that afternoon, sitting with me at the piano and exhorting me constantly to brilliance. I don't think she really believed in that fortune, but she managed to fill me with enthusiasm and inspirational joy. We had the greatest fun and were very close and happy. I still have the song in manuscript for it was not one of those I have had published, and I am still very fond of it for Sylvia's sake and my fond remembrances of her. She would sometimes invite me to her personal rooms, where the conversation would always be on religious topics. Hers was a private faith–she was a Christian Science practitioner–which she felt no call to preach, but was always happy to answer my questions. Her talks saved me much lonely thinking on my road from Mother's dogmatic teaching to the belief that sustains me now. For all her eccentricities, I remember Sylvia as a bright and beautiful woman.

Frank Thomas had always been an admirer of Mame's, and when her husband died, he adopted a role toward her that caused some scandal in the family. There was much discussion as to his motives. My mother, of course, suspected motives of sexuality despite their ages. (She might have been referring to their younger acquaintance which had fond memories for them both.) The others generally suspected he was after her money. As he was in his late seventies (he was a few years younger than the women) and fairly well off financially and as Mame was then practically entirely dependent upon her brother Theodore, both theories seemed unlikely to me. I prefer to think that he was a courteous and chivalrous old gentleman who wanted to do what he could to bring comfort to the lady he most admired. Perhaps my view was colored by the belief that Mame was a perfect object for courteous and chivalrous admiration, I, too, considered her a great lady.

Mame, at her advanced age, was tall, erect, and where she had once been quite large, she was now much thinner and more elegant. She wore her white hair in ringlets and dressed exquisitely, roselike, fresh, and she looked out at the world through her immense, peaceable eyes. She received a great many visitors at her home, most of them my own generation, for she loved to talk with the young and to discuss the subjects we were studying at school. Entering her parlor, the visitor had the immediate feeling of becoming a part of her personality and being made welcome. She was both physically and spiritually a big human being. She had sympathy for all and would eagerly share our youthful enthusiasms, yet she was by no means a passive listener. She contributed to our conversation and her contributions were often crucial. Her sound common sense, a sort of innocent wisdom, helped us put our new-won knowledge into perspective.

Many older people find enjoyment in pin-pricking the ballooning ideas of youth. Mame never deflated our theories. She did her best to fill the hollow spaces with solid sense from her own wide experience with life. She was, in a way, like those staid old bankers who financed the merchant adventurers on their voyages to the New World. She assumed a share of responsibility for the daring of our ideas without laying any claim to their originality. If, on discussion, one small mental venture failed, she was ready to listen to the next. Because she had shared our loss, she never made us feel that sense of inadequacy which is so terrible to youth and which often springs from having some wonderful idea that later proves to have some obvious flaw. Mame made "being wrong" a vital part of learning to "be right." Many a young person turned half-formed theories or ideas into useful knowledge or opinion just by talking to Mame. She was neither a teacher nor a confidante. She was, in virtue and truth, a wise and tolerant friend.

During these years I was closer to her than either my mother or father, although we had always visited back and forth and there was no strain on our relations. Mother, in her distant way, approved of her sister-in-law, Mame. She often spoke of the way Mame had handed over the use of her Rochester home to my mother and father on their extended honeymoon. It was the type of gesture Mother admired, but would never have been able to make herself. As a consequence I never heard my mother speak ill of Mame as she often did about other members of the Dreiser family.

In retrospect, I have often asked myself about the charisma Mame possessed. What was this element which held the world at bay, while summoning it? What was this ingredient which set a limitation, a kind of clause against completion, against any relationship which demanded responsibility, allowance for individual freedom? It was not so destructive in Mame, who reached some degree of happiness in her marriage to Austin Brennan, although Uncle Theo never did realize this or accept it. But I believe it was the same grace, an amazing grace, which in Sarah Dreiser did a double twist and kept the world in abeyance. Sarah projected fantasy in the face of dissatisfaction, and while this may be seen as a protection against vulnerability, it teaches a child that the world is cruel, not to be trusted, and the only hope for happiness lies in self-deception. This implies that everywhere lies potential disaster, a crippling conviction, and a belief that the wild nature of the world precludes having any measure of control of your own fate, thus resulting in feelings of ineptness and inadequacy. Such had been Sarah's maternal gift to her children.

The scepter of death had already appeared to the Dreiser clan. Aunt Claire, who had been ill for many years, was now dead. Her son, Paul Gormley, and I, who had been very close friends as small children, were separated after his mother's death in 1918. In later years he wrote to me concerning his mother's feelings toward Uncle Theo:

> Mother [Claire] had virtually alienated herself from all contact with Ted, even when I was a small boy. She and Jug and Ida, Jug's sister, were on excellent terms and I know that her sympathies were with Jug. Mother was *strait-laced.* Dreiser was far in advance of the mob.

In 1933 Emma began showing signs of senility (in fact, she was the only member of the family who was quite obviously afflicted with this geriatric debility). Her daughter, Gertrude Hopkins (whom Helen, in her book, erroneously confused with me), waited on her hand and foot at the expense of her promising singing career. Finally, in 1936, when Gertrude could no longer carry the burden of a business career (she was a successful woman executive for Con Edison in New York) and tend to her mother's constant bodily needs, Emma went to live with Mame, Sylvia, and Frank Thomas. There she died in 1937.

Aunt Jug, too, was failing. She was living at 92 Grove Street, in New York City. After the success of *An American Tragedy* Uncle Theo was persuaded to settle a monthly allowance on her, although he never sought a divorce. At the time he was living with Helen, and most of their acquaintances assumed they were married, despite their constant bickerings and separations. In 1938 Uncle Theo gave up his Mt. Kisco home and made plans to move to California permanently to live with Helen. Before he made this final break with the East he took time out to attend the Paris Peace Conference. Upon his return he and Helen took up residence in Glendale, California, where Louise Dresser was living. Later Louise told me when she learned that Theo and Helen were living in the same community, she would cross the street rather than encounter Theo. Like my mother she disapproved of the life style of Theo and Helen—a style which caused them to embrace new friends in new situations, removing themselves from the past and the associates they had made. Finally they moved from Glendale to a home they purchased at 1015 North Kings Road in Hollywood, where Uncle Theo lived until his death in 1945.

In 1939 I married Alfred E. Scott. We had planned to go abroad on our honeymoon, but that summer Europe became the spearhead of war. With Hitler on the advance and conditions unsettled we decided to tour the United States instead.

When we arrived in California, we contacted Helen and Theo who had sent us a beautiful silver tray for a wedding gift. Helen was most cordial and apparently delighted with my groom, while Uncle Theo was stiff and formal and insisted upon calling Alfred "Mr. Scott," something I could never understand.

The early 1940s were a very difficult period for Theo. He was upset by world conditions and openly discussed his hope that America would remain neutral. His position was an extremely unpopular one, and he was thought to be pro-German because of his outspoken views on World War II. Because of his compassion for so many different causes Uncle Theo often antagonized those with whom he was unable to communicate his real sentiments. In later years he tried to explain to me his ideas which were indeed very unpopular—as were those of leaders and others who lived beyond the period and were seen in a different light as time wore on and history, as history is wont, altered in its perspective. In a letter of Uncle Theo's which I later read, he seemed to have been seriously disturbed by the situation. He wrote:

> All decency seems to have gone out of government life. . . . But down among us little people it's not so bad. We're like the Irish fairies or "good people" in the grass across which the giants of circumstance pass, never knowing we are there. . . .

In 1941 Uncle Theo came to New York. Although Helen had been writing to me in regard to the film being made of Paul's life, she never mentioned that Theo was to be in New York; but she added to a letter which arrived almost at the same time as he, "TD sends his best wishes!" He called my father at Mallinson's and the three of us met for lunch before he returned to the coast.

It was not long after this visit that Aunt Jug died in Missouri. The notice of her death caused considerable embarrassment among Helen and Theo's California friends because they had not been informed as to the relationship of Theo and Helen. That there existed another Mrs. Theodore Dreiser who was still recognized as *the* Mrs. Theodore Dreiser called for enormous tact on the part of their acquaintances. Now Theo was free to marry Helen but he did not do so. In fact his interests among women did not diminish and the death of Jug did not alter his relationship with Helen. It was two years later that he decided to marry Helen.

In the meantime the story of Paul Dresser had been made into a film featuring Victor Mature and Rita Hayworth. It opened at Radio City Music Hall and we were invited to the opening preview showing. The film was a lavish musical which was a highly fictionalized version of Paul's life. It was not the story of Paul Dresser, a man whose very name could conjure such adjectives as "lovable," "generous," "good-natured," "big-hearted," "kindly," and "impossible to dislike," words which came from people in all walks of life. I had been fed on stories of Paul since birth. One of my favorties was the story my father told about Paul, the free-loving man of the world of the theater, who remained a Catholic until his death although he was not overly observant in his religious duties. Paul was constantly met by a Catholic priest, Father Van–short for Van Rennsalaer–at the corner of 42nd Street and Broadway where he would hear Paul's confession in passing. Paul's confession was, "Father, I've committed every sin in the book–except murder!" Then he would smile and give the priest a contribution and gaily go about his merry way.

The Paul Dresser story involved every member of the Dreiser family. I was completely and especially committed, as I had maneuvered the releases necessary from my parents in order to make the film. Ironically, I never received any credit as it became propitious for Helen to establish a communication with my mother and credit her with the cooperation. Helen must have sensed that my mother's devotion to respectability was a trump card she could use in her playing hand to become Mrs. Theodore Dreiser before Uncle Theo died. If she could be on friendly terms with Mai, she felt (correctly so) she would accomplish her life's desire. With Aunt Jug deceased, there was really no reason why her relationship should not be legalized, and with my mother's friend Jug no longer an emotional consideration, Helen felt she could gain some headway. The making of the film and the necessary legal papers the Ed Dreisers had to approve made it possible for Helen to resume contact and to be regarded in a more appreciable light.

The film evoked memories of the stormy Dreiser family history, and although it was a well-put-together Hollywood vehicle, it bore little resemblance to either Uncle Theo's story, "My Brother Paul," or to Uncle Paul's life or achievement.

Actualy it was not until 1971 that Uncle Paul was given his proper status when his peers elected him along with Sigmund Romberg to the Songwriters Hall of Fame of the American Society of Composers, Authors and Publishers.

Had my daughter, Sheri Dreiser Scott, been born a boy my husband and I had planned on naming the child "Theodore Dreiser Scott." We even toyed with the idea of naming our baby girl "Theodora," but we settled on "Sheri." (She subsequently called herself "Tedi.") My personal life was so involved with my marriage, my child, and my own career that my interest in Uncle Theo, Helen, and even my own parents became of secondary importance.

In 1944 Uncle Theo came to New York to accept an award from the American Academy of Arts and Letters. The award was to be presented in the month of May, but just before Uncle Theo arrived, Aunt Mame had to be hospitalized. I visited her frequently, and sensed her condition was terminal. One day my mother and father accompanied me to Kew Gardens Hospital where she was confined. We had left Sheri with a cousin in Jackson Heights. While we were waiting for the "visitor's hour" call, I became interested in the activity around the reception desk in the lobby of the hospital. My spirits were very low and gloomy for I wondered if this visit would be the last, and as I watched the briskness around the desk, I wasn't certain whether I was dreaming or hallucinating, for I saw my Uncle Theodore standing at the desk talking to the head nurse. I felt a quickening of my pulse and simultaneously a sense of fear over the consequences of this unexpected encounter between my mother and Uncle Theo. We knew he was expected in New York, but it never occurred to me that the first meeting would be so dramatically staged. I feared what my mother might say. Much to my surprise—and probably to Uncle Theo's too—she was most cordial. After greetings had been exchanged and the nurse informed us she could allow only two persons at the same time to see the patient, my mother spoke up and suggested that Uncle Theo and I go in first to visit—together!

I was almost frozen to the spot but managed to walk in a state of somnambulism. I could not believe what had just transpired between my mother and my Uncle Theodore.

Uncle Theo led the way along the hall. His inquiries at the desk must have been very precise, for he knew exactly where to go. Mame's room was in the extreme west wing of the building and we had quite a length of hallway to navigate. He walked slowly and more heavily than Dad and all the time we both were aware we were each doing our very best to make conversation—but we failed. Our talk was inconsequential chitchat and I was relieved when we reached Mame's room. Uncle Theo opened the door in such a way that I was well inside the room before he appeared. Overnight Mame seemed to have shrunk. Her halo of curls was now thin, straight hair pulled tightly back revealing the contour of her skull. Her face was the ugly blanched white of the hospital gown she wore. But her voice was still strong and confident when she greeted me. "Vera," she began and then suddenly she saw Uncle Theo. "Theo," she cried, and then she was unable to continue her speech. Uncle Theo walked around and stood between her and the window. He reached down, kissed her, and took her hand in his.

She smiled and then said, "You didn't come all the way from California—" she stopped and rubbed her brow with one frail transparent finger. I knew she was thinking that such visits are usually made only at deathbed scenes. Uncle Theo beamed at her. "I was in New York on business. The Academy of Arts and Letters decided to honor me. I think they must have known I wanted to see you again, Mame."

She lay quite still, looking at him. They were both constrained as if there was so much to say, yet they both sensed it would never get said. Uncle Theo squeezed her hand. "You'll be up and about soon again, Mame." Mame again smiled wanly, but shook her head. Then she spoke. "I want to go home, Theo [her pet name for him] to die. It is only right. Poor Em came home to me to die, as did Rome." She sighed in remembrance. "It's the expense," she continued. "If I should get sick again, fall . . . and there would have to be an ambulance, more hospital bills. . . ."

I was jittery because I had been told so often by my mother that Uncle Theo was not very generous as far as his family was concerned, and I was afraid Mame's words would cause him to depart abruptly.

"There, there, Dearie," I heard Uncle Theo say comfortingly, using the same word, "Dearie," my father was accustomed to use. "This is no time to think or talk about money. Everything will be taken care of."

Mame clutched his hands. "You've always been so good to me. I can never repay you. . . ."

It was obvious that Uncle Theo was embarrassed. He soothed Mame by saying, "Now . . . now. Ed and Mai are waiting to see you and we mustn't monopolize your time. I just wanted to look in and see that you were comfortable and had everything you need."

Mame smiled and motioned to Uncle Theo to bend over closer. She said, "Get to know Vera, Theo . . . get to know her well, she'll be your good friend." Uncle Theo nodded and smiled at me standing on the other side of the bed. "There are so few of us left," she whispered. Uncle Theo acted as if he were taking orders from Mame and walked around to the side of the bed where I was standing and took hold of my hand. Mame smiled, her incredible smile of warmth and belief. I walked out of the room feeling more confidence and inner security. If I were to lose Aunt Mame, she had arranged for me to have a replacement in Uncle Theodore. It is never easy to explain one's need for another person except when that need is simple and physical. My need for Mame and her sympathy was very special, one I had never been able to explain to my parents, nor to Dr. Lawton, my associate who had helped me adjust my personal talent toward my work. It would be hard to explain to anyone, I thought, how Mame had helped me to adjust to life itself.

When the visit was ended, Uncle Theo said good-bye and promised to be in touch. I wanted to step forth and ask him if we could meet again, talk, hoping he would understand my need for someone to fill the breach–if Mame should die. But there was something formidable in him, and something frightened in me that made me reticent, self-conscious, once again a child in the presence of a living enigma. Would he reject me, mock me, or simply dismiss me curtly? I could not afford the chance. I knew he had to take the initiative if we were to know one another. As I watched him walk down the corridor, for a moment he was not my uncle but the shadow of the controversial man, Theodore Dreiser. I returned home in silence.

The ringing of the telephone the next day answered my questions. It was Uncle Theodore. Paul Robeson had given him two tickets to *Othello* and he wanted me to join him. I had already seen the production but under no set of circumstances could I have told him and refused his invitation. I went to the Commodore, parked my car, and Uncle Theo and I went to the theater in a cab. From the moment the curtain rose, I became aware of Uncle Theo's labored breathing—especially during the silences on the stage. At intermission I mentioned to Uncle Theo that I was associated with Dr. Shailer U. Lawton and that I had great respect for his medical opinion. I told Uncle Theo I would like to have him have a complete check-up by Dr. Lawton. He didn't refuse, and I sensed he didn't want to, but he seemed somewhat pleased in my concern about his health. During the next act, I felt his hand slip upon my knee. I became very uncomfortable as I associated the gesture with overtures made in a dark movie house when I was a teenager and would be obliged to get up and change my seat. In retrospect I am embarrassed to realize what a fool I was. There was nothing in Uncle Theo's gesture, as his hand never moved, and after a very short time he removed it. It was almost as if he had reached for my presence as a sense of security, a realization that I was there, his flesh and blood, beside him, concerned for him.

Our plan was to take Paul Robeson out for a private visit and some food and drink after the performance, but when we went backstage Paul was most friendly but said if we wished to be together we would have to go the Village as he would not be served in any of the restaurants in the neighborhood of the theater. I was floored! Here was his name in bright lights on the marquee; he was the star of the production but he could not be served in a first-class cafe. Uncle Theo was too tired to travel to Greenwich Village so I took a cab with him, picked up my car, and drove home. I have often thought what important observations might have been made by those two friends in my presence—comments on Russia, on racial prejudices, on the life of the artist.

The next day I made arrangements for Mame to leave the hospital as she wished. Poor Frank Thomas, whose entire life at that point seemed to center around Mame—in cooking for her, tending her needs, and listening to her talk—was not liked by anyone except me in the family despite his kindness. The few times Uncle Theo came to see Mame, it was clear that the well-meaning but disliked man had to disappear.

My insistence brought Uncle Theo and Dr. Lawton together for Uncle Theo's complete physical. Dr. Lawton, who was respected by everyone in his profession and adored by his patients and students, was obviously excited by meeting a man whom he had admired all of his life for his writing, his courage, his honesty, his onslaught with conventional society—Theodore Dreiser. Uncle

Theo, on the other hand, kept the appointment, pouting like a small child and somewhat resentful of Dr. Lawton whom I almost idolized. His attitude toward him is clearly evident in his letter to me. The battle of the giants!

COPY OF LETTER TO FRANKLYN THORPE, M.D. (California)
FROM SHAILER UPTON LAWTON, M.D., F.A.C.P.–SPRING 1944

Dear old Franklyn,

Thank you so much for your wonderful letter. Believe me, I am happy that Theodore Dreiser, of whom I am extremely fond, is in your hands. When he was here his Blood Pressure was 112/60, pulse regular at 98, Blood Chemical Sugar 88.2, Icterous index 8.4, Blood Calcium 9.3, Basal +16. EKG he has with him and so I will not give you data on this since he can show tracings. Was interested in getting X-Ray of chest. Wanted all abscessed teeth out and, if possible, vaccine made from pus. Would like to have EKG checked again. Medication suggested was Ascorbic Acid, 100 mg. T.I.D.; Ahmend's solution, 5 drops per day; a high potency of Vitamin AD capsule and Dicalcium phosphate with Viosterol capsule (Squibbs) of which he is supposed to take 1 a day. We suggested less meat and definitely less liquor and spices, with more fruit, vegetables, and dairy products. We told him it was more important to be under the wing of a good M.D. like you, as a matter of insurance, than any other single thing he could do.

Please give my best to the charming gentleman and tell him to be a good boy and do what you order.

This is not a letter, old pal. I'll write later. As far as I'm concerned I'm nothing but a cash register and one of those creatures that lives in the treadmill grinding out the tripe. I think of myself as being an intellectual prostitute, which means whore to you. The older I grow, the less I know of what it is all about, so if you have any answers handy in 10 easy, monosyllabic words, please enlighten your benighted, ignorant, uncouth, and humble servant.

Ever, ever faithfully yours,

As we were leaving and Uncle Theo was grumbling about "subjecting myself to this damned medical nonsense . . ." I sensed that he did not want to be left alone, but wanted to remain with me. We went for luncheon to a small French restaurant in the neighborhood of our office which was at 65 East 55th Street. Over luncheon, as our conversation was getting more interesting, I suggested we go for a drive to Fort Tryon Park. Knowing all of the Dreisers' love of natural beauty and their reaction to an outdoor environment, I felt that it would be good for Uncle Theo to get away from the city sounds and sights and relax as we drove along the Hudson River. He began to unwind as the city disappeared behind us and he told me how pleased he was in getting to know me, complimented me on my patience, and then said, "How would you like me as a patient?" Knowing he wasn't serious, and also having some knowledge from his writings as to his attitude toward Freud, Jung, and other psychiatrists, and knowing how he could have received treatment, if he had so desired, from Dr. Brill, I laughed and said, "I'm afraid it would be too hard a job!"

While I was with him I became conscious of the problems of our situation. Ever since my school days I had admired him even in the (to him, I am certain) casual and probably meaningless ways in which our paths had crossed. But now the picture had projected itself into another dimension. I was an adult woman, a wife, a practicing therapist, a mother! I was too conscious of the sexual tension (on my part), the hero worship, the challenge of mental gymnastics, not to recognize that our relationship was fraught with too many problems for sheer comfort. I could not be relaxed and as I watched him suffering through the compulsive ritual of making his "mouse" while we sat, parked, trying to find peace, comfort, and companionship, I felt a deep inner sorrow for him. I knew he needed something he had lacked all of his life and how I wished as I sat beside him that I could help. I knew that lack of acceptance and love is present in the early years of an obsessive-compulsive neurosis, but I knew talking to him about his youth and his mother would be impossible. We sat in silence for quite a while, admiring the view, when suddenly he said, "You know, I don't think I have ever really known love." I thought before I answered and said, "Well, even so, if a need is satisfied, one can be happy. One must feel needed and loved through kindness and consideration." He shook his head and replied, "I have never had a need satisfied." I wondered if he meant a sexual need, but he did not pursue his meaning. Gingerly, I tried to bring up the subject of his mother, my grandmother, but he withdrew into himself and suddenly seemed very tired. He took refuge in contemplating the blue sky and the beautiful woodland scene. Watching his heavily browed eyes absorb the surroundings, I could not help but think that this man who wrote of bitterness and suffering also wrote of hope and that those critics who saw him only as a pessimist, a believer in mechanical fate, should have sat there with me and almost heard coming from his lips his words in *Sister Carrie* when she sits all alone: ". . . hearkening to the sound of beauty, straining for the flash of its distant wings."

> I was probing gently, I thought, because I had sensed deep seated problems where men and women were concerned. I know he truly believed he adored and needed women. Any other suggestion to him would have brought about a dreadful reaction. After all he was in his 70's so why make him any more unhappy than he was. I felt that would have been cruel, and he was such a giant in his own way why should I destroy him–and it would destroy him had I said what I already knew "Uncle Ted, you have latent homosexual tendencies." He was not the kind of man you could say this to. It would not challenge him to argue the point. It would hurt him and sear his already badly damaged self-image. He was so like a child in many ways, which was both wonderful and yet difficult at the same time. Talk about his mother would have to follow and he would not participate I knew.

On the return drive, I asked him if he was a communist at heart and he answered me, "Only insofar as it is relevant to the dignity of man." He then continued talking as if he were addressing a group of young students. "In my book on Russia [1928] I went down the middle of the road. I witnessed firsthand a great deal to be admired, and yet I don't believe I could live under the system. I am too much of an individualist. However, you must remember that was in 1927 when I was there and all eyes were watching the economic and social development of Russia. I was glad that I was invited to visit and observe there, but I received a firm promise that I would be free to evaluate it as I saw it."

He went on to say that it was difficult to write or discuss sex freely in the United States and in this respect he felt he would be more comfortable in Russia because of the more realistic attitude there in regard to man's relations toward woman. The freedom of a man or woman to walk away from a relationship was what he felt most keenly about. When I asked what the communist system would do to our responsibility to our children, he replied that such a plan could not exist in the United States. In Russia, he pointed out, they had already established the state's responsibility toward children, their education and support. I gently suggested that he and Helen had more or less lived their lives in such a manner for twenty-three years and I bluntly asked if he thought he would have married Helen if he had been free when he met her. He was obviously a bit annoyed at my "prying" but he thought for a moment and then answered, "It is true that my first marriage was not as happy as it could have been. I was not the most successful sexually of young men when I married Jug. I often felt inadequate when around women yet along with this I had a keen desire. As a boy I always believed I had absolutely nothing that a girl would find attractive." I asked point-blank, "Is that why you had so much hostility toward women?" He looked amazed, his mobile brows rising and then falling. "Hostility?" he paused and then said, "I asked you earlier if you would consider taking me on as a patient. . . . Well, now, I've changed my mind. Let's talk about something else."

I took advantage of this suggestion and I blurted out, "Do you believe in God, Uncle Theo?"

There followed a voicelessness and then he spoke with more assurance than I had previously observed. Indecision, fear, anxieties vanished and he said, "Do I believe in God? That's quite a question. I have never abandoned a belief in God. You have only to read what I have been writing all my life to know that I believe in certain things, forces, nature creations that are above and beyond the ken or power of any human being as we know it. Let me say this: that along with a lot of other myths and misunderstandings about my way of life that time and time again I have written about this. When you read the book I am in the process of completing, *The Bulwark,* you will see what I say in the character of Solon Barnes . . . a philosophy is there that I have believed all of my life. One is labeled, pegged and pigeonholed as I have been, and I suppose I have been branded atheist and many other things, *but, not only do I believe in God,* but I will go into any scientific laboratory and prove it to you."

When we returned he took me to dinner at Luchow's with his friend, Edgar Lee Masters.

When I left him at his hotel that night I suggested a long weekend on Long Island with all of us. He was delighted with the idea and put his arm around me and kissed me good night for the first time in my life. I drove off anxious to put his exact words in my book of personal notes. I could hear again his saying "I've been in love a thousand times . . . . or maybe never at all. . . . most likely never at all. . . ."

Every time I had chauffered Uncle Theo we had been in my little "blue Chevvie" to which he sent *love* in his letters, but the day we picked him up for the long weekend we were in Dad's big car. Alfred was with us, and as we were driving home, we began singing songs, which was a custom of ours. We sang "Indian Love Call" and Uncle Theo, who didn't know the words, hummed the tune. He seemed delighted, a perfect one-man audience, when suddenly he broke into song, singing "There Was An Old Woman," which he followed with "The Bold Fisherman." They were delightfully silly songs and we all laughed at Uncle Theo's gusto and abandon. When I asked him who had taught him these songs, he blushed and confessed, "Jug . . . ." We changed the subject and Uncle Theo talked to me about some of my songs which I had sung and suggested that I pursue the writing further. When I told him of the complications I had encountered with music publishers, he told me he would see what he could do. (Which he did upon his return to California.) As we approached Far Rockaway, I could see he was getting nervous. He asked, "How is Mai?" and then, "Has she changed any?" In my own mind I could still see him leaving the porch of the same house on that hot summer's day at my mother's insistence. I, too, became apprehensive. Had I done the wrong thing, inviting him for a long weekend? What would explode? What skeletons would emerge of which I was not aware?

To ease the tension, I decided to tell a risqué joke. I thought I had brought it off with aplomb, sophistication, and all of the other applicable adjectives. But Uncle Theo suppressed his laugh and seemed uncomfortable. I refrained from telling the second when he turned to me and said, "What a memory for low stuff! You remind me of Paul." I was baffled. The realist, the first really honest writer was actually embarrassed! I thought about his attitude toward an off-color joke and decided it must trigger off unconscious memories of his chagrin at his sisters' capers when he was a boy. Jokes dealing with sex could have had painful memories of his shortcomings in this area. He could write about it seriously and with compassion, but to laugh at it was another matter.

When we arrived, I was amazed at my mother. She looked exceedingly attractive, more so than I had seen her appear in quite some time. Actually, she was in her element–housing and feeding people, entertaining *at home.* Here she was always comfortable because she could take refuge if the situation got out of hand by excusing herself and retreating to the kitchen to see if all was going well.

That evening everything went with the smoothness of a Broadway production. Mai, instead of being "Ed's Wild Irish Catholic" in Uncle Theo's eyes, was charming. "Mai has mellowed," he commented and then added, "She's still lovely." We were all weary and retired early. Uncle Theo was put to sleep in the "pink bedroom."

In the morning Dad and Uncle Theo went for a long walk along the beach. When they returned I had my tiny baby daughter all prettied up for her meeting with her Grand-uncle Theodore. The baby, only months old, was in an enchanting mood. Uncle Theo's eyes opened in wide surprise as he stared at her. "Why, she's beautiful! What's her name?"

"Sheri," I said; "we liked the sound with Scott." I told him we had prenamed her as a him "Theodore" and almost selected "Theodora Dreiser Scott" as the family name was dying out. Uncle Theo raised his beautiful hand in interruption. "Nonsense–I don't think one has to worry about perpetuating a family name if one leaves enough ideas behind."

I, like any proud mother, placed Sheri in his arms; and he was terrified. He was awkward and afraid that he would drop her. Since babies sense this feeling in the manner in which they are held, Sheri set up her security wail, her huge blue eyes staring at him as if he were a monster. He thrust her back in my arms, amazing me as he said, "Take Her! She doesn't like me!" At the time, his words did not carry the insight they now do to me.

That afternoon and evening were spent in narrating forgotten family stories and a great deal of singing. For the most part I was merely an interested spectator. Uncle Theo referred to Dad as a "hero. . . he was no mollycoddle, work was his forte . . . any kind of work that had lots of exercise in it and Ed was willing." Observing the "banquets" my mother was setting before him, he asked Ed how he managed to stay so slender. For the first time I realized that Dad looked at least fifteen years younger than Uncle Theo although they were less than two years apart in age. "Exercise, exercise," replied Ed, and Uncle Theo laughed and said, "That's Ed–a study in perpetual motion, running around with a baseball in his hand, his shirttails dragging."

Almost as if none of the rest of us were present, Uncle Theo and Ed marched backward in time to their boyhood days in Indiana and Illinois. Uncle Theo talked as if he were narrating a film clip, while Dad supplied complementary documentation.

"Ed and I constantly pestered our mother for as much as fifteen cents a week in order that we might see the strolling repertoire shows which occasionally arrived, staying as long as a week at a time playing *East Lynne, Uncle Tom's Cabin, The Octaroon. . . .*"

Dad sang many of Uncle Al's funny songs and recited "The Little Senator," Uncle Al's poem:

The Little Senator

When I was but a little lad, the neighbors used to say
As they'd pat me on the head "You'll be a Senator someday".
And it got to be so common, that I could hardly stir
Without a hearin' someone say "Why there's the little Senator".
As time went on, and I grew older, it kinda seemed to me
As everyone expected, why that's what oughta be.
The notion it grew with me, and it made me sorta vain
And I felt above the other lads, with that stamped on my brain.

I was only eight years old when mother took sick and died
How I lingered, 'round the coffin in the parlor, by her side
And wondered why the silver plate tacked on the coffin breast
Was lettered so, and what it meant by saying "she's at rest"?
I remembered that she told me human bein's never died
Just went to live in Heaven with the angels in the sky.
But I had the strangest feelin' when they shoveled in the sod
I wondered how all covered up, she ever got to God?

My father was a laboring man with horny hands and brown,
Who bought through honest toil our home at the outskirts of the town

And when his work was over, through the bustle and the stir
I used to run to lead him home, his little Senator.
We struggled along together, I kept house and went to school
Father's heart was charity, his life the Golden Rule.
He'd a notion of hereafter, but never preached, n' prayed, n' stole
Then swapped the plunder with his God, for mercy on his soul.

We got along together, and kept poverty at bay
'Till father lost his job, and then things went the other way.
The money changers took our home, foul fiends of human kind
Like vultures shrieked around their prey, 'till father lost his mind.
I was left alone and destitute, an outcast in the street
No friendly hand to cling to, no friendly heart that beat
For the little wandering stranger, save the heart that beat in her
Who watched him from the clouds above, her little Senator.

I draw the curtain here and close, the struggles of a child
For trails more cruel and bitter, up-on life's stormy wild.
Would to God I could have died a child, and never lived to stain
A soul once pure and spotless, with the blighting curse of Cain.
But of all the Devil's conjurings, and demoniac tricks
The worst of all was when he led me into politics
T'was there I struck the fatal blow, that severed every ban
Of human right, and left me cursed–a wandered in the land.

T'was the evening of election, I was watcher at the poles
They were counting out the ballots, in the dingy, dirty holes
And I saw the deal was crooked, one was cheating in the count
And I called a halt and asked him, Why he kept those ballots out
They said that I was crazy– "had softenin' of the brain
Took it from my father, heard that he had gone insane"
The sting was more than I could bear, and quicker done than said
I grabbed a chair, and like a flash, I up and struck him dead.

For life behind the prison bars, the Judge gave his decree
But penitentiary bolts and bars, were never made for me.
For I was born on freedom's soil, and take it him who can...
I scaled the walls and claimed the God of nature's gift to man.
A homeless wretch, I wander, shunned by everyone I meet
But always 'neath this ragged vest, a manly heart will beat.
Trodding on, through rain and snow, naught but a mockery and a slur
To that once vain conceited lad, the little Senator.

When Dad sang the German folk song their father used to sing when he would gather all of his children around him when the family was about to be separated, Uncle Theo shed tears.

Obviously he had repressed all of the memories of this action of his father and the remembrance came back to him in a rush of pent-up emotion. I heard him gulp and ask, "Ed, how do you remember all of these things?" Yet it was Uncle Theodore who vividly remembered the bedtime stories Sarah used to tell them—most of them blood-curdling and fear-inspiring. Mai reminded them of the days she and Ed spent in Rochester with Mame and Austin Brennan and their father, John Paul Dreiser. They discussed his religious fanaticism, but time had also summoned to them other memories of his inner strengths, untouched potentials. As they were now getting older, they viewed him with much keener insight.

The moment had to come when Uncle Theo reminded Mai of the day she "tossed him off her front porch" because of Jug. Aunt Jug had now been dead for two years and Uncle Theo and my mother were able to talk about her and their ill-fated marriage with a reasonable degree of detachment. Obviously whatever bitterness Uncle Theo had expressed from time to time had passed. He appeared to be taking in a new perspective on marriage as he sat with his brother and his wife. Undoubtedly he was thinking of how he had spent a great deal of his life flitting from one woman to another, while his brother Ed and his wife, Mai, had remained constant and apparently still devoted.

On Monday morning we decided to stop over at Mame's en route to the city. Over the weekend Frank Thomas had called and said she seemed to be sinking very rapidly. When we arrived at her home it was decided that each of us would go in and say good-bye separately. Since Dad had business to attend to and had to ride the subway from there on to the city, he went first. When he came out of the house he was looking very grave. He said quite calmly, "I'm afraid the end is near." Dad knew he had to continue about his daily affairs, and yet he seemed reluctant to leave, sensing, perhaps, that it would be the last time he and Uncle Theo would be together. Neither man appeared willing to say that final word, "good-bye!" They stood speechless for several minutes when suddenly Uncle Theo reached out and put his arm around Dad's neck, pulling him close and kissing him on the cheek. "Long life, Ed" was all he said. They embraced in silence and Dad had tears streaming down his face as he hastened away. Uncle Theo looked after him and almost as if he had forgotten I was within hearing distance he mumbled, "So many things I've missed!"

Uncle Theo next went in to see Mame and returned very shortly without making any observation. I entered, expecting to see her semiconscious, but she startled me by saying clearly, "Is that you, Vera?" Her mind was unclouded and I could scarcely act out my role of pretense knowing that shortly I was going to lose my wonderful aunt and good friend. She was eighty-four and had lived a very full life.

Uncle Theo and I drove on in to New York. With Mame's death hovering over us, out talk concerned life, death, the hereafter. Uncle Theo expressed his desire to be buried simply, close to nature, not to be cremated. He talked about his work–completing *The Bulwark* and writing *The Stoic,* the last of *Trilogy of Desire.* He told me of his meeting with Anna Tatum many years before. She was a young girl who had written him glowingly of *Jennie* and, after much correspondence, they met and she told him the story of her father, a Quaker, a man of nobility and character whose religious faith, rather than bringing him happiness, plunged him and his family into despair and ruin. The girl's story, plus her intelligence, had intrigued Uncle Theo. The more he thought about it, the more he found similarity in the story of his own father and his religious obsessions. The story, he said, would not leave his mind, and he had returned to it again and again. As we approached the Commodore, he turned to me and said, "Won't you come to California and help me finish *The Bulwark?"* I explained to him I could not leave my husband, my child, and my work with Dr. Lawton. He stared at me and said, "If you wanted to, you could." I didn't answer his words, but told him Dr. Lawton was planning to go to California in August to visit his mother and sister in Beverly Hills and possibly I could accompany him. The idea pleased him and as he stepped out of the car, he made me promise to do so.

After he left I did considerable reminiscing on our first serious adult encounter and I recorded the following in my diary:

> He seemed to believe that his sexual life was perfectly normal, as it should be. I tried to explain to him that a good healthy sex drive was fine provided that's what it was. He listened attentively when I told him from what had been said about him coupled with his own admissions, he had too many going at once to be healthy, and that it would bring him unhappiness in the end. I asked him what he was trying to prove? "TO

PROVE?" he repeated. "The only thing I can prove is that I need women. One doesn't seem to be enough." Yet you say "I have not love," "I am lonely" etc. so something is wrong.
If we were able to spend lots of time together explaining some of these things, do you think you'd go for it? Yes. It wouldn't all be easy or pleasant. Some answers we don't want to hear.
"I want to hear them & I'd be content with you anywhere" "and for any length of time because you are stimulating mentally to me and I like that."
"Come back with me to Calif. I need someone like you."
You know I can't do that. I have my practice, Alfred and the baby here. "If you really wanted to you'd arrange it. You have your mother & Ed. They'd help you." I'll think about it.
"No you won't."

On June 2, Mame died in her home as she had wished. Uncle Theo stayed over for the funeral but as soon as Mame was buried he left for Oregon. (I knew he was not going to California.)

After he was gone I thought over his request for me to come and work with him and my decision to remain with my husband, child, and career. Had I made the correct decision? As the years have passed, it has been one which I consistently questioned and one which I have regretted making.

II

Theodore and Vera

"... and I shall run with you."

It was June 5, the day before D-Day, that Uncle Theodore boarded a train headed for California—or so others thought. When he left, immediately after Mame's funeral, he was too depressed and exhausted to carry through a planned visit to Philadelphia. New York had been "almost too much" for him.

Unbeknownst to anyone in the family, he had contacted Helen and agreed to marry her, providing there would be no big ceremony, no publicity. Helen had located a small town fifty-three miles from Portland where they could be married without much fanfare. When Uncle Theo got off the train he was coughing and so fatigued he collapsed. Helen put him to bed and went to Portland where she bought herself a gold wedding band and applied for a marriage license in the names of Helen Richardson and Herman Dreiser. On June 13, with Helen's sister and her fiancé as witnesses, Helen and Theo were married by Justice of the Peace Gertrude Brown, who had no idea that the groom was a prominent author who had just presented his bride his recently accepted Academy of Arts and Letters gold medal.

It was several weeks after his return from New York that we learned of his marriage. His first note was brief, complaining about "germs" he had acquired "in an unfumigated berth on the miserable train." "I am the loneliest man in the world," he had confessed to me. When I learned of his marriage I wondered if the legal state of matrimony would alleviate his loneliness. When he had been in New York he had become convinced that it was most important that he complete *The Bulwark* for both monetary and artistic reasons. I wrote reminding him of Dr. Lawton's referral of Uncle Theo to Dr. Franklyn Thorpe (former husband of Mary Astor) in California for further medical check-ups on his thyroid condition.

Six weeks after his return on July 17, 1944, I received a letter from him which read:

1.
1015 N. Kings Road
Hollywood - 46
Calif.

July 17 - 44

Vera Dear:

What a nice brisk, ambitious healthy attractive neice it is that I have fallen heir to;—mentally and physically so alive and comprehending and so anxious to be up and doing. Really you are not only charming mentally but physically and I keep wishing that I had such an industrious as well as attractive maiden beside me—at my elbow. For most assuredly you would have me up and doing in connection with the things I should be up and doing about instead of myself complaining of this and that. In fact *I think of you all the time,*—your thoughtful and energetic and considerate approach toward everything—your friendly and helpful desire to get things done. I do not wonder that your Dr. Lawton wants you to take charge of his psychosomatic—research laboratory for without such a wise and willing and energetic girlie dynamo as Vera D I doubt whether he would get by with it. It is sound enough and ambitious but back of an ambition and soundness of idea must be a stirring human dynamo and that same is none other than my attractive Vera. Don't think I didn't gather his dependence on you that morning that he threw the new patient across your capable and graceful shoulder. If I had you here I'd be having you write my next book for you have the mind and the will and the delight in life and energy to

Helen with Theo, Vera, and Hilary Harris

make you capable of almost anything. For I noted that when I was with you anywhere—with and near you—I felt better for your being there, my girlie genius, just radiating energy—and good will and faith in the successful outcome of whatever task it was that was before us. And so I feel that your Dr. Lawton is just super-lucky. He's grabbing off a personality that can and could do wonders for itself and that can and will do wonders for him, even make him believe in himself . . and that is going some as you probably know yourself deep down in that attractive personality of yours. But it's so and you know it. And so luck to you Baby and to your Dr. Lawton, only I wish I had such a charming whirlwind attached to my humble little go cart. Would I go places? I'd retire to my writing room lie down and wait for you to bring the places to me, and as they came there you'd be along with smiles and good cheer and all the latest news. In fact my graceful girlie niece refusing to even be complimented. (—Oh, the hell with Lawton. Why didn't I draw my Vera D.) As for your songs sweet—never mind that tricky son of God who wants to share the profits. Send me four of the best-printed or copied. I know some one here who is a real judge and furthermore, if she likes them, can do something toward placing them and I'll take them to her and get her to move in the matter. Furthermore I'll write Deems Taylor and he'll tell me what if any move to make.

Meanwhile here's love and best wishes for my pet niece. You were so nice to me dearie and I won't forget. Also here's love to Ed, your mother, Alfred, the Baby, even the car. And luck to everything you choose to be interested in, from yours,

George Washington Dreiser

Your letter with Eds song was darling.

I later received a second letter dated August 3, 1944, following his visit to the California doctor, in which his antagonism to Dr. Lawton was veiled and not as overt as in the previous letter:

Thursday—Aug. 3—

Vera Dear

What a gay, enthusiastic letter. Plainly life goes well

enough for one with your physical and mental vigor for you sound like one who practices the "Have Faith Darling" Poem you wrote although no doubt you were addressing the world in general not anyone in particular. But somehow just the same the words and the melody of it bring you close to me and I got the feeling that if you did live near me it would be fun for all of the times I saw you in New York or was with you rather, I couldn't get close enough because there was so much that was warm and encouraging and affectionate about you—your voice, your smile, your cheerful and welcoming eyes I was drawn to you, and still am of course.

But one thing I wish you would do is tell me the tale or true story you referred to in this charming letter of yours—the one you want kept secret: It stirs my curiosity and I would love to share a secret like that with you, particularly since you feel that it would make a good story and the more so since of your own accord you thought of sharing it with me. I would (n't) betray you nor it ever unless you wished me so to do. I have the feeling that it must be something worth while or you would never mention it. More I feel as if it would bring us closer together and that I would like. Do write it out for me sweet—and if anytime later you say destroy it I will.

Well, yesterday morning, honey, following your advice I went to Doctor Olson whom Lawton Los Angeles doctor recommended and had tooth number one extracted. Its the last but one on the upper right jaw and took some pounding and pulling to make it let go. Two weeks from yesterday I'm to go and have the second removed although I hate to do it. This tooth looked so clean and strong and firm. There was no pain attached to the extraction nor was there any pain after and very little bleeding. In fact an hour afterwards at the doctors recommendation I had a bowl of thin soup, a cup of coffee and some ice cream. That was due to the fact that I had to attend a luncheon at the Authors club and he felt sure a little nourishment would do me no harm even if I didn't need it.

Well, Babe, this letter is dragging out and I'm afraid I'll bore you. But just the same I keep thinking how nice you are & how clever & so I'll tell you that. Meanwhile I'll be wishing to hear from you. If you lived around here I'd be walking around now to see how you were. So write me.

Affectionately,
TD

Thanks for the promise of the song records–I'll take them over

These letters are an example of Uncle Theodore's oedipal longing in full operation, the force that had drawn him to all the women that he had known intimately over a lifetime. The world reading this letter might accuse him of incestuous desires, but as a therapist I am in the position of knowing better. The very suggestion of intimacy with me would have frustrated and nullified his attraction. The dynamics of his attraction had a different emotional emphasis. Uncle Theo was borrowing strength to enhance his own security. To us it was security but to him it was unconsciously maternal, which is almost synonymous. He turned toward me at a very confusing period in his life, as one does to a physician, making in me an object for transference. I then became the supportive, maternal surrogate which was the image sought by him in a love relationship.

Of course I never explained the nature of these desires to my uncle. He had spent a life continually denying their existence in himself until they had become so built into the forces that relegated his mind that such explanations would be disregarded, scorned.

I had made plans to visit Uncle Theo in California in August and our correspondence substantiated this date. One day I received a letter from Helen (one of the few she wrote to me although she took many occasions to write to my mother, always thanking her profusely for her congratulations upon learning of the long-delayed marriage), asking me to please postpone my visit until September. In a busy practice such as that of Dr. Lawton scheduling a vacation is no minor task, and rescheduling is an effort one scarcely dares to request. However, when I told Dr. Lawton that Helen felt my visit would be more convenient for Uncle Theo in September, he understood how important this trip was to me and agreed to alter his plans to suit my convenience. As

Vera and Uncle Theo at 1015 North Kings Road

the date for our departure arrived, we decided to take my car since I would be having more use for a car than he. We drove across the country, arriving much later in the evening than I had expected. After dropping Dr. Lawton in Beverly Hills with his family, I managed to get lost in trying to find the Dreiser home on North King's Road. When I drove up it was quite dark and I could not see the beautiful street nor the houses of splendid architecture which graced the area, houses which were occupied at that time by some of the most prominent people in Hollywood. (Today King's Road is comprised almost totally of luxury high-rise apartment buildings. Opposite the site of Uncle Theo and Helen's house is a mansion which is now a seminary for orthodox Hebrew rabbis and scholars. The contrast between the yarmulke-wearing, bearded men of religious heritage, men from all parts of the world, with the swinging stylish young singles who occupy most of the apartments is incongruous, to say the least. And the physical alteration of the once wooded, beautifully cultivated, secluded neighborhood is almost unbelievable—even to longtime residents of Los Angeles. The houses had been the creations of some of the finest architects in the West—Frank Lloyd Wright, Neutra, and others.[1] Practically all that remains are memories of the past, summoned for the nostalgic who recall that "once upon a time" the best minds in the "art" colony lived there, walked the streets, and gathered in one another's homes for talks.) I drove into the driveway of the Spanish-style house that was the home of my Uncle Theodore and his "new" wife, Helen. Upon greeting me Uncle Theodore babbled forth as to how worried he had been, but Helen cut through with a cheerful but firm observation, "Oh, I knew Vera would get here okay!" Much to my surprise they had kept dinner for me and I was most grateful as I was starved, having driven for several hours without stopping in order to keep my arrival date. Uncle Theo was like a little child—a quality which endeared him especially to women. He was excited with his guest and puttered about to be certain of my comfort and urged Helen to hurry with my food. She came out of the kitchen with a delicious chicken dinner she had prepared and as she set a place for me at the table she explained they did not keep a live-in maid because the presence of one annoyed Uncle Theo—and besides, she and he ate out several nights a week.

It had been many years since I had seen Helen and I was somewhat surprised at the change in her appearance. She was now fifty-one years old, plump, and a little faded, but there was still evidence of her earlier good looks and she carried herself with the assurance of a woman who knows she has once been "a beauty." Her one remaining feature that time had not altered was her beautiful legs. These had remained the same. She still dressed in the flashy style of a Hollywood "star," wearing "at home" lounging pajamas trimmed in sequins, and her hair, which was still shoulder-length, was dyed in dark henna. Marriage seemed to have given her more poise, more self-assurance. I was to learn, in time, she supplemented this with studies in Near Eastern religions, yoga, and associations with men and women of sundry cults which were then flourishing in California. I looked about the beautiful home and saw the familiar objects that had always been associated with Uncle Theo—Uncle Paul's rosewood piano, now converted into a writing desk, his ever-faithful rocking chair where he sat and rocked and thought and wrote. When he sat rocking back and forth in front of the open fireplace he seemed so simple, so humble. Until he would begin to speak I found it difficult to believe that this quiet, childlike man was the giant artist who had written *Sister Carrie* and *An American Tragedy,* that this contemplative man of such apparent spiritual reckoning was also the explosive, controversial, antagonistic man whose enigmatic personality was unfathomable to all who had known and been associated with him. In a very short time it was easy to discern that Helen had, to a degree, won her long-fought battle. She treated him as a child and as an aging man—a genius, who was her special charge.

I was exhausted from my long trip and retired early. Helen had given me her room in the tower—one flight of stairs over the dining room. It was a large bedroom, decorated in white satin and lace. There was an adjoining dressing room and bath. The rest of the house sprawled in Spanish design on one floor. Uncle Theo had built a studio over the garage to which no one had access except himself—not even Helen was permitted there if he chose to be alone and work.

When I awoke after a good night's rest, I was amazed to discover that Uncle Theo kept a rigid schedule. He was immaculately dressed, had already consumed his breakfast, and was ready for the workday. His literary assistant had arrived in August before me. She had taken a cottage in Cadet Court in Hollywood Hills and it was here she and Uncle Theo were working on *The Bulwark.* It was then Uncle Theo asked me why I, too, hadn't come in August. He told me of the birthday party Helen had given him—his seventy-third, of which he did not care to be reminded—and the many friends who had celebrated the occasion with him—not his birthday, but the soon-to-be-birthing of *The Bulwark,* which had been so long in a gravid state. I said nothing, for not until then did I know that Uncle Theo had expressed no desire to have my visit postponed until September. It was not his wishes that were being catered to; it did not suit Helen for me to arrive in August. "It's a shame you weren't here," he commented, patting me affectionately, "I would have been so proud to have shown off my niece. But then I didn't know about the party to be certain you were here. As usual, Helen surprised me."

He arranged for me to visit the various studio heads, asking that they see me and give my musical compositions some consideration. When I came home the first day and told Uncle Theo the very special treatment I had received when they heard his name, he was genuinely surprised. I don't believe he ever had any real sense of his own importance among the movie executives. This was, of course, an example of his perpetual sense of inadequacy, his deeply rooted feeling of inferiority. He could not believe that anyone was really interested. He had to be reassured constantly, by word, by deed.

The evening after my day at the studios we went to the Brown Derby for dinner where we ran into Jimmy Durante. Uncle Theo was truly delighted to see him, and as they sat and chatted I could not help but think to myself, "What a funny combination, Jimmy Durante and Theodore Dreiser." But they were most compatible and enjoyed many laughs. The following night we were invited to a screening of *None But the Lonely Heart,* a Cary Grant film. To a person in my profession, even though I had always had one foot in the life of the theater, it was a rare experience. I had never seen so many stars gathered together. In New York one rarely sees a large gathering of stage celebrities. Sardi's or Toots Shore's, the meeting and eating places of Broadway celebrities, were about the only places where one might see the subject of one of the famous caricatures seated on a banquette beneath his or her image. But one seldom saw more than a half dozen at a given time. On this occasion there must have been a hundred. I remember sitting next to Hedy Lamar with Helen on my other side next to Uncle Theo who was engaged in conversation, before the picture commenced, with Clifford Odets. In addition to star-gazing like a child, I found myself, coming from the East, appalled at the informality of dress. I must confess to a moment of shock upon seeing the lordly Charles Laughton stroll down the aisle wearing neither a coat nor a tie and with his shirt-sleeves rolled up to his elbows! I was acutely aware that Hollywood and Broadway were miles apart. (At that time black tie and formal dress were not uncommon in evening attendance at the theater in New York—in fact, until the fifties such attire was more the rule than the exception. And no one would appear at a Broadway opening without wearing formal attire.) I learned in Hollywood such protocol had already gone with the wind.

Uncle Theo thought I should see Baja California, Mexico, and suggested that Helen take me to Ensenada where we could stay overnight and shop. While driving down with Helen I came to understand her partially. At the time she was concerned that *The Bulwark* be completed and that Theo finish *The Stoic*—the last Cowperwood novel,—and find some spiritual faith with which to sustain himself. She was apparently quite preoccupied with many religious movements in her search for something which would also intrigue Uncle Theo. She assured me and reassured me that she had been a "privileged woman to have had such a companion." And she confessed to "mothering" him, adding that it had been her experience "that all *great* people are like children." I knew that this LOVE, this undying, passionate, forevermore love Helen had for Uncle Theo must have originated in pure, unadulterated sexual appeal or attraction. I was also aware that people who are deprived of the closeness it brings, even if temporarily, become ill—sometimes emotionally, sometimes physically. I could see in Helen's possessiveness, her well-controlled but obvious jealousies, her frustrations over the years, her long abstinences from sexual love, definite signs of an inner sickness which could (and did) bring about collapse. In September of 1944 she was functioning—under duress but functioning—but when the final shock of Uncle Theo's death would strike, I knew she would be vulnerable and weak.

We were quite late in arriving home and Uncle Theo was up and about in his pajamas and robe, with his hair standing on end—from running his hands through it in nervous despair. He literally screamed, "Where were you? I was going to call the police in another few minutes. I was worried sick!" Without another word he stalked off to bed in a fit of anger. Helen shrugged her

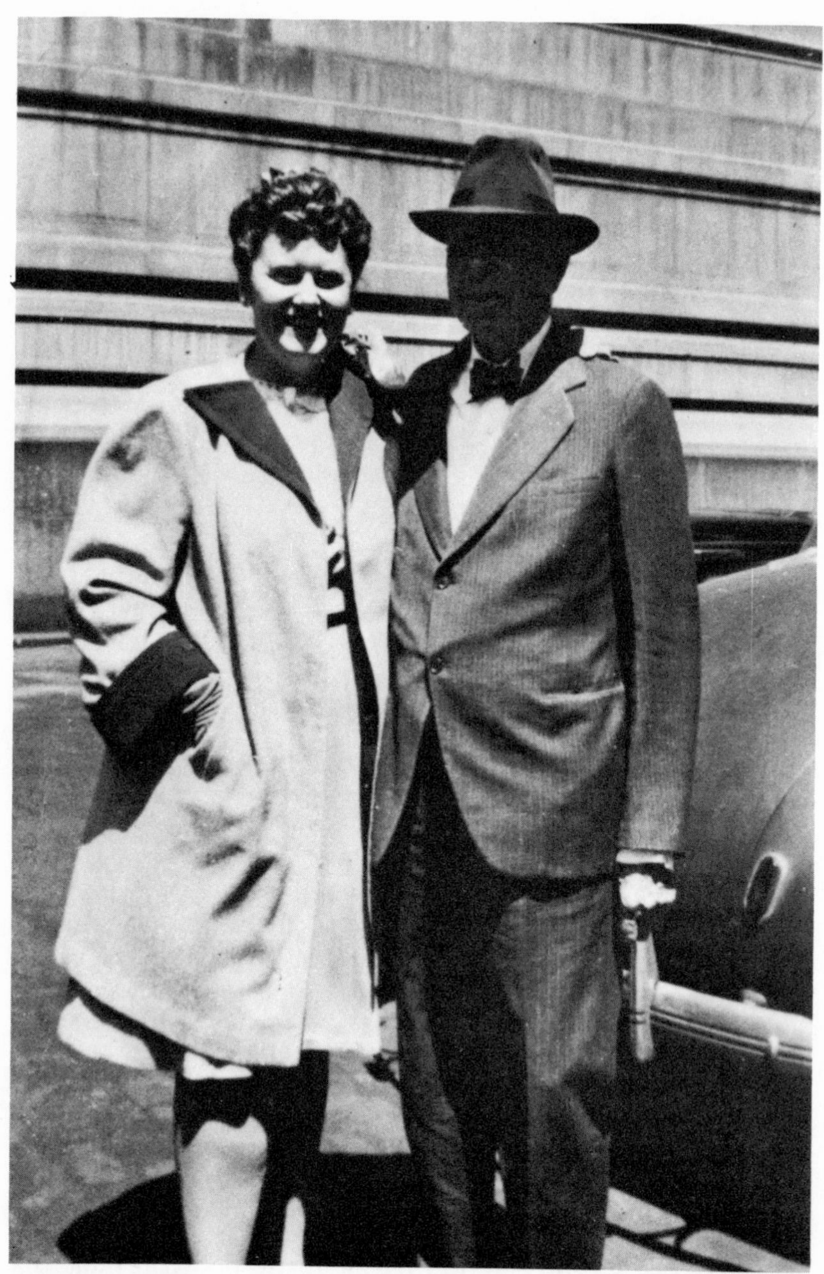

Vera and Uncle Theo at the Commodore Hotel,
New York City

shoulders and laughed. . . . . I said good night, and as I walked up the stairs, I thought of the emotional strain he had been subjected to. The next morning I tried to make light of the situation, warning Uncle Theo I was going to buy him a "worry-bird."

At this period he was deeply engrossed in his work and even though it took a great deal out of him physically he was a slavemaster to himself. He worked as if he knew the deadline for final publication was close at hand.

One of the few breaks he allowed himself was a jaunt to Palos Verdes. Helen was driving and she told me to get in the back seat which I did, and Uncle Theo got in beside me. As we began our journey, I felt sorry for Helen. It was as if she were not present. He held my hand all the way there and back and he talked to me while Helen chauffeured us in silence and, I am certain, martyred annoyance. I was uncomfortable. . . .

> I wanted to slip my arms around him and hold him tight. He seemed so all at sea. I don't know why I had such a need to let him know he was not alone . . . that I understood. I wanted to be close, to talk and talk because I sensed his need and knew that I could feel part of it. I knew that sharing my knowledge of people, emotions, causes, etc. would open some doors which needed to be opened. . . . But was it too late? Instead of doing this and expressing what I felt (as I would have done now, years later) I let fear take over. Fear of it not working out my way, of being misunderstood. I could not bear the thought of a romantic embrace or implied sex. It repelled me. His eyes were so like my father's that I over-reacted. In the end he might just have let it be the affectionate closeness for his niece. I didn't know, but I pulled away every time he reached for me to try to pull me close to him. Was it my problem? Had my mother's words really penetrated so deeply that I had never let go of them? I couldn't understand why they had done so only in this instance. She had warned me over and over again that as an attractive girl I had to look out for men! Still, I had no inhibitions sexually. As a matter of fact, I seemed to bend over backwards to outwit her and did so. So why was I panicked by this show of possibly innocent affection that I wanted, yet I feared?[2]

It was a few nights after this trip when Helen was in the

kitchen and Uncle Theo was sitting and reading a magazine. As I walked by he grabbed my hand and tried to pull me down to kiss his upturned face as he hugged me. I pulled away and froze. I was terrified that Helen might walk out of the kitchen and witness the scene, misunderstand, and create another type of scene. If Uncle Theo's gesture was as innocent as I think it was, he must have been cut to the quick. Today my action seems downright cruel on my part and I have never ceased to regret it.

Once when we were alone Uncle Theo told me a story which I thought was fiction. It was the story of a writer-architect and her lover who was an artist. Neither had very much money or worldly goods. They were squatters on a beach, nibbling stale crackers and sitting on wooden crates, sleeping on bare floors or the sandy shore. She became ill, suffering from malnutrition and the agonies of poverty. Her lover, who had been ill for some time, died. Later she met a man much older who fell in love with her, whisked her off to Mexico, and married her. He was very good to her and built her a house with a soundproof room, overlooking the ocean. In time her health improved, as did her writing. A lovely fantasy I thought, until one day Uncle Theo took me to the lady's house in Santa Monica. She was brilliant, charming, sensitive. Her husband took me aside and told me since he had known Uncle Theo he had never talked about anyone as much as he had talked about me upon his return from New York. I looked at him. He looked weary, ill. I wondered if he were following Dr. Lawton's advice.

I watched him carefully for a few days and became convinced that he was not doing any of the things Dr. Lawton had ordered. We were going out to visit a composer friend and were waiting for Helen to drive the car out of the garage. As she sauntered to the automobile I heard Uncle Theo say under his breath, "Strange girl!" His eyes were following her as if even then he did not understand her. For a moment I almost asked him if he had ever asked my father what he thought of Helen, but I didn't. Instead, I asked him if he were having physical check-ups with Dr. Thorpe as Dr. Lawton had suggested. I pointed out that with his thyroid condition, if he did not get proper medication he would continue to suffer the fatigue he seemed to be enduring, and that he was putting an abnormal strain on his heart. Helen had picked us up by then and immediately interrupted the conversation. "Doctors and medicine," she said, "nonsense!" She went on to say how yoga and her religious faiths had helped her, and if Uncle Theo would follow her suggestions he, too, would be renewed in physical strength. I felt a sudden chill come over me, and looking at Uncle Theo's tired face I had a dreadful fear for him. Fortunately, the evening was a happy social occasion and my mood altered. The next day everyone was more relaxed, and as Helen had some chores, Uncle Theo and I were alone. We drove to the beach and had our first real talk together since my arrival. He said that his reunion with Ed had given him cause for some deep thoughts that had seriously affected him. He had been thinking of their early life, off and on, ever since. He confessed he had let early scars distract him and that since meeting me he had begun to feel strong; with me he had renewed strength. I recognized this and other similar allusions he had made as more of a doctor-patient relationship than a sexual overture, although in all male-female relationships some of the latter exists.

Uncle Theo confessed to me he did not like—and had never liked—to be completely alone, but at the same time he could not stand to have someone hovering over him. He liked to know there was someone in the background. I knew that the threat of abandonment by his mother was still constantly gnawing at him, and this was the factor that had linked him to Helen. She was the one person he could depend upon to be present when he needed her. I knew that other persons reading his letters to me would never understand, nor would they understand his talks. The strange, intangible feeling he was getting was the beginning of a psychological transference. I've heard similar thoughts expressed over and over from patients; it is a part of a treatment process, a phase that, when handled properly, finally dissipates itself. I knew I had developed a manner of transmitting strength to people from observing Dr. Lawton. I had always admired his approach to his patients and the magic it seemed to perform. Dr. Lawton swore I had always possessed the same power. I don't know and I am not certain that I could have transferred it on to Uncle Theo.

His unhappiness filled the car. I knew he had never known peace, that he never would. I told him so. He asked me, "Do you think Dr. Lawton has ever known peace?" I asked what made him think of Dr. Lawton at this time and he said, "Because I know you two will be going back East together very soon, and will be working together as partners." I felt compelled to tell him that there had been only "electricity" between Dr. Lawton and me; never anything physical. He seemed surprised and asked how this was possible. I knew I could never explain to Uncle Theo so I settled with a plebian response: "Because he had several other women in his life that he made commitments to and by whom he has children."

I know my answer did not satisfy or even whet his curiosity but after we completed our talk and returned home his attitude toward me changed slightly. It was warm and more quiet, more controlled and less urgent. I tried to analyze it later, writing in my diary:

> He has been called fearless; plodding through a wilderness of lies; speaking about things others dared not speak of, yet I sensed he knew fear. He realized and said he was handicapped and thought he might have achieved so much more in his lifetime were he free! Free of what, one asks? I don't think he actually knows himself what got in his way, but he kept repeating that he felt more secure and stronger when he was with me. If this were anyone else it would be easier to accept. "When I am full of fear or struggling with myself to gain composure, I think of you and visualize you beside me, encouraging me and I feel stronger." Strangely enough this confession coming from Uncle Theo I had heard many times before *but* in this case it reacted on me as therapy, an ego builder, since it came from one whom I considered mentally superior to myself. I felt quite minute and humble in the face of this intangible quality. . . whatever it was . . . that made a great man like Theodore Dreiser feel more secure when he was with me. Yesterday, I would have passed it off as flattery but somehow I know what he was feeling and that he was being truthful. Dr. Lawton had said the same thing and he was my great teacher. If I told uncle Theo how much strength I also pulled from Alfred [my husband, Alfred Scott] he wouldn't believe me nor would he believe that I was what I was because of two great men in my life. But alas, my own limitations got in the way of greater spiritual fulfillment for both of us, for whenever he had reached out to touch me, I would pull away. I never did with anyone else. Was mother unconsciously getting in my way?

A few days before I was to leave, Uncle Theo said he wanted me to have a copy of *Moods.* I was delighted. He picked up his pen to autograph the book and said aloud, "To my favorite neice." Helen, who was standing by, said, "I wouldn't write that. If Gertrude saw it her feelings would be hurt." He thought for a moment and then wrote, "To my gifted neice, Vera, from her favorite uncle . . . I hope." This episode was quite humorous since he was now the only uncle I had, and Gertrude had long since become disenchanted with both of them. She had thoroughly disapproved of *Dawn* and had told me so. I thought, how many other ways has Helen influenced him erroneously?

We had one more brief period alone the following morning when Helen was busy shopping. Once again the subject of love came up, and I asked him if he had ever really liked any of the women with whom he had love affairs. He did not answer, so I told him to think about this because if one did not have a liking for a love object one did not have anything. I am certain he was aware of this fact, but he had never thought about it in just such a manner. He told me he was having difficulties with *The Bulwark.* I suspected that his problems were arising over his identifying his own father with the character in his trials and tribulations. He also was suffering from self-identification, which happened with all of his writing. To create the Quaker, Solon Barnes, he had to identify with his compassion, his tenderness. At the same time he was having a conflict with himself not to make his character "too religious."

When the time came for me to leave, I tried to control my emotions so the parting would not be a tearful one. It was a difficult situation, filled with frustrations. The weeks spent with Uncle Theo were almost a period of self-inflicted cruelty–to get so near, yet still be so far. I had to return to my world and leave Uncle Theo in his. As I drove away, the many years we had been separated, years in which we could have been so close, so valuable to one another, were spent. The thought of "what might have been" was too painful for reality. His work had to be finished. My work had to be done; it lay ahead.

When I left Hollywood, I was cognizant of the fact that I had left behind my uncle who was obviously not a very happy man, who was "a virtual prisoner in his own home," and not in the best state of health. As to the latter, it had become apparent that neither he nor his wife was going to follow the regimen prescribed by doctors of medicine, and they were not going to tolerate any outside interference in this matter–not from me or from well-meaning friends. For the years ahead, in regard to Uncle Theo's health, one had to place his life expectancy with the loving-living Dreiser family and hope for the best. His unhappiness with Hollywood was rooted in his frustration. He was dismayed at Hollywood's interpretation of his books (the magnificent George Stevens' version of *An American Tragedy* had not yet been filmed; nor had the memorable *Carrie* in which Sir Laurence Olivier enacted one of the great roles of his career as George Hurstwood), and he was almost in a state of disgust with that "damn movie version of Paul's life. . . .'

I later reconstructed a conversation I had had with him while riding in the car on the way home to New York. I wrote in my diary:

> What do you think of Helen, Baby? I really don't know she shies away from me, so I have just an impression. I don't think she helps stabilize and support you emotionally.
> She is too unrealistic in her thinking, too impressed by what I call junk. Swarmis and stuff like that.
> I think you are just as bad for her! But I know you need her and depend on her. You couldn't be alone. After all, she's always been there, always came back, hasn't she?
> However sick the relationship was (and to me it was a sick one) her need-your need, you know. For this you owe her something. "She got in my way a lot though." True but you still had a need for someone didn't you, and she accepted what you gave her and was there. "Helen has a warm, affectionate side to her that is very likable." I know that. "There are times when I want her not to come back. I get tired of it." Do you like the companionship of men? "Yes, they are more stimulating mentally. I haven't met many women with your looks who were also brilliant. So outside of making love, I prefer male companionship."

I had seen clearly the need Helen and Uncle Theo had for one another. Their mutual dependency, whether it was a "sick relationship" or not, existed and had existed for much too long a period of time for either to withdraw and walk alone. It would and did endure to the end despite constant bickerings and disagreements such as occurred when Uncle Theo wished his present literary assistant (he had had many) to continue to work

Vera Dreiser in the 1940s

with him on *The Stoic* and Helen interfered. Her argument was that Uncle Theo was now too ill, too feeble to leave his home for his writing. It was better that it be accomplished at home, where she could be in personal attendance. So *The Stoic* was completed with Uncle Theo sitting in his rocking chair, while Helen took dictation. To Helen this was the situation she had always desired, and in her own words, "Never have we been more close, mentally, spiritually and physically than we were this last year of his life."

In July of 1945, five months before his death, I was somewhat shocked to learn that Uncle Theo had finally asked to join the American wing of the Communist party. It was hard for me to believe in view of his words to me. The full explanation will always be a mystery, but I feel he was pressured. I feel that he was also motivated by his feelings of intellectual honesty and an effort on his part to take what he considered a stand on behalf of the "underdog." His joining was a surprise to practically everyone who had ever been identified with him. After publication of *The Bulwark,* Mencken predicted Uncle Theo would return to the fold of the Roman Catholic Church as Heywood Broun had done on his deathbed. But there was still no place in organized religion for Uncle Theo, so to some of his acquaintances his membership in the now dying Communist party seeded to be a form of religious conversion interwoven with his individual form of mysticism.

Our correspondence shortened, as did his correspondence with most of his friends. He was too old, too tired, and too engrossed in completing his last book to take the time for any other form of writing. The usual Christmas greeting the year of my visit was a formal card addressed by Helen and signed "Mr. and Mrs. Theodore Dreiser" by an engraver. However, I also received a personal card from Uncle Theo, obviously mailed without Helen's knowledge.

In September of 1945, Aunt Sylvia died. The original Dreiser clan had diminished to my Uncle Theo and my father, Ed. On December 28 at 6:55 P.M., Uncle Theo faced the last of his "many kinds of death are necessary. . . ." From this there was no return. He had suffered a kidney attack two days earlier, but the real cause of death was a heart attack–the organ had simply been used beyond its physical capacity, and the strain induced by medical neglect had produced the death.

In the six weeks following the funeral when I stayed with Helen I learned that Alan Hunter, the Congregationalist minister,

Tedi (Sheri) Dreiser Langdon

had paid Theo a visit on the afternoon of his death. For no apparent reason, Dr. Hunter, who was not a usual visitor at the Dreiser household, had a compulsion to call—almost as if he heard a voice ordering him to make this unexpected visit. Esther McCoy (Tobey) likewise paid a visit. When she left to drive to her home in Santa Monica the bright warm sun of the day clouded and an almost invisible fog dropped like a curtain over the Pacific Coast. She remembered Uncle Theo's description of death being like an enveloping fog—"a wooly fog that blocks one's course and quenches all." She told me later that at that moment she sensed that her friend's death was imminent.

The six weeks spent with Helen trying to give her moral support and assist her in the many complexities that followed Uncle Theo's death, in the estate planning, the coping with his publishers, made me conscious of how much she had leaned upon his strength. In his final absence I saw Helen's own deterioration take on visible physical manifestations. In her helplessness and confusion she too became suspicious, at times paranoid. To sustain her waning spirits she leaned heavily upon alcohol both as a stimulus and as a sedative. At times she suffered hallucinations[3] and I felt guilty about leaving her, but I had no choice. She begged me to return and live with her, bringing Alfred and baby Sheri. But by the time I reached New York there was a letter awaiting me in which she wrote she had decided that she needed to be alone to do her life's work—to write her memoirs of her life with Uncle Theo. She never knew that I took the suggestion with a grain of salt, as at that time we were too much involved in the New York scene, both professionally and socially.

In 1947, my mother, father, husband, child, and myself paid a visit to California to see her. She was busy handling the estate and she had aged considerably. Shortly after our return my husband, Alfred, died of cardiac insufficiency after a bout with pneumonia, during the winter of 1948. In 1951 Helen suffered a cerebral hemorrhage and was from that day until her death on September 22, 1955, an invalid. She was buried beside Uncle Theo at Forest Lawn.

The same year, my mother, Mai, died, leaving only my father, Ed, of the characters in the Theodore Dreiser saga. He died in 1958, the last member of the original family. On January 31, 1958, The New York *Herald Tribune* carried a notice and picture entitled "E. M. Dreiser dies; actor, last of a Famous Family." He and my mother are buried side by side in the family plot in Calvary Cemetery in the same plot from which Aunt Mame removed Uncle Paul's body many years before.

My Uncle Theo had probed the stormy lives of the Dreisers—the reason they were born, lived and died, why they knew too late what was right and did what was wrong, why they yearned for light and groped in the darkness, why they passionately admired good and enjoyed evil. His quest, put into writing, made the Dreiser family famous. His summing up was probably best expressed in *The Bulwark* in Solon Barnes' words: ". . . faith in divine love, a faith which is constant in nature itself, everywhere the same, in sunshine and in darkness. . . . It was an intimate relation to the very heart of being."

12

The Misunderstood Dreiser

"No song sparkles in my glass, something has been taken from me."

Since the publication of *Sister Carrie* in 1900, the character and personality of Theodore Dreiser have been subjected to persistent attacks. Many of the disparagers have never studied his books nor did they have the advantage of knowing him personally; more often than not their charges have grown out of their own limitations. Dreiser has been maligned as no other prominent American in the twentieth century has been. I think it is time to take a careful look at the dedication and integrity he brought to his career, and to seek the motivations that gave meaning to his actions. I cannot bring my story to a conclusion without an attempt to examine and clarify Dreiser's personal record in view of the many accusations, distortions, and the facts that have been overlooked. Dreiser's critics are concerned, for the most part, with such questions as: 1) Was Dreiser "inactive" between the writing of *An American Tragedy* (1925) and *The Stoic* (1945)? 2) Was Theodore Dreiser a Communist–in the real sense of the allegation? 3) Is it true that Theodore Dreiser, both as a man and an artist, was totally humorless? 4) Is *The Bulwark* a dying old man's return to organized religion, the work of a frightened, former communicant of the Roman Catholic Church, who was seeking support from some acceptable form of organized religion which coincided with his political views, and who subsequently sought a compromise in the faith of the Quaker religion?

In *Dawn* Uncle Theo wrote, "No one ever wanted me enough." From this pitiful thought which developed in the mind of a child grew a lifelong pattern of overcompensation of which Uncle Theo was never aware.

During the period between the writing of *An American Tragedy* in the twenties and *The Bulward* in the forties, it was erroneously believed that Dreiser had gone into retirement. While it is true that his writing became more diversified after he gained fame with *An American Tragedy,* a cursory look at his career after 1925 indicates that he continued to be a prodigious writer. In 1927 he published *Chains,* a volume of short stories, followed by a volume of poetry, *Moods* (1928). Following his trip to Russia in 1927 he published *Dreiser Looks at Russia* (1928). In 1929 came *A Gallery of Women,* a collection of fictionalized portraits of women he had known. His autobiography, *Dawn,* was published in 1931, along with his first politically orinented volume, *Tragic America.* In 1939 he wrote a long preface for *The Living Thoughts of Thoreau,* and in 1941 he published his second volume of political thought, *America Is Worth Saving.* Returning to creative writing in the last year of his life, he completed *The Bulwark* and *The Stoic,* both of which were posthumously. His writing record during this period is certainly ample proof that he had not retired to a much earned mental and physical retreat.

In reality, this period was probably the most active and exhausting stage of his entire career. He was lecturing for the first time (after having overcome a natural timidity that had made his initial appearance at the lecturer's podium a personal triumph), writing broadsides on numerous social, political, and economic issues, and becoming more involved in matters of science. In addition, he initiated a massive piece of philosophic writing which he tentatively titled *The Formulae Called Man.* This work was to have been the embodiment and crystallization of his lifetime thinking about Death, Religion. Life, and Reality. He envisioned it as his *magnum opus* and wrote many essays to be included in the work, but he died before the project had taken final form. Throughout the thirties, as he worked for social causes and formulated material for *The Formulae Called Man,* his publishers and close friends pressured him for news about his next novel; his answer was always, "How can I work on a novel when the world is in such a condition?" He felt very deeply the tragic course of world events during this period, and his sense of personal commitment and integrity would not permit him to retire to a life of luxury and ease.

In April and May of 1930, he traveled through the West delivering speeches that called for reform in birth control,[1] religion, penal codes, news reporting, and employment laws.

In 1931 Dreiser accepted the chairmanship of the National Committee for the Defense of Political Prisoners; in October the International Labor Defense asked him to exercise this chairmanship by establishing a committee to investigate labor injustices in the coal district of Harlan County, Kentucky. For more than six months, the Harlan and Bell county areas had been terrorized by a bloody struggle between mine operators and officials of the United Mine Workers and its members. Both sides had lost men in open bloodshed, newspaper reporters had been openly attacked, and communist efforts to set up soup kitchens had resulted in explosions of dynamite. Dreiser, along with a committee that included novelist John Dos Passos, conducted hearings under the surveillance of the National Guard at the Lewallen Hotel in Harlan. Every effort was made to publicize the horrible conditions of mining families who were reduced to living on meager food supplies, often nothing more than pinto beans and fat pork gravy. Mine officials, searching for a way to retaliate, found it on November 9 in a trumped-up charge of adultery against Dreiser and Marie Pergain, an attractive blonde whom he had seemingly brought from New York.

Known as "the toothpick episode," because mine operators had leaned toothpicks against Dreiser's hotel door after Miss Pergain entered late one evening and found them undisturbed the next morning–proof positive of adultery–the incident made headlines throughout the country, many of them comic and derisive. "I am with you to the last toothpick," wired William Lengel, Dreiser's secretary. Bruce Crawford, originally a member of Dreiser's investigating committee, found less humor in the incident. "It is a terrible commentary on newspapers and public that a sex scandal can obscure such inhumane and tragic conditions that exist in Harlan," he lamented. Crawford was only partially correct for–humorous as it was with the legendary boudoir hero Dreiser announcing to the press that adultery was impossible since he was "completely and finally impotent"–the incident brought nationwide attention to Dreiser and the committee's fight for the miners. The publicity he gained in Harlan also established him as a nationally known champion of social causes, a fame that he would use to the benefit of many civil rights causes throughout the thirties.

A few years ago when I began to organize material for this volume, I wrote to John Dos Passos and asked about Dreiser's role in the Harlan investigations. Answering that from boyhood he had always admired my uncle "as an opener-up of forbidden trails," Dos Passos commented, "What I mostly remember is his unperturbable gall. He conducted the hearings like a United States Senator."

Some Americans became so accustomed to Dreiser's raging political stance in the thirties that they found it difficult to equate the gentle Dreiser of the earlier novels and short stories with the warrior they read about in the daily news accounts. "How did a swashbuckler like you who goes through the world making bellicose noises–how did you ever come to write that lovely story 'A Doer of the Word'?" wrote T. S. Martin in September, 1934. Dreiser reminded Martin that in its own quiet way "A Doer of the Word" was "a bellicose noise disguised in a soft word." Dreiser continued, "I object to stupidities which can be really easily swept away and which are tolerated by the smug, calm-minded, precedent-minded, traditional and authority-minded superior so-called classes. . . . Under those circumstances if I make bellicose noises I feel fairly well justified."

An inveterate letter writer, he attacked many social problems by writing directly to those individuals most intimately involved. When the Scottsboro case made national headlines, Dreiser began to organize his N.C.D.P.P. committee to insure a fair trial for the nine Negro youths who were accused of raping two white girls. Meanwhile, he wrote a letter seeking the assistance of The Association of Southern Women for the Prevention of Lynching. In his request Dreiser stated, ". . . the Negro as well as the white person should, before the law, be treated with understanding and liberality, in other words, humanely. . . . Because Negroes are not, at present, a dominating race, some unthinking members of the white race manifest petty prejudice toward them . . . not only laws unduly severe concerning the human relations of Negroes have been made, but these laws in the eyes of the unified Southern population have become so near perfection itself that the people almost justify mob rule to enforce them." He added that "The whole southern attitude toward the Negro has become a national ill."

In July, 1938, he attended an international peace conference in Paris as a delegate of the League of American Writers. Speaking to the delegates, he warned, "More fair play must come into life. We are co-heirs of all that is. We should find ways and means of sharing peacefully what has been given us by nature." When the conference concluded, he traveled to Spain to see at close range the revolution in which he ideologically supported the Loyalists in their battle against Franco. He returned home deeply disturbed by the human suffering he had observed in Spain. When he wrote to Franklin Roosevelt asking to confer with the president about a plan to aid Spain, a nonpartisan plan based on "grounds of plain humanity," he was granted a fifteen-minute appointment which was later changed to a luncheon meeting aboard the presidential yacht *Potomac.* President Roosevelt, unyielding in his neutral position on the Spanish Civil War, suggested that Dreiser organize a citizen's committee to raise funds for the victims of the Spanish war. It was during the development of this committee that Dreiser met Rufus M. Jones, the well-known Quaker who was to have a profound influence on Dreiser's completion of *The Bulwark.*

Tragic America and *America Is Worth Saving* are the two books Dreiser wrote during this period of social and political action when he was at the peak of his writing powers.

America Is Worth Saving (1940) is a thoughtful examination of American politics and life. Much of the book is a criticism of American tolerance of English imperialism, as well as English aristocracy. In the "strutting vanity" of the English imperialists, Dreiser saw the ideological roots of dictatorships that permit the rise of a demagogue like Hitler. In a radio speech given during World War II, he repeated his theory:

> An honest review of my personal thoughts concerning the present world war and world politics can only bring me into conflict with the varying opinions of thousands of people, no one of which I fancy agrees exactly with my own. For one thing, as much as I despise Hitler and all of his works and hope to see him and his Axis allies now completely defeated, yet I have never felt that a Hitler or any such type of creature could have appeared anywhere in Europe save for the strutting vanity of the ruling class in England and its determination to

> rule not only the seas, but Europe, and in addition to that if possible the entire world. ("Rule Britannia.")

In tone and subject, *America Is Worth Saving* appears strikingly contemporary; today, Operation Breadbasket is seeking to eradicate the injustice that Dreiser identified in 1941 when he wrote, "In California, nature's mountain ranges are rapidly being rivaled by the man-made mountains of 'surplus' oranges and potatoes which we carefully spray with poison so that the hungry may not eat." Overall, some measure of the contemporaneity of this volume is indicated by the numerous ideas it has in common with a 1972 movie entitled *The Ruling Class.*

I have studied every page of this book *(America Is Worth Saving)* and find it to be direct, honest, and accurate, from the opening "Consider uranium 235" to the closing "We must make the Constitution work." In pointing out the defects of the labor situation, Dreiser states,

> Today, on the contrary, blood flows fresh and bright from the battles for free expression of the agricultural workers, laundry workers, ten-cent store clerks, waitresses, Southern mill workers, who take the place of the black slaves. In sum it is a new set of obscure people, unimportant people, the lowly who do not count, who have risen and who, more and more of them, are rising up to ask for their liberties under the Bill of Rights.

Is he not speaking of the genesis of a civil rights and labor movement which every American recognizes—from the strikes of the California grape pickers to those of the New York garbage collectors?

(It is inevitable that any individual who is outspoken and fearless in defending his beliefs will gain more enemies than friends, and is usually misquoted or misinterpreted either by design or honest mistake.)

Elsewhere he exhorts, "Democracy is at stake here because you cannot by any known means make the masses of the people indefinitely submit to want in the midst of plenty, and if you don't let them have their share of the wealth by democratic means they will eventually take it by violent means." How many civil rights marches and violent riots might have been avoided in the sixties if this problem had been faced in 1941? A writer who in January, 1941, decried, "America's cool raising billions for destruction" in "Europe's destruction orgies" while denying "American people who want a decent living" shares a common vision with more contemporary civil rights leaders who insist that it was morally wrong to spent $50,000 to kill a Viet Cong soldier.

In his plea for a better life for all Americans, Dreiser proposed a social structure based on abundance—"a society in which nobody went without the basic needs. . . ." To those who doubted that such a society could be effected, he made a statement that from our present vantage point in history appears prophetic:

> Hell, does that make it any less worth trying? But somehow, worth trying or not, your question is directed into the empty air. Because for one thing it is going to happen in the end and you can't stop it happening, for nature says so. And if you can realize that, you can see it's better to do something about it now—this minute—so that it may not be ushered in with a bath of blood that will make the 1914-1918 war look like a Girl Guide's Field Day.

That bath of blood to which he refers started with a blood-soaked limousine in Dallas and has cost the lives of three other American leaders and uncounted American citizens. In retrospect, the course of modern civil rights history gives added impetus to Dreiser's basic theme which he reiterates in closing:

> We must make the Constitution work—all of the Constitution—or we will never have a democracy. We must do it in a fully conscious and methodical and speedy way, because if we don't it will come to fighting in our streets between brother and brother. *(America Is Worth Saving.)*

Can such a statement now be challenged with Watts, Kent State, and many similar incidents of the sixties part of our history? Although involvement in social causes became Dreiser's primary concern in the thirties, it was not the first time he figured prominently in social welfare efforts. This total involvement was, in fact, directly related to the 1907-1910 period, when, as editor of *The Delineator*, he participated in a number of humane causes.

"No one ever wanted me enough"–Uncle Theo and Nick

One of the legends arising from Dreiser's involvement in liberal causes in the thirties was that he was a member of the Communist party during the "Red Decade," as this period has been called. A part of the misconception may be attributed to the fact that many prominent American writers were avowed Communists or Communist sympathizers—hihgly respected writers such as John Dos Passos, Upton Sinclair, Howard Fast, John Steinbeck, Archibald MacLeish, Edmund Wilson, and Clifford Odets. All of these men shared a common faith in the communist ideal of a brotherhood of man; unfortunately, each was destined to experience the destruction of the Utopian dream as the democratic ideal became a totalitarian nightmare. By the end of the thirties, all had returned to the "bourgeois liberties" which they had ostensibly sacrificed to the common cause of communism.

Theodore Dreiser has often been placed among this group of intellectuals whose conversion to Moscow politics reached hysterical dimensions in the 1930-1939 period. All the facts of Dreiser's relationship to the communist cause repudiate such an interpretation. As might be expected, his associations with this movement, like his association with all movements, were tenuous and highly individualistic. He never subscribed to party doctrines—as did many of the authors who wrote the proletarian literature which the party dictated—nor did he ever support the party for doctrinaire reasons. He remained an individualist throughout his life; as such, he would never have submitted to party discipline. No one acquainted with Dreiser's investigative mind and intransigent manner could imagine his ever being intimidated by the communist hierarchy of America or Russia.

In determining the roots of Dreiser's socialistic affinity, one must first of all realize that political faith, like its religious counterpart, is seldom the result of reasoning or rational persuasion. All faiths have their origins in the believer's past, more often than not in the individual's social environment—especially the all-important childhood environment which molds lifetime attitudes. Dreiser's childhood environment—characterized by poverty, social rejection, and perpetual change—created in him an ambivalent attitude toward money and the economic base of life, a conflict which remained an intergal part of his personality even after he attained financial security with the publication of *An American Tragedy* in 1925. Because of his improverished childhood, he began early in life to overrate the personal satisfactions and happiness that attend the possession of wealth. As a young man he developed an insatiable craving for the material comforts of life—stylish clothes, luxurious surroundings, and sensual pleasures. This aspect of his personality manifests itself most vividly in his novels as the recurrent image of the outsider—the "waif amid forces" who is lured by the splendor of wealth. The indigent young man who stood outside the Terre Haute House in the 1870s—spellbound by the meretricious display of wealth—becomes fictionalized in the pitiable character of Clyde Griffiths who longs to share the bacchanalian delights in the Aladdin-like realm of the Green-Davidson Hotel, that "twelve-story affair" that was "the quintessence of luxury and ease."

But at the same time that young Dreiser was drawn to the gospel of wealth, the seeds of what would later become a decidedly anticapitalistic philosophy were implanted in him, along with a growing compassion for the poor. This compassionate nature evolves as his most consistent attitude toward the human condition; it appears as a strong force in his earliest pieces of fiction, "Nigger Jeff," now a classic and one of his first short stories, which perhaps establishes a point of origin for this trait in his writing. It is an impassioned condemnation of the maltreatment of the black man in white-dominated America—written, of course, at a time when it was unpopular to speak out in behalf of the black American. The story describes a lynching as it was experienced by a fledgling newspaper reporter, undoubtedly Dreiser himself. The vivid account of the lynching is humanized by the depiction of the "cruel sorrow" of the guiltless mother who mourns the "still black form" which once was the source of maternal joy. For the young reporter, the experience constitutes an initiation into the injustices of American racial life; for the first time he knew ". . . that it was not always exact justice that was meted out to all."

"There is something . . . about poverty and squalor that is as depressing and destructive as a gas or a chemic ferment." Dreiser wrote in *The Color of a Great City,* "Poverty has color and odor and radiation. . . . It speaks. It mourns, and these radiations are destructive." But poverty alone does not destroy the individual who suffers the pangs of impoverishment; his final destruction results from a delusion perpetuated by society that wealth is the salvation for the poor–the delusion that would later form the American tragedy of Clyde Griffiths. Among the teeming, foreign-born population of New York City's East Side and the Bowery, Dreiser discovered that a desire for money rules all levels of American life; it especially dominated the poor. "Nearly the only ideal that is set before these strugglers still toiling in the area is the one of getting money," he wrote. This "doctrine of wealth," he observed, was the "shabbiest and most degrading doctrine that can be impressed upon anyone."

In September, 1927, Dreiser received an official invitation from the U.S.S.R. to visit Russia and observe firsthand the Soviet experiment. Although he remained skeptical about the possibility of translating the Utopian dream into a social reality, he accepted the invitation. However, he requested a firm agreement with the Soviet leaders that he could write freely and without censorship about what he saw and felt. He was given a solemn promise to this effect and on returning wrote *Dreiser Looks At Russia.*

Throughout his trip he remained unconvinced that the communist ideal could be realized, even though he admired the efforts being made.

To his guide, he expressed concern that the communist experiment would not better conditions. Would the doctrine of "plenty for everyone" not eventually lower the standard of living for everyone? What would be the effect of such a lenient philosophy on art and culture? On a visit to the Black Sea ports, he was nauseated by the contrast between the elegant mansions and places of pre-Bolshevik times and the slovenly masses of workers who now used them as rest homes. Everywhere he observed the harshness of life for peasant families living in deplorable conditions at subzero temperatures.

When he left Russia on January 13, 1928, he openly criticized the Russian experiment, especially the "national indifference to sanitation." Finding much to praise in what "the superior group of idealists" had done for Russia thus far, he nevertheless was unwilling to align his own thinking wholeheartedly with the cause. *"I am an individualist and shall die one,"* he wrote, "In all this communistic welter, I have seen nothing that dissuades me in the least from my earliest perceptions of the necessities of man."

On his way home, Dreiser was interviewed by a London journalist who praised his loyalty to America. "Dreiser is a complete American," wrote Thomas Burke in *T. P.'s Weekly* on

June 9, 1928. "Unlike the shallow intellectuals of his country, he does not sneer at America or turn his back on it and seek sham culture in the cafés of Paris. He is proud of being an American and he is as American as Mark Twain."

One of the American principles that Dreiser was not ready to relinquish was the belief in free enterprise. For all his condemnation of the capitalistic system—the aggregation of great fortunes and the inevitable usurpation of power—he had seen too many cultural and social advancements brought about by the so-called robber barons of American industry to accept a totally negative representation of their role in history. He had already established in his Cowperwood trilogy, begun two decades earlier, that Machiavellian financiers like Charles Yerkes (Frank Cowperwood) have many admirable and redeeming qualities, the most admirable being that each had retained his individuality. But how could the ideal brotherhood of man be achieved if individuality were permitted? Unable to reconcile the matter, Dreiser wrote his statement of belief for a prominent magazine soon after arriving home from his Russian visit.

> I can make no comment on my work or my life that holds either interest or import for me. "Nor can I imagine any explanation or interpretation of any life, my own included, that would be either true—or important, if true. . . . In short I catch no meaning from all I have seen, and pass quite as I came, confused and dismayed.

From the beginning of his involvement in social and political causes, Dreiser accepted as empirical fact the theory of the eighteenth-century economist Adam Smith who stated, "Civil government is maintained for the defense of the rich against the poor. . . . For one very rich man there must be at least five hundred poor." In his personal life and in his profession as a journalist and writer, Dreiser had observed a greedy struggling world that had much need for change; he respected the Soviet experiment because he felt an attempt was being made in Russia to effect this change. When he was faced with the possibility of defending the communist efforts, he did so because he believed that at the core of the communist belief was a genuine desire to create an equitable world wherein men might lead fruitful, harmonious lives.

The Dreiser of 1945 was a tired warrior for human rights; he had fought the battle vigorously and faithfully for many years. His decision to ask for official party recognition in July, 1945, was not a failure of mind, nor was it a stamp of approval of party doctrine. His request to the party was a final tribute to the political ideal which he had shared with the communist movement in its earliest history when he had observed its efforts firsthand. It must be noted that exactly 30 years ago in 1945, American and Russian troops had a friendly handshake at the Elbe River to celebrate the triumphant Soviet-American alliance. It was also exactly seven months before Dreiser died. It is certain that if he had been totally welcomed into the party and had lived longer than the five months after his formal gesture for party recognition, he would have been ousted on the grounds of insubordination.

Shortly after he exchanged letters with Party President Foster, he was scheduled to speak before a California political group. An official from the party called to suggest that Dreiser cancel the engagement since the group was comprised of undesirables. When he persisted in keeping his speaking engagement, the official politely explained that the party could not permit him to speak there. Immediately enraged, Dreiser bellowed, *"I'll speak wherever and to whomever I choose . . . Go to Hell!"* "Belief in the greatness and dignity of man has been the guiding principle of my life and work."

Most of Dreiser's adult years were spent in brooding over and attempting to alleviate the plight of society's outcasts; obviously such situations did not engender a humorous approach. Similarly, when he was depressed because of the rejection of his work in America, he could not be expected to laugh. Nevertheless, it is unfair to accept this serious aspect of his personality without acknowledging that, in spite of personal struggles, Dreiser possessed a unique sense of humor—generally known only to his close acquaintances. It is possible that he cultivated his somber image in the public press in order to give impetus to the seriousness of his purpose. I also think a part of his solemn public image resulted from a natural reticence and repression which kept his sense of humor from surfacing in social situations. I am not sure of the cause, but I do know that he had a sense of humor.

One of the ways in which his humor was manifested to his

friends was in his letters; his communications, especially to H. L. Mencken, were often a barrage of puns and witticisims. Throughout his life, he showed his appreciation for the comic by clipping humorous articles from newspapers and magazines, many of which he would send to his friends. He evidently initiated this custom early in his career, for among his letters to Sara Osborne White appears the following short article to which he had added, "Read the attached clipping. Isn't this dog funny?"

Likewise, in another letter, he included a cartoon which he had considered amusing. Of it, he commented, "Say Jug! Isn't this funny?" It was a piece entitled "These Skeeters No Spaniards," in which a report of a plague of mastodon mosquitos descending on Hoboken, N.J., was presented, and it was one of the funniest articles I have ever read. Included was a life-size picture of the mosquito measuring one inch and a quarter, and it was reported that it could easily pass for a humming bird!"

Dr. Max Rosenthal, his New York doctor who had known the Dreisers when they lived in Terre Haute, remembered Dreiser's humorous way of showing his appreciation. For "old times sake," as Dr. Rosenthal termed it, the doctor did not charge Uncle Theo for his medical examinations or routine visits. Never missing an opportunity to inject a comic note in his close friendships, Uncle Theo would wait in the outer office until Dr. Rosenthal had advanced to another patient; then he would give the secretary a ten-cent check on which he had written, "This is on account, Max, since I haven't received a bill from you in quite a while."

The aspect of his humor that I appreciated most was his ability to laugh at himself, especially his reputation. He was always aware of the disparity between the way his friends knew him and the way in which he was depicted in the public press. This recognition of this dual image is apparent in his contribution to a 1935 volume entitled *So Red The Rose,* a collection of comic cocktail recipes submitted by well-known individuals. The ingredients for Uncle Theo's *American Tragedy Cocktail*[2] labeled "This is definitely the end," were preposterous:

1 t.	nitroglycerine
1 T.	heavy ground gunpowder
2 jiggers	ethyl gasoline
1	lighted match

In the directions for mixing the cocktail, he cleverly undercuts his reputation as an irascible grouch:

> Please accompany the above by horrific series of eccentricities, aversions and drinking habits, all based upon my notorious and incurable alcoholism.
>
> In case I deny, any American Publisher or Movie Picture Corporation will verify.
>
> Truthfully,
>
> Theodore Dreiser

At times, especially when he was in a relaxed mood, Uncle Theo was capable of producing clever parodies such as the one he sent to his journalist friend Claude Bowers. On a rainy April evening in 1926, Bowers called at Dreiser's apartment for dinner and an evening of conversation. As he departed late in the evening, after the rain had stopped, Bowers left his new umbrella in Uncle Theo's closet. A few days later, the journalist received the following clever notification:[3]

> Proof of Special Divine Intervention in Behalf of the Righteous
>
> I said to the Lord–Lord–I need an umbrella very badly. I can't afford to buy one & my old one blew up in the last wind.
>
> And the Lord said, my well beloved Son, I see your need & will satisfy it. There's an unworthy Editor & author named Bowers who has one and he's coming to see you Sat., April 3rd. So just as he's departing I'll cause a deep sleep to fall upon him & the umbrella is yours.
>
> And as the Lord said, so He did. And I am now in full possession of a very decent umbrella. Praise be the Lord.

As a postscript, he added:

Dear Bowers,

If you think you have any drag with the Lord now is the time to exercise it.

Dreiser

Dylan Thomas once wrote, "No one can deny that the most attractive figures in literature are always those around whom a world of lies and legend have been woven, those half mythical artists whose real character becomes forever cloaked under "a veil of the bizarre." While it is true that the "world of lies and legend" serve to heighten public interest in any artist, nevertheless, the legend must not be premitted to assume the mask of truth in the accounting of history. In some small measure, I hope that these personal memories and comments about my Uncle Theodore may have helped to reveal his true character, for certainly he was too honest and genuine as a person to have ever been flattered by "a veil of the bizarre" that too often continues to cloak his personal history.

One of the oldest and most enduring of the accusations hurled at Theodore Dreiser was that he did not believe in God.

In essence the charge is a misjudgment stemming from his pronounced rejection of religionists. He certainly was conditioned against this as a child by his father's attitude of strict adherence and his mother's more or less indifference to it. Throughout his entire writing career he maintained that life was not organized according to the compact social and moral theories expounded in the organized religions of the day. He looked closely at the shifting patterns of life in the urban growth centers of industrial America, and he was able to share the prevailing faith that "God's" in his heaven; all's right with the world." But this lack of dogmatic acceptance does not mean that he did not believe in God. His disagreement was not with God, nor religion, but with the narrow conceptions of God which were propagated by organized religions.

The distinguished American psychologist and philosopher William James once stated that religion is the faith which men have in the existence of an unseen order that exists beyond this world but which helps to explain actions that take place here. Such was the manner in which Dreiser viewed religion; his greatest concern as a student of science and philosophy was to know the ultimate forces that control our lives. Such an inquiry cannot be confused with an abandonment of hope in God; in reality, it is an attempt to explain the omnipotent force which we call God in such a manner that our faith may be deepened. Dreiser's intellectual determination and his insatiable desire to know the facts of existence were never to become lost in the facile rejection of God.

When I had asked Uncle Theo about his belief in God he had answered that he had scientific proof and invited me into his "laboratory," his novel of spiritual affirmation, *The Bulwark.* This novel, which was completed in 1945 had its origin in 1912 when Uncle Theo met Anne Tatum, a young woman of Quaker stock. The story took shape immediately in his imagination, but it required many years of broadening experiences and spiritual growth before he had resolved the theme of acceptance which dominates the novel. The religious affiliation of Solon Barnes was Quaker, but it might have been any other religion for, in reality, Solon Barnes is Grandfather Dreiser whose religious intolerance had caused the disintegration of the family circle. Like Solon Barnes, the elder Dreiser had become too indoctrinated and restricted in his thinking to understand the secret dreams and longings of his sensitive and artistic children. Too often, he had offered his children stern rebuke in the place of much-needed guidance. By spending the last years of his life with Aunt Mame, who had once been the victim of his pious scorn, Grandfather Dreiser had also learned humility; like Solon Barnes, he was to find that tolerance and love are the most important ingredients of a man's faith. "Daughter, I know now that it is not for me or thee to judge or forgive anyone," states Barnes to his wayward daughter, Etta . . . but it is also the sentiment which Grandfather Dreiser might have uttered to his wayward daughter Mame who taught him the need for forgiveness.

Similarly, Uncle Theo's choice of Quakerism was undoubtedly affected by his knowledge that the Quaker faith was another of the religions of the plain people, like the Mennonite faith of Grandmother Dreiser. When Dreiser writes of the affection existing between Solon and his mother, Hannah Barnes, the reader feels again the influence of Dreiser's own mother and the conscious admiration he had for her throughout his life. His description of Hannah Barnes is literally a description of my grandmother as she was remembered by all of her children: "Her face and body, if not wholly physically attractive, were truly esthetically and spiritually arresting. For her thoughts were mostly, if not entirely on the needs of others . . . never on her own. And her deep, dark, wide-set eyes and her fairly firm and yet kindly mouth, the lips of which sometimes moved as in silent prayer . . . caused all to think well of her." Certainly, a reader would have to be far removed from the strife and failures of everyday life to miss the fact that *The Bulwark* speaks honestly about real problems that beset American families, not only in the forties, but especially in the sixties.

In the development of his story, Dreiser is careful to present the total picture of the conflict that exists between Solon Barnes and his children; he presents both sides without condemning either. He does not reproach the characters who are involved, nor does he attempt to influence the reader to conclude wherein the fault lies. The reader knows the compelling reasons for Barnes's attitudes, and he accepts Barnes's interpretation of himself as a "righteous man" with many commendable qualities. The question facing the reader is one that had puzzled Uncle Theo for many years: If one accepts the goodness of the spiritual bulwarks like Solon Barnes and John Paul Dreiser, what then must be said about their children who do not follow the path of their righteous fathers? Surely these children who yearn for more than life has given them cannot be condemned for the longings which they did not create in themselves.

In this Quaker novel with the nineteenth-century setting. Dreiser convincingly depicts a family conflict which we have in the last decade referred to as "the generation gap." But the labeling of a conflict, as we have learned, is not a substitute for its resolution, nor does it answer the lingering questions. What type of guidance, understanding, parental attitudes would have helped Stewart Barnes to cope with the restlessness, the yearning, and the hunger for life—the insatiable urge that would eventually result in his suicide? It is a question of great importance to any society, but especially to one such as ours where the suicide rate of young people is a haunting reminder that we have failed as parents and have been remiss in our obligations to our fellowman.

Even more satisfying than Barnes's renewed religious

experience at the end of the novel is his realization of the unresolved conflict at the root of his family misfortune. In creating Barnes's recognition of his inability to communicate with his restless son, Dreiser has exhibited genuine insight into the psychologically sound parent-child relationship. For unlike the dictatorial father who ascends the pedestal of parental authority whenever a family crisis arises, Barnes seeks first to question his own role in the failure:

> What if in so urgently seeking to sway him to the right, he had, after all, failed to do all that he might have done. . . . Or perhaps . . . might he not have been more gentle, loving, persuading, as the book of Discipline of his faith so earnestly cautioned parents to be? Had it not been his bounden duty to exhaust the last measure of tenderness and liberality in seeking to save his son, rather than to drive him, spy on him, irritate him with his constant queries, trying to compel him, by sheer strength and will, to do this or that, when love, love and prayer . . . might have done so much more?

Most important of all, Solon Barnes is vastly different from other Dreiserian protagonists; he is the first of Dreiser's characters to rise from the ashes of destruction and create meaning from the tragedies of his life. The insight that Barnes gains through suffering and the reunion with his prodigal daughter enables him to reaffirm his faith and thereby avoid the bitterness which might have been an outgrowth of his defeats. He achieves a spiritual height, as his past with all its shortcomings is translated into a future with meaning; to Etta, he remarks, "Daughter, until recently I have not thought as I think now. Many things which I thought I understood, I did not understand at all. God has taught me humility . . . and His loving charity, awakened me to many things that I had not seen before. One is the need of love toward all created things."

From his reading in the *Journal* of the colonial Quaker John Woolman, Dreiser also gained insights into the power of universal love and had strengthened his own faith in the God which he had never in any way denied. Nevertheless, for the first time in his spiritual searching, the elevating power of his spirit had triumphed over the desires and demands of the flesh, and he experienced a comforting sense of belonging to the greater family of man.

The Bulwark has been overlooked by the critics as a superficial, pious depiction of spiritual struggle; too often, the critics who found this novel superficial were the intellectual descendants of those who found *An American Tragedy* too ponderous—all of which indicates personal reading preferences more than a standard of literary merit.

The Bulwark is not an old man's return to faith, nor is it a "failure of mind and heart," as one well-known critic has labeled it. It is a simple, but inspiring, narrative which gives new meaning to all that Dreiser had written before; it proposes love and understanding as a palliative which can alleviate the inevitable tragedies of the human condition. The tragedy of Uncle Theo's life was that he had never experienced the effects of this gratifying love relationship with those who had shared his life intimately, but his loss does not invalidate the faith which he had in the efficacy of human love. Any modern psychologist, marriage counselor, or spiritual advisor could cite numerous case studies to validate the soundness of Dreiser's theory.

Prologue

1. Letter is in the Charles Patterson Van Pelt Library, University of Pennsylvania.

Chapter 1

1. The quotations at the beginning of each chapter are Theodore Dreiser's own words taken from his volume of poems *Moods, Cadenced and Declaimed*.

2. In Helen Dreiser's book she has the year 1924, and me as the same age as my cousin Gertrude.

Chapter 2

1. Theodore Dreiser, *Dawn* (New York: Liveright, 1931).

2. *Ibid.*

3. *Ibid.*

4. It is interesting to note that of the ten, only two boys married and only one had an offspring; three girls married and only two raised children; one rejected her child who later committed suicide.

The strict Catholicism of their father's heritage held no allure for most of the children, who in later life adhered to a variety of religious faiths, including Christian Science, Unitarian, Presbyterian, and a lukewarm Catholicism. However, none of them were without some form of religious belief.

Chapter 3

1. *Dawn.*

2. *Ibid.*

3. Impotence–the failure to achieve an erection when sexual desire is present. Sometimes this occurs with one woman and not another. Partial Impotence–premature ejaculation.

4. *Dawn.*

5. See *Sister Carrie.*

6. *Dawn.*

7. *Ibid.*

Chapter 4

1. John Cowper Powys' letter to Vera in the Charles Patterson Van Pelt Library, University of Pennsylvania.
2. *Dawn.*

Chapter 5

1. *Newspaper Days*

(All letters of Dreiser's to Sara White are in the Lilly Library, Indiana University, Bloomington, Indiana.)

Chapter 6

1. Letter is in the Charles Patterson Van Pelt Library, University of Pennsylvania.

Chapter 7

1. *Newspaper Days*
2. *Ibid.*
3. *Ibid.*
4. And Theodore Dreiser dedicated his first novel to him:

DEDICATION

Sister Carrie New York 1900

To my dear father—with a sort
of inheritance proviso by which
I manage to inscribe it—also
to Mame and Austin.

If any of you fail to read and
praise it the book reverts to me.
With love according to precedence

Theodore

(All letters cited are in the Lilly Library, Indiana University, Bloomington, Indiana.)

Chapter 8

1. "My Brother Paul."

Chapter 9

1. *My Life With Dreiser* by Helen Dreiser.
2. *Ibid.*
3. *Ibid.*
4. *Ibid.*
5. *Ibid.*
6. *Ibid.*

Chapter 10

1. Edna St. Vincent Millay, *Sonnets* (New York: Harper & Row, 1945).
2. Direct quotes from Vera Dreiser's personal diary.
3. *Ibid.*

Chapter 11

1. There were many efforts to keep some of civic monuments but to no avail.

2. Direct quote from Vera Dreiser's personal diary.

3. An example of her hallucinating was at the time of Uncle Theo's death before the funeral service when she and I had to go to Forest Lawn for some of the last-minute details. She kept running to the window every few minutes swearing that Uncle Theo's literary assistant was parked outside in her car, "spying" on her. I looked out of the window. There was a car, but no person anywhere in sight. Try as I might I could not convince her that she was seeing things. Without physically struggling with her, I somehow managed to coax her from the window, and got her dressed to go to Forest Lawn where she was needed. But until my final departure these scenes would recur, and she would remain unconvinced that other of Uncle Theo's women acquaintances and literary helpers were "bugging" her.

(All of Theodore Dreiser's letters to Vera are in the Charles Patterson Van Pelt Library, University of Pennsylvania.)

Chapter 12

1. Newspaper reports of his trip.
2. Original in Lilly Library, Indiana University, Bloomington, Indiana.
3. Ibid.

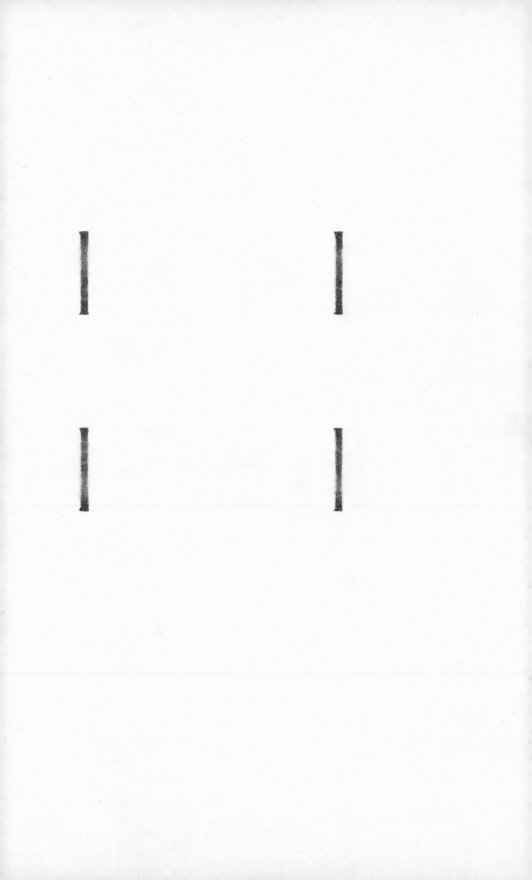